SHAKESPEARE ON SCR

M000284937

The first volume in the re-launched series Shakespeare on Screen is devoted to *Othello*, offering up-to-date coverage of recent screen versions as well as new critical essays on older, canonical films. An international cast of authors explores not only productions from the USA and UK, but also translations, adaptations and appropriations in Québec, Italy, India, Brazil and Mexico. The volume takes part in the ceaseless cultural investigation of what *Othello* says about Shakespeare, the past and our present time, supported by an invaluable film-bibliography. Accompanying free online resources include a fuller version of the bibliography and an additional contribution on YouTube versions of *Othello*. This book will be a valuable resource for students, scholars and teachers of film studies and Shakespeare studies.

SARAH HATCHUEL is Professor of English Literature and Film at the University of Le Havre and the President of the Société Française Shakespeare. She has written extensively on adaptations of Shakespeare's plays. She is the author of *Shakespeare and the Cleopatra/Caesar Intertext: Sequel, Conflation, Remake* (2011) and *Shakespeare, from Stage to Screen* (Cambridge, 2004). She also edited *Julius Caesar* and *Antony and Cleopatra* in *The New Kittredge Shakespeare* collection (2008), and co-edited, with Nathalie Vienne-Guerrin, the *Shakespeare on Screen* series (from 2003–13, PURH, Rouen).

NATHALIE VIENNE-GUERRIN is Professor in Shakespeare Studies at the University Paul-Valéry Montpellier. She is Co-general Editor (with Jean-Christophe Mayer) of *Cahiers Élisabéthains* and co-director (with Patricia Dorval) of the *Shakespeare on Screen in Francophonia Database* (shakscreen.org). She is the author of *The Unruly Tongue in Early Modern England, Three Treatises* (2012), and co-edited, with Sarah Hatchuel, the *Shakespeare on Screen* series (from 2003–13, PURH, Rouen).

Shakespeare on Screen is unique in Shakespeare studies. Each volume is devoted to a single Shakespeare play, or a group of closely related plays, and discusses how it has been adapted to the medium of film and television. The series ranges far beyond the Anglo-American sphere, paying serious attention to European perspectives and combining discussion of mainstream Shakespeare cinema with broad definitions of adaptation and appropriation. As a result, each volume redefines the limits of the field and of the play. The series provides the finest writing on screened Shakespeare by scholars of international significance.

Originally published by Presses universitaires de Rouen et du Havre (PURH), Shakespeare on Screen will now be extended by Cambridge University Press to provide fresh emphasis on new media, multimedia and the evolution of technologies. A special feature of each volume is a select film-bibliography, which will be augmented by a substantial free online resource.

VOLUME IN THE SERIES:

Shakespeare on Screen: Othello

FORTHCOMING VOLUME:

Shakespeare on Screen: The Tempest *and Late Romances*

SHAKESPEARE ON SCREEN
OTHELLO

EDITED BY

SARAH HATCHUEL
and
NATHALIE VIENNE-GUERRIN

CAMBRIDGE
UNIVERSITY PRESS

CAMBRIDGE
UNIVERSITY PRESS

University Printing House, Cambridge CB2 8BS, United Kingdom

One Liberty Plaza, 20th Floor, New York, NY 10006, USA

477 Williamstown Road, Port Melbourne, VIC 3207, Australia

4843/24, 2nd Floor, Ansari Road, Daryaganj, Delhi - 110002, India

79 Anson Road, #06-04/06, Singapore 079906

Cambridge University Press is part of the University of Cambridge.

It furthers the University's mission by disseminating knowledge in the pursuit of education, learning and research at the highest international levels of excellence.

www.cambridge.org
Information on this title: www.cambridge.org/9781107525238

© Cambridge University Press 2015

First published 2015
First paperback edition 2017

A catalogue record for this publication is available from the British Library

Library of Congress Cataloging in Publication data
Shakespeare on Screen : Othello / edited by Sarah Hatchuel and Nathalie Vienne-Guerrin.
pages cm. – (Shakespeare on Screen)
Includes bibliographical references and index.
ISBN 978-1-107-10973-5 (Hardback)
1. Shakespeare, William, 1564-1616. Othello. 2. Shakespeare, William, 1564-1616–Film adaptations. I. Hatchuel, Sarah, editor. II. Vienne-Guerrin, Nathalie, editor.
PR2829.S49 2015
822.3′3–dc23 2015004114

ISBN 978-1-107-10973-5 Hardback
ISBN 978-1-107-52523-8 Paperback

Additional resources for this publication at www.cambridge.org/9781107109735

To friendship, again

Contents

Illustrations

Notes on contributors

VICTORIA BLADEN has published three Shakespearean text guides in the Insight Publications (Melbourne) series: *Romeo and Juliet* (2010), *Julius Caesar* (2011) and *Henry IV Part 1* (2012). She co-edited the *Macbeth* volume (2013) in the *Shakespeare on Screen* series, and has published articles in several volumes of the series (*The Roman Plays, Hamlet, Macbeth*). Other publications include articles on tree and garden imagery in the poetry of Andrew Marvell, representations of Zeus in early modern culture and the pastoral genre in Joan Lindsay's *Picnic at Hanging Rock* and Peter Weir's film adaptation. Currently she is working on a book project *The Tree of Life in the Early Modern Imagination*, and co-editing volumes on *Supernatural and Secular Power in Early Modern England* (2015) and *Shakespeare and the Supernatural*. She is on the editorial board of *Shakespeare on Screen in Francophonia* (www.shakscreen.org).

FLORENCE CABARET is a lecturer at the University of Rouen. Since her PhD on Salman Rushdie, she has written several articles on Indian Anglophone writers and film makers, on British TV series with an ethnic perspective, as well as on translation in human sciences and children literature. She has recently co-edited with Nathalie Vienne-Guerrin a volume entitled *Mauvaises Langues!* (2013) and co-organized two symposiums: TV Series Redux (Rouen, September 2012) and Re-translation in Children's literature (Rouen, February 2013). She is also the translator of Hanif Kureishi's and Chloe Hooper's latest novels.

JOSÉ RAMÓN DÍAZ FERNÁNDEZ is a senior lecturer in English Literature at the University of Málaga (Spain). He has published articles in *Early Modern Literary Studies*, *The Shakespeare Newsletter* and *Shakespeare Bulletin* and has contributed essays to the collections *The Reel Shakespeare: Alternative Cinema and Theory* (2002), *Almost Shakespeare: Reinventing His Works for Cinema and Television* (2004)

as well as all the volumes in the *Shakespeare on Screen* series edited by
Sarah Hatchuel and Nathalie Vienne-Guerrin. In 2001 and 2006 he co-
chaired the 'Shakespeare on Film' seminars at the World Shakespeare
Congresses in Valencia and Brisbane. His volume of revenge tragedies
by Thomas Kyd, John Webster and John Ford was awarded the
Translation Prize by the Spanish Association for Anglo-American
Studies in 2007. He is currently the principal investigator of a
research project on Shakespeare in contemporary culture.

JENNIFER DROUIN is Associate Professor of English in the Hudson Strode
Program in Renaissance Studies at the University of Alabama. She has
published essays in the journals *Theatre Research in Canada* (2006),
Borrowers and Lenders: The Journal of Shakespeare and Appropriation
(2007), the volumes *Shakespeare Re-Dressed: Cross-Gender Casting in
Contemporary Performance* (2008), *Native Shakespeares: Indigenous
Appropriations on a Global Stage* (2008), *Queer Renaissance
Historiography: Backward Gaze* (2009), and on the website of the
Canadian Adaptations of Shakespeare Project (2005, 2007). Her book,
Shakespeare in Québec: Nation, Gender, and Adaptation, was published
in 2014.

KINGA FÖLDVÁRY is a senior lecturer in the Institute of English and
American Studies at Pázmány Péter Catholic University, Hungary.
Her main research interests, besides a close reading of William
Harrison's *Description of Britain*, include Shakespearean tragedy,
problems of genre in film adaptations of Shakespeare's plays, together
with twentieth- and twenty-first-century British literature. Her work in
screen studies focuses on the ways the adapting cinematic/televisual
genres or the oeuvres of auteur-directors define our interpretation of
film adaptations of Shakespeare's plays, as opposed to traditional
fidelity-based taxonomies. She has co-edited four volumes of essays,
and published several articles in edited collections and journals,
including 'Postcolonial hybridity: The making of a Bollywood Lear in
London' in *Global Shakespeares*, a special issue of *Shakespeare: Journal of
the British Shakespeare Association* (2013).

SARAH HATCHUEL is Professor of Early Modern Literature and English-
speaking Cinema at the University of Le Havre (France), where she is
the director of the 'Groupe de Recherche Identités et Cultures'. She has
published several articles on the aesthetics of Shakespeare on screen, and
is the author of *Shakespeare and the Cleopatra/Caesar Intertext: Sequel,*

Conflation, Remake (2011), *Shakespeare, from Stage to Screen* (Cambridge University Press, 2004) and *A Companion to the Shakespearean Films of Kenneth Branagh* (2000). She co-edited, with Nathalie Vienne-Guerrin, seven volumes in the *Shakespeare on Screen* series (Presses universitaires de Rouen et du Havre); she also edited the plays *Julius Caesar* and *Antony and Cleopatra* in the New Kittredge Shakespeare collection (2008). She is currently working on a volume focusing on dreams in US TV series.

PETER HOLLAND is McMeel Family Professor in Shakespeare Studies in the Department of Film, Television, and Theatre, and Associate Dean for the Arts at the University of Notre Dame. From 1997 to 2002 he was Director of the Shakespeare Institute in Stratford-upon-Avon and Professor of Shakespeare Studies at the University of Birmingham. He is Editor of *Shakespeare Survey* and Co-general Editor of *Oxford Shakespeare Topics* (with Stanley Wells) and *Great Shakespeareans* (with Adrian Poole). Among his recent publications are *Medieval Shakespeare* (edited with Ruth Morse and Helen Cooper, Cambridge University Press, 2013) and *Coriolanus* (3rd series, 2013).

DOUGLAS M. LANIER is Professor of English and Director of the London Program at the University of New Hampshire. His published work on early modern British writing includes articles on Shakespeare, Jonson, Marston, Middleton and the Jacobean masque. He has also written widely about contemporary adaptation of Shakespeare, including articles on Shakespeare adaptation in film, television, audio performance, radio, comic books, and advertising. His book *Shakespeare and Modern Popular Culture* appeared in 2002; his articles have appeared in many journals as well as *Spectacular Shakespeare, The Cambridge Companion to Shakespeare and Popular Culture, The Cambridge Companion to Literature and Film, The Blackwell Companion to Shakespeare in Performance,* and *Shakespeares after Shakespeare.* He currently serves as a trustee of the Shakespeare Association of America and on the editorial board of the journals *Shakespeare* and *Adaptation.* He is currently completing a book-length study of screen adaptations of *Othello,* both faithful and free, and an edition of *Timon of Athens.*

SÉBASTIEN LEFAIT is a lecturer in English at the University of Corsica. He completed a PhD on Shakespeare and Orson Welles, in which he treated Welles's works as adaptations *of* and *to* Shakespeare's thought.

Besides articles about films and about Shakespeare's plays, he has published several articles about film adaptation. He is the author of *Surveillance on Screen: Monitoring Contemporary Films and Television Programs* (Scarecrow Press, 2012), and has co-edited a volume entitled *In Praise of Cinematic Bastardy* (2012). His current research focuses on the use of surveillance in TV series, in the theatre and in the context of cinematic adaptation.

RONAN LUDOT-VLASAK is a lecturer in English at the University of Le Havre (France). He holds an MPhil in Renaissance literature from the University of Cambridge, and a PhD in American literature from the University of Paris Diderot. He has published a monograph on Shakespeare in nineteenth-century American literature (*La Réinvention de Shakespeare sur la scène littéraire américaine, 1798–1857*, 2013) as well as articles on the use of Shakespeare in American literature and culture. He has also co-authored *Le Roman américain* (2011) and co-edited two volumes on science and American literature.

AIMARA DA CUNHA RESENDE is a retired professor from the Catholic University of Minas Gerais, and an associate professor from the Federal University of Minas Gerais; co-founder and President of Centro de Estudos Shakespeareanos (Shakespeare Studies Centre), in Brazil, General Editor of Selo CESh/Tessitura; Associate Editor of the *Cambridge World Shakespeare Bibliography*, forthcoming; and Editor of *Foreign Accents: Brazilian Readings of Shakespeare* (2002). She has published several articles on Shakespeare in books and journals both in Brazil and abroad. Her present research is on Shakespeare and Popular Culture in Brazil and Latin America.

PETER J. SMITH BA (hons), MA, PhD, is Reader in Renaissance Literature at Nottingham Trent University. His publications include *Social Shakespeare: Aspects of Renaissance Dramaturgy and Contemporary Society, Hamlet: Theory in Practice* and *Between Two Stools: Scatology and Its Representations in English Literature, Chaucer to Swift*. His articles and reviews have appeared in *Cahiers Élisabéthains, Critical Survey, Renaissance Quarterly, Review of English Studies, Shakespeare, Shakespeare Bulletin, Shakespeare Survey, Speech and Drama, The Times Higher Educational Supplement* and *Year's Work in English Studies*. He is UK correspondent of *Cahiers Élisabéthains* and a trustee of the British Shakespeare Association.

JESÚS TRONCH is Senior Lecturer at the University of Valencia where he teaches English literature and creative translation. His main research interests are textual criticism (specifically on Shakespeare and early modern drama) and the presence of Shakespeare in Spain. He has published *A Synoptic 'Hamlet'* (2002), and *Un primer 'Hamlet'* (1994), co-edited bilingual English-Spanish editions of *The Tempest* and *Antony and Cleopatra*, and, with Clara Calvo, a critical edition of *The Spanish Tragedy* for the Arden Early Modern Drama series. He has also published commissioned essays in book collections and articles on journals such as *TEXT: An Interdisciplinary Annual of Textual Studies*, *SEDERI* and *Shakespeare Survey*.

NATHALIE VIENNE-GUERRIN is Professor of Early Modern English Literature at the University Paul-Valéry Montpellier (France) and head of the 'Institut de Recherche sur la Renaissance, l'âge Classique et les Lumières' (UMR 5186, research centre of the French National Centre for Scientific Research, CNRS, IRCL). She is Co-general Editor, with Jean-Christophe Mayer, of *Cahiers Élisabéthains*. She has published a number of articles on insults, the evil tongue and the war of tongues in Shakespeare's plays. She co-edited (with Claire Gheeraert-Graffeuille) *Autour du* Songe d'une Nuit d'été (2003). She co-edited, with Sarah Hatchuel, seven volumes in the Shakespeare on Screen series (Presses universitaires de Rouen et du Havre). She is the author of *The Unruly Tongue in Early Modern England, Three Treatises* (2012). She is preparing a pragmatic dictionary of Shakespeare's insults (2015).

Series editors' preface

'Shakespeare on Screen' is a series of books created in 2003 by Sarah Hatchuel and Nathalie Vienne-Guerrin. Until 2013 the books were published by the Presses universitaires de Rouen et du Havre (PURH). Each volume is a collection of essays aiming at exploring the screen versions of one play (or a series of plays – such as the history cycles or the Roman plays) by William Shakespeare.

Volumes published by the Presses universitaires de Rouen et du Havre, available from 'le comptoir des presses d'universités' (www.lcdpu.fr/), are as follows:

Shakespeare on Screen: A Midsummer Night's Dream (2004)
Shakespeare on Screen: Richard III (2005)
Shakespeare on Screen: The Henriad (2008)
Television Shakespeare: Essays in Honour of Michèle Willems (2008)
Shakespeare on Screen: The Roman Plays (2009)
Shakespeare on Screen: Hamlet (2011)
Shakespeare on Screen: Macbeth (2013)

The series thoroughly interrogates, through a diversity of viewpoints, what Shakespearean films do with and to Shakespeare's playtexts. If one film cannot render all the ambiguities of the playtext, the confrontation of multiple versions may convey a multiplicity of interpretations and produce a kaleidoscopic form of meaning.

Films based on Shakespeare fall into categories whose boundaries are always being transgressed. This collection encourages scholarly examination of what 'Shakespearean film' encompasses. It not only provides readers with diverging explorations of the films but also deploys a wide array of methodologies used to study 'Shakespeare on screen' – including all types of screen (cinema, TV and the computer – with digital productions and internet 'broadcasts') and all kinds of filmic works, from 'canonical' adaptations using Shakespeare's text, to derivatives, spin-offs and quotes.

This series acknowledges Shakespeare as a repository of symbolic power and cultural authority in 'mainstream', English-speaking adaptations, while also showing how the plays' words and themes have travelled to other non-English cultures, and can be transacted freely, no longer connected to any kind of fixed cultural standard or stable meaning. The series shows how Shakespeare's western, northern, English-speaking 'centre' has been challenged or at least revisited through geographical and trans-media dissemination.

The books emphasize new media, multimedia and the constant evolution of technologies in the production, reception and dissemination of 'Shakespeare on film', especially at a time when so many Shakespearean filmic resources can be accessed online, whether it be on open platforms such as YouTube or cinema/television archives.

Each volume offers a select film-bibliography, which is expanded in a free online version within the Cambridge University Press website, where the reader can also access links to new media forms of Shakespeare.

SARAH HATCHUEL
NATHALIE VIENNE-GUERRIN

Acknowledgements

We first and foremost wish to thank Cambridge University Press for welcoming this book and the volumes that will follow as part of a new Cambridge 'Shakespeare on Screen' series. We are particularly grateful to Sarah Stanton for her invaluable support and patient advice throughout the preparatory work that has led to this publication.

This book stems from an international conference that took place at the University Paul-Valéry Montpellier in June 2012, in the wake of a series of 'Shakespeare on Screen' conferences that we organized at the University of Rouen and at the University of Le Havre from 2003 to 2010, as well as of two seminars that were held at the International Shakespeare Conference in Stratford-upon-Avon (2006) and at the World Shakespeare Congress in Prague (2011). This volume is the result of a long-term collaborative work with colleagues and friends who have come to constitute a dynamic international community of specialists examining the forms that screen Shakespeare can take.

We wish to express our deepest gratitude to the University Paul-Valéry Montpellier and to the University of Le Havre, to our research centres, the GRIC (Groupe de Recherche Identités et Cultures, EA 4314, Le Havre) and to the IRCL (Institut de Recherche sur la Renaissance, l'Âge Classique et les Lumières, UMR 5186, CNRS Montpellier), to the Centre National de la Recherche Scientifique (CNRS) and to the 'Société Française Shakespeare', who helped us financially, logistically and morally in this venture, from the initial Conference to the publication.

Our thanks also go to the international advisory board of the 'Shakespeare on Screen' series: Pascale Aebischer (University of Exeter), Mark Thornton Burnett (Queen's University of Belfast), Samuel Crowl (University of Ohio), Russell Jackson (University of Birmingham), Douglas Lanier (University of New Hampshire), Courtney Lehmann (University of the Pacific), Mariangela Tempera (University of Ferrara), Poonam Trivedi (University of Delhi) and Michèle Willems (University of Rouen).

We are very grateful to the six anonymous colleagues who reviewed the proposal we submitted to Cambridge University Press: their invaluable feedback helped us immensely to improve the coherence of the project and widen its scope.

Special thanks go to Russell Jackson and Samuel Crowl for their extra work on this particular volume, as well as to Victoria Bladen for her assistance and useful suggestions.

We warmly thank the contributors to this volume for their unfailing patience, reactivity and support, which have made our work on this book a truly collective venture.

We finally wish to thank wholeheartedly our respective families and friends for letting us spend so much (demanding but fun) time together to prepare this volume.

Quotations from Shakespeare's works are taken from *The Norton Shakespeare*, based on the Oxford Edition. General Editor: Stephen Greenblatt; editors: Walter Cohen, Jean E. Howard, and Katharine Eisaman Maus (New York: W. W. Norton, 1997).

CHAPTER I

Introduction
Ensnared in Othello on screen
Sarah Hatchuel and Nathalie Vienne-Guerrin

Othello kills Desdemona. At the end of Shakespeare's tragic play, a Moorish general murders his white Venetian bride after having been convinced of her unfaithfulness by Iago, a dissatisfied officer. The play, thereby, raises issues of race and gender, dramatizing the very processes in which stereotypes are culturally built, conveyed, questioned and internalized. One of Iago's efficient stratagems, as Stephen Buhler remarks, is 'to persuade Othello that his very blackness – as well as his older years, his lack of "gentility," and his status as foreigner – makes him an unnatural mate' for Desdemona.[1] Othello is led, in Frantz Fanon's words, to 'epidermalize' – i.e., accept at the level of his skin colour – his racial inferiority.[2] Iago's machinations depend on the prejudiced beliefs, shared by characters inside the play, that black men are monstrous Others and women are harlots; but for spectators too, the sight of the fair Desdemona with her black general has, through centuries of performance, motivated and challenged culturally conditioned responses to race and gender.

Othello's final scene is known for blurring the frontiers between illusion and 'reality', affecting the audience profoundly but also, in Lois Potter's words, making them 'feel less like spectators ... than like bystanders at a traffic accident'.[3] The power of that scene is evident in the alternative French and German translations that have offered happy endings, and in the numerous anecdotes of outraged spectators shouting in disgust or intervening to stop the action, as if it were inappropriate for a fictional murder to stir such powerfully real emotions. Actors themselves apparently did not escape the effects of this blurring between life and art. Stories abound of Othellos who actually killed their Desdemonas. For Potter, 'the history of playing Othello is the history of a desire for a degree of identification between hero and role that might almost seem to rule out the need to act at all'.[4]

Paradoxically, despite this constructed 'identification' between actor and role, the part of Othello was in the hands of white men for nearly three hundred years, starting with Richard Burbage at the Globe theatre (who, let's remember, faced a boy as Desdemona). Ira Aldridge was the first black actor to enact Othello in the nineteenth century. He was followed by Morgan Smith, Edward Sterling Wright and the famous, politically conscious Paul Robeson, who performed the part to great acclaim on the London stage in 1930, on Broadway in 1943 and in Stratford-upon-Avon in 1959. Decades of activism were necessary before black actors were cast in the part on a regular basis. The role of Othello bears the weight of a long (and ongoing) history of discrimination and racism, of years of struggle for equality of opportunity, which questions the very possibility of 'colour-blind' casting.

However, the praise for black actors as 'natural' choices for the part – as if they were good only because they did not have to act – is certainly double-edged, since it has denied them both artistry and intelligence.[5] Moreover, casting a black man in the role may prolong a cultural practice that labels the black man as arch-villain, reinforcing the racial clichés. Hugh Quarshie from the Royal Shakespeare Company even stated in 1999 that Othello might be the one classical role an actor of colour should *not* perform.[6]

In the early modern period, the term 'black' was generally opposed to 'fair' – read 'beautiful', with a special moral resonance in the case of women, evoking innocence and virginity.[7] 'White' skin was desirable in the (noble) English women, but not in men, whose complexion had to be 'ruddy' or 'brown' to be considered healthy.[8] In practice, as Kim Hall points out, 'this means that the polarity of dark and light is most often worked out in representations of black men and white women'.[9] As Othello embodies the enemy of the white race, he encapsulates what Arthur L. Little calls 'an iconographic truth', conjuring up, as he does, a prominent cultural picture of 'the dominant society's sexual, racial, national and imperial fears'.[10] The myths about black men's sexual rapacity and the dangers of racial 'pollution' were used to ensure the control of white women – who might tarnish their own sexual or racial 'purity'. This recurrent fascination with narratives centred on a black male and a white female has been explored by Celia Daileader, who coined the term 'Othellophilia' to address the critical and artistic 'habit of casting black actors in "color-blind" roles that uncannily recalled the role of Othello' (pointing out, for example, that inter-racial productions of *Romeo and Juliet* almost inevitably cast Romeo – not Juliet – as black).[11] The practice of Othellophilia, she argues, should be considered in the context of Anglo-American culture: from the Renaissance onward, the 'canonical' narratives of inter-racial marriage and sex have told the story of black men and white women – not of black women and white men, thus suppressing its counterpart – 'the more historically pertinent if more ideologically troubling story of white male sexual use of black females, the slave-holder's secret'.[12] Casting a black actor as Othello may, therefore, contribute to exorcize the slave-master's sexual guilt.[13] Nevertheless, because of the fight to achieve recognition and legitimacy and to secure job opportunities for black actors, it has now become very problematic to cast a non-black performer, whether on stage or on screen.[14] In silent films, black actors were limited to the eye-rolling-'coon' stereotypes established by D. W. Griffith in his *Birth of a Nation* (1915) and were not even allowed to touch the white heroine. Cinema employed white actors to play black protagonists for a very long time, until worldviews and acting codes started to change. As Pascale Aebischer contends, 'A white actor blacking-up … is almost inevitably racist in his performance of racial Otherness and in his suggestion that these characters' race, rather than the racist attitudes …, is the reason for their savage outbreaks of violence.'[15] Similarly Neil Taylor observes: 'now, blackface no longer convinces. The mask has ceased to be a convention and become an outrage.'[16]

How have films of *Othello* negotiated the delicate pitfalls of what – albeit anachronistically[17] – seems to be the racist and sexist agenda of a play in which a foreign dark lord murders a weak white girl? In the short feature *Che Cosa Sono Le Nuvole?* (1967), Pier Paolo Pasolini appropriates *Othello* as an inset play performed by full-sized human puppets before a working-class audience. Increasingly upset by the plot, the audience invades the stage and changes the story. As the spectators reveal their lack of sophistication, seeming to mistake fiction for reality, they also heroically stand up against the patriarchal, racist and sexually masochistic subtext by saving Desdemona and killing Othello and Iago. By showing the string-pulling puppeteer and giving the human puppets (and the spectators) agency of their own, Pasolini dramatizes, as Sonia Massai argues, the tension between Shakespeare's powerful authorial discourse and resistance against it.[18] Forty-three years later, in the 2010 'Sassy Gay Friend: Othello'[19] video on YouTube (which has been viewed more than 3.5 million times since its uploading),[20] Desdemona is saved by her hilarious 'sassy gay friend', who advises her to leave before Othello's murderous arrival. He informs her of her husband's suspicions by deconstructing the gender politics of the play: 'What? Some guy ends up with your handkerchief, so your husband gets to murder you?! No!', thus preempting the reactions that may (too often) be heard among spectators or students of the play – 'her murder is so unfair – she was innocent and faithful to her husband'. But what if she had been 'guilty' of infidelity? Would she, then, have deserved to die? In both scenarios (Pasolini's and the Sassy Gay Friend's), opposing what the play seems to advocate ultimately implies changing its ending. Can productions of the tragedy that follow Shakespeare's playtext or plotline escape a racist and sexist stance and denounce prejudiced responses? What are the challenges Shakespeare's *Othello* raises when it is adapted, appropriated or cited on screen? And can there be such things as 'post-racial' films?[21]

Much has already been written on *Othello* screen adaptations and derivatives, as attested by José Ramón Díaz Fernández's select film-bibliography at the end of this volume and its extended version in the online resource for this book; yet, this collection of essays offers analyses of new filmic objects as well as original critical stances to review older ones. By revisiting 'canonical' versions, their making-ofs and translations (including amateur clips posted on YouTube), by analysing free retellings in the Anglophone zones but also those beyond the US/UK axis, in Québec, Italy, Brazil or Mexico, and by examining 'mirror' metanarrative films, their genres and receptions through time, the essays all take part in the ceaseless investigation of what the play continues to say about 'Shakespeare', of the past and of our present time. The adaptations, appropriations, spin-offs, quotes and misquotes invite us to reflect upon what 'Shakespeare on film' signifies or engenders, and upon the way *Othello* has been circulating and received in our contemporary cultures. The exploration of racial issues in *Othello* has made it an enabling text for racially segregated cultures and more generally for colonial and postcolonial readers, adapters and performers of Shakespeare. Othello's character has, indeed, provided a mouthpiece for the consciousness of denigrated[22] peoples in their unequal and exploitive cultural encounters with Europe.[23]

Whether one considers Shakespeare's text as conveying or condemning racial segregation, *Othello* puts these issues to the fore, exploring the ways notions of Otherness are constructed and calling for adaptations to other contexts – which reflects Othello's own traveller's tales inside the play. Othello has journeyed to liminal exotic places and even encountered 'the cannibals that each other eat,/ The Anthropophagi, and men whose heads/ Do grow beneath their shoulders' (1.3.142–4). In the opening chapter to this collection, Victoria Bladen examines how eight screen adaptations, dating from 1952 to 2004, have inventively inserted motifs of peripheral places and figures. Bladen shows how the films have dealt with the intersections of race and gender with the marvellous and the

Figure 1:   Othello in Stuart Burge/Laurence Olivier's 1965 production.

monstrous, showing how Othello the 'voyager' is in turn framed by, and entrapped within, narratives of Otherness.

As early as the pre-sound film era, films of *Othello* have sent mixed messages on racial issues. In Dimitri Buchowetzki's 1922 German adaptation (in which Othello heroically succeeds in killing Iago before committing suicide), Emil Jannings's Othello's very black make-up, marking him as a racial Other, is challenged by intertitles that present him as the noble son of an Egyptian prince and a Spanish princess. Yet his Otherness is reinforced by Krauss's Iago's use of the handkerchief to wipe himself in disgust after having touched Othello's brow.[24] However, the scene also emphasizes the artificiality of the mask. As Judith Buchanan notes, Iago's 'expression of interest in what comes off on the handkerchief cannot help but also register the fact that in their *performance* of this scene at least, it was very probably boot polish'.[25] The attempt of a white actor to 'racially' impersonate blackness peaked in Laurence Olivier's performance for the National Theatre in 1964, which was recorded by Stuart Burge in 1965 (see Figure 1).

This blacked-up, histrionic performance, which was probably more suited to the stage than to the 'realistic' medium of cinema, heavily emphasized Othello's Otherness through skin colour, exaggerated gesture and accent, and has often been received, especially in the light of the civil rights movement taking place at the time, as condescending and, to quote Aebischer, as 'the infamous key example of extreme racial stereotyping'.[26] But offensiveness may be precisely part of the performance's point. Peter Holland's chapter in this collection asks that we think again about Olivier's bravura performance, relocating it in its historical moment but also seeing it as the nearest we can now come to the ambiguities of early modern constructions and representations of Othello's blackness.

To avoid addressing the issues raised when Othello is portrayed as a black African, some critics and directors have, as Buhler points out, 'denied that race is a major factor in the play' by claiming that 'Othello is classified, after all, as a Moor, a term that could describe any number of peoples from the Mediterranean and beyond'.[27] In Jonathan Miller's 1981 BBC version, Othello was played by a white man, Anthony Hopkins, against Bob Hoskins's Iago; but, contrary to Olivier, Hopkins impersonated a hardly tanned-up North African. Kenneth S. Rothwell notes the coincidence that links the two names 'Hopkins' and 'Hoskins', suggesting that the production's emphasis was less on racial Otherness than on volcanic macho jealousy, class conflict and 'the *Doppelgänger* relationship between hero and villain'.[28] However, in a different cultural context, even the 'North African' option may bring the racial matter to the fore with a vengeance. This was the case in France with Claude Barma's TV production, which was broadcast in January 1962,[29] just a few months before the end of what was called the 'events' (to avoid saying 'war') in Algeria – by that time a French colony. Daniel Sorano, who plays Othello, had a father who was born in Algeria; he experienced racism and, in his youth, was called a 'nigger', a word that actually often replaces the term 'Moor' in the French translation for this TV version. Sorano stated in an interview that *Othello* was definitely less a tragedy of jealousy than a racial tragedy,[30] before completely identifying himself with the role in the tradition highlighted by Potter ('Yes, it's true, admits Sorano, I am Othello')[31] and tragically dying at forty-one, just a few months after the film was made. Interestingly, Sorano's North African origins did not prevent him from using make-up to darken his skin, making even more visible the difference and segregation that the actor felt throughout his life. Not considered white in France, Sorano was yet positioned, by a TV magazine at the time, in the line of blackface actors, from Orson Welles to Serge Bondartchouck.[32]

In 1988, in the explosive context of apartheid South Africa, Janet Suzman filmed, for Channel Four (UK), a production of *Othello* performed at the Market Place Theatre (Johannesburg) that addressed racial politics frontally, challenging the South African audience with black actor John Kani embracing a white Desdemona. A year later, Trevor Nunn's filmed stage production in Stratford-upon-Avon cast the black Jamaican opera singer Willard White as Othello. This casting choice may retrospectively be read in the light of opera's ongoing tradition of casting white tenors in blackface in Verdi's *Otello*, causing 'considerable controversy in recent years'.[33] In Nunn's production, the Moor is no longer isolated as the only Other on stage since Bianca, Cassio's lover, is also black; however, Bianca's blackness reinforces the idea of racial hierarchies since Cassio may worship the white Desdemona but 'relieves' himself with a 'black harlot'.[34]

Oliver Parker's 1995 version is the first general-release film in which the title-role is played by an African American actor, Laurence Fishburne, whose body often becomes an eroticized spectacle. Buchanan notes how, on the night of the arrival in Cyprus, it is 'his undressing, not hers, upon which the camera lingers with the most intimate and detailed appreciation'.[35] The motif of the chessboard that pervades the film with its black-and-white colour pattern evokes colonial narratives in which Othello is envisaged as a servant owned and controlled by Venice. Mark Thornton Burnett also sees, in Iago's appropriation of the chess pieces, the sign of 'a position of political dominance or, at least, imperial power'.[36] If the film attracted African American audiences,[37] it also exploited stereotypes of the black man and black male sexuality, notably through Othello's slightly menacing, almost stalking, attitude during his first scene of lovemaking and through Fishburne's previous role as Tina Turner's brutal husband, Ike, in Brian Gibson's *What's Love Got to Do With It* (1993).[38]

On screen, Desdemona has generally been framed by a patriarchal gaze she cannot escape. The Italian *Othello* filmed by Arturo Ambrosio and Arrigo Frusta in 1914 was sometimes refused exhibition because Desdemona was killed at the end,[39] but, paradoxically, this silent film is perhaps the less voyeuristic in its depiction of the murder: it takes place out of shot while the camera focuses on a candle that is extinguished, as a mere visual equivalent to Othello's line 'And then put out the light'. Other productions have, on the contrary, revelled in the sado-erotic cruelty of the murder. As Aebischer notes, the murder in Orson Welles's 1952 film takes place slowly with 'explicit eroticisation' and even 'panic-stricken collaboration' from Desdemona (Suzanne Cloutier).[40] What is first a fetishized, unsullied, passive 'white' icon becomes a lurid vision of expressionist shots in which she is monstrously fragmented and 'dis-membered'.[41] Iago (Micheál MacLiammóir) turns, in Carol Rutter's words, a 'Madonna into [a] gargoyle'.[42] Desdemona is the victim of both Othello and the montage constructed by the all-controlling male *auteur*. In this volume, Sebastien Lefait's chapter addresses this wish for absolute control and considers Welles's *Othello* making-of (*Filming Othello*, made in 1978) as the attempt to manipulate the spectators' reception (in a very Iago-like way), to modify his former film and rerelease it in an updated version. *Filming Othello* certainly proclaims 'the need for *Othello* to be remade over and over' but as long as Welles may have 'the final say in the field of *Othello* adaptations'.

As a rather light-skinned Othello, Welles does not put alterity to the fore but identifies the hero with himself, the powerful actor-director who rejects Otherness, like a prestidigitator, onto Cloutier.[43] Welles's fascination with magic and forgery, as Rothwell suggests, influenced his whole world view (one of his last filmic essays was *F for Fake* in 1973).[44] His *Othello*, which aesthetically influenced so many other adaptations, marked his turn away from the filmic long take and towards the 'magical' effects of juxtaposed, quick shots (the film includes some five hundred of them).[45] The rhythmic montage, the chiaroscuro lighting, the tilted camera angles offering differing perspectives and the recurring motifs of cages, bars and the mosaic reflect Iago's scheme of entrapment, of 'enmesh [ing] them all' (2.3.357), but also 'map female unknowability or perhaps male anxiety'[46] according to which women are aloof and deceitful.

Othello's misogynistic environment has spurred discussions about the relation between Othello and Iago. Do the film productions emphasize what could be read as a homoerotic relation? The debate peaked when reviewing Parker's 1995 film. While the story was meant to focus on the sexual union of Othello and Desdemona (the film was advertised as an 'erotic thriller'), the critics repeatedly commented on the interplay between Othello/Fishburne, who was labelled a newcomer to Shakespeare, and Iago/Branagh, whose experience with the language was emphasized. On homosexuality, critics and scholars alike were divided. For Rothwell, 'Parker pays no attention to the fashionable vogue for a homoerotic attraction between Iago and Othello.'[47] Hodgdon compares Othello and Iago's bloody handshake as they take their vow with the 'close-up of Desdemona's and Othello's hands against the flower-strewn wedding sheets' but eventually concludes that 'any suggestion of a homosexual coupling' is 'avoid[ed]' in favour of stressing a 'military code of honor' where 'justice' against women 'becomes the provenance of men'.[48] Douglas Lanier reads Branagh's Iago's motivations as stemming from 'homosocial jealousy, not racism', as made clear by the 'homoerotic joy' he seems to feel during their 'blood bond' embrace; violence against women is thus linked to the 'seductiveness of homosocial male bonding'.[49] This is in keeping with Richard Burt's observation that 'in Parker's 1995 Snoop-Doggy-Dog-style *Othello*, Branagh plays Iago as a gay man who loves Othello but cannot admit it and so destroys him and his wife'.[50] Burnett, too, perceives a homoerotic subtext in Iago's 'visual contemplation' of the Moor and in his lovemaking with his wife Emilia, which suggests 'a barely suppressed imaginary of male-on-male consummation'.[51] Iago's fascination with Othello's body can also be found in his blackening of his own hand with charcoal, a gesture that Buchanan identifies as 'simultaneously of mock-derision and of intimate identification with the black Other whom he professes to hate'.[52] As regularly in *Othello* productions, identity is elusively hybridized and slides across and between racial categorizations.

In Parker's *Othello*, the tragedy explicitly happens through a gaze that is manipulated by Branagh's Iago, the master-director. As Iago catches a glimpse of Cassio and Desdemona (Irène Jacob) on the blade of his knife, he discloses his strategy to the spectators: he will 'interpose himself as a distorting mirror through which Othello may observe the world',[53] thereby identifying himself as the film's inset director who guides Othello's (and the audience's) gaze and acknowledging Branagh's own experience as a filmmaker. In his regular addresses to the spectators and his awareness that he is filmed and observed, Branagh's Iago uses the camera as the very net that 'enmesh[es] them all', since, as Buchanan remarks, the camera embodies the 'subjectivized gaze, and a failure to acknowledge the limits of one's own subjectivity'.[54]

Films of *Othello* dramatize the power that words have to transform our gaze but also to engender mental images. Sergei Yutkevich's 1955 version shows visually how Desdemona imagines and romanticizes Othello's tales of adventure and captivity. In Buchowetzki's 1922 film, Othello's thoughts of his wife's unfaithfulness are projected, during his epileptic fit, onto the curtain behind his bed, turning verbal accusations into visual ones. Parker's 1995 film also literalizes Othello's fantasy as he imagines his wife in bed with Cassio. These literal, soft-porn visions are, for Buchanan, 'insidiously persuasive' since the slander 'assumes a degree of quasi-photographic truth'.[55] As the spectators see what Othello sees, Iago's innuendoes about Desdemona's infidelity are written onto Desdemona's body, which, according to Rutter, serves to 'validate the misogynistic stereotypes . . . that Shakespeare's play circulates'.[56] As the camera goes back to the epileptic Othello, his back is against the wall, his head shaking in pain, and his hands attached to heavy, handcuff-like chains (see Figure 2).

These shots prolong the sado-masochistic imagery as well as portray Othello as a tied-up slave. Moreover, Othello's suicide through self-strangulation at the end of the film evokes, for Burnett, 'photographic images of lynchings of blacks in the American Deep south'.[57] The chains and the strangulation may also suggest, as Buhler contends, that the character is 'enslaved not only by his jealousy but by the racist categories Iago has led him to internalize'.[58] Again, we witness, in the film's reception, the tensions that the play itself arouses. *Othello* productions can be explored as reflections, in various contexts, on the unstable processes leading to the construction of racial identities, documenting how the blackness of each

Figure 2:   Iago and Othello in Oliver Parker's 1995 film.

specific Othello is 'defined within and against white value systems and beliefs'.[59] Films may be best approached as sites of negotiation where stereotypes are at once created and challenged, reinforced and exploded.

Free adaptations that rewrite Shakespeare's text are also confronted with these tensions. In the ITV/PBS 2001 *Othello* directed by Geoffrey Sax (following a script by Andrew Davies), which takes place in London, with John Othello as a member of the Metropolitan Police Force, Jago (the production's equivalent of Iago) is not punished at the end and is even promoted to a position from where he can continue to endorse racist policies. The PBS website claims that 'Shakespeare's classic tale of jealousy, love and obsession enters the millennium'[60] but, for Barbara Hodgdon, this 'millenium' appears more as a 'memory of the past than a symptom of present-day hopes ... for an equitable future of race (and gender) relations'.[61] Davies/Sax's *Othello* would result 'in white blindness' and reflect on the fact that 'whiteness' is invisible, never has to be defined, while constituting a norm linked to masculinity and power, against which Otherness is created.[62] In this volume, Peter Smith's chapter offers a reading of Davies/Sax's version within the context of current racial tensions in the UK – contemporary legal cases, instances of racist abuse by the police, and the Euro 2012 football tournament – and shows how 'the adaptation is preternaturally prophetic of the condition of the Met at the present time'. His critical approach is that of a presentism 'tethered' to a particular time, which, by acknowledging its own transitoriness, demonstrates the topicality of particular readings and the integration of pressing sociopolitical concerns.

Critics have regularly commented on the intersection between the timing of an *Othello* film's release and topical events. Parker's 1995 *Othello* and Tim Blake Nelson's 2001 *'O'*, in particular, have been received through the scandals and tragedies of their time, and have also addressed general issues of cultural integration/exclusion in contemporary western societies.[63] Parker's *Othello* opened in the United States in December 1995 and interacted with the media frenzy around the trial of O. J. Simpson, the African American football player who was accused of murdering his white ex-wife whom he suspected of having a relationship with a white man. Like Othello, Simpson also threatened to take his own life. The extra-cinematic world guided responses to the fiction which, in turn, influenced 'real' events in a reciprocal relation, since Simpson started (subconsciously or not) internalizing the part of Othello in interview: 'Let's say I committed this crime. Even if I did do this, it would have to be because I loved her very much, right?', as if Simpson aligned himself with the Moor that loved 'too well' and continued to convey a view in which men may rule over women's fates.

'O', which recontextualizes the play in a prep school in South Carolina, was first experienced through the prism of the real-life 1998 Columbine High School shooting in Littleton, Colorado. Although the massacre delayed the release of the film (because the lonely, alienated Hugo/Iago so closely resembled the supposedly harassed real shooters), it also lent 'plausibility to the film's implausibility', as noted by Rothwell.[64] *'O'* fully engages with the ambiguities of racial construction. As the school's basketball champion, O(din) embodies a social and cultural recognition that might only come through physical achievement and which implies becoming the school's 'property'. The black athlete may win games and soar professionally, but he also remains a 'captive object'.[65] Race is, therefore, challenged and reinforced at the same time. Through O's last words to Hugo (the Iago figure), 'You tell'em, where I came from didn't make me do this', the film 'dreams itself' as a cry away from essentialism and a denunciation of the racist stance, openly addressing the ambiguities generated by its own re-location in a contemporary high school.[66] Ronan Ludot-Vlasak's chapter in this collection explores the question of intertextuality in *'O'*, arguing that the relations between the film and Shakespeare's works do not merely constitute the migration and updating of a plot in a different social and cultural context, but involve complex transcultural

transactions where Shakespearean imageries are revisited, disseminated, literalized or displaced. A postmodern avatar of Shakespeare's wooden O, the title of the film recalls the basketball hoop but also points to several key issues in the film such as gazing, gender, sexuality and the representation of bodies.

The two 2001 *Othello* productions – '*O*' and the Davies/Sax *Othello* – have been regarded by Lanier as notable exceptions in a recent trend that, on screen (as opposed to the stage), tones down the racial (i.e., black vs white) issues at work in the play.[67] Since 1996, film productions have been less racially oriented at the same time as the *Othello* narrative has become attractive to filmmakers beyond the US/UK axis. Adaptations such as Richard Eyre's 2004 *Stage Beauty* puts sexual/gender politics to the fore; *Huapango* (Mexico, dir. Iván Lipkies, 2003) and *Omkara* (India, dir. Vishal Bhardwaj, 2006) emphasize culturally constructed ethnicity and class; and *Othello: The Tragedy of the Moor* (Canada, dir. Zaid Shaikh, 2008) focuses on religion (Christianity vs Islam). Taking into account this 'shift away from race towards some other forms of identity politics', Lanier asks whether *Othello* is now becoming a 'post-racial' tale. Since, only a few decades ago, cultural politics and film 'realism' started to demand a black actor in the role of Othello, films concentrating on race have reproduced a tale of racial victimization, often through a racialized Anglo-American lens – which could explain why the two 2001 films from the United States and the United Kingdom have escaped the new trend. Thereby, the worldwide shift to *Othello* films that are 'post-racialized' and 'indigenized' may testify, according to Lanier, to the way cinema is resisting Anglo-American ownership of Shakespeare, 'rebrand[ing him] as a global author'. This change is ambivalent – it may be greeted as a postcolonial, maybe even post-Obama, sign of tolerance and acceptance, but also seen as a disquieting obliterating of the racial issues, as it makes the play 'about just difference'. This globalized trend has certainly produced an irony since, to quote Lanier, 'just as the role of Othello has become available to American and British black film actors, it is becoming no longer theirs again'.[68]

Many essays in this volume suggest, indeed, that there are many ways of 'unmooring the Moor' and of going beyond the 'black vs white' reading of the play. Florence Cabaret's contribution on Vishal Bhardwaj's *Omkara* (2006) shows how this film addresses several Indian domestic issues, more than a postcolonial view of the relations between the former colonizer and colonized people, by choosing an all-Indian set of actors. *Omkara*, Cabaret notes, 'transposes a race issue into a caste issue' and translates Othello's jealousy into an 'honour crime'. The point of her study is to demonstrate that the film is representative of 'a post-independence way of approaching Shakespeare rather than a postcolonial reclaiming of Shakespeare'. She shows that the 'black vs. white trope' is transformed into an 'Indian appropriation of colour stigmatization' in a film that is inscribed in the historic evolution of the 1970s 'angry young man' film in India.

Aimara Resende's study of Iván Lipkies's Mexican film *Huapango* (2003) and of Paulo Afonso Grisolli's Brazilian TV production *Otelo de Oliveira* (1983) is in keeping with Lanier's contention that world cinema seems to manage to do without race, and that globalization allows de-racialization; in the two productions, the 'transmuted' Moor is 'not a Negro' even if he bears the marks of an outsider. Race seems to be lost in translation through a process of appropriation that conforms to the different media used, but also to the cultural constraints and the contemporary demands of the global market.

Jennifer Drouin studies how *Une histoire inventée* (dir. André Forcier, 1990), which she defines as both a 'parallel' and 'meta-narrative' film of *Othello*, adapts the racial and gender politics of Shakespeare's play to a Québécois context. The adaptation partly displaces the racial issues onto the evocation of the debate over 'multiculturalism' vs 'interculturalism', with the latter constructing ethnicity based not only on racial but also on linguistic difference. The film, Drouin notes, is more '*about* Shakespeare than an adaptation *of* Shakespeare' and raises important questions 'about Québec society and the Bardbiz more broadly'.

Nevertheless, do such appropriations mean race erasure? Referring to 'post-racial' *Othello* suggests that 'race' remains the inescapable landmark when it comes to studying *Othello* on screen. It is as if race, even when it is 'dis-integrated',[69] could continue to screen, blur, mask, not to say stifle, the other features of the play. Lois Potter distinguishes various angles of entrance into the play through chapters she entitles 'Othello's play', 'Iago's play' and 'Desdemona's play'.[70] It seems difficult so far to do the same with screen versions and to delineate 'Othello's films', 'Iago's films', and 'Desdemona's films', as if contemporary screen culture were 'ensnaring' us by or into focusing on the central issue of race, illustrating the overwhelming 'ocular' impact of a play that leads us to ceaselessly question what Michael Neill calls 'the look of Othello'.[71] Yet, when you look for 'Iago' and not 'Othello' on YouTube, the film that overwhelmingly appears is Disney's 1992 *Aladdin* in which Iago is a villainous parrot. *Othello* may, partly, momentarily or subjectively at least, be 'e-raced'.[72]

Looking at what Rothwell has termed 'mirror movies' may help in seeing other aspects of *Othello* and of its screen life. Cinema has been attracted by backstage narratives involving Othello and murder as early as the pre-sound era, with films such as Harley Knowles's *Carnival* (1921). As Lanier argues, these metanarrative films constantly negotiate with the theatre, the cultural authority of which must either be 'purged or repressed'.[73] Via the threat that a staged murder could become real, cinema discloses its strive for the realism that comes with 'total acting' (in which the actor is erased behind the role) but also demonizes and 'pathologizes' theatre, showing how the role can eventually 'play' the actor and trigger excess and madness. In this volume, Kinga Földváry looks at *Othello* through two 'mirror movies' that use a theatrical setting in which actors' offstage lives mirror the roles they are performing on stage. Comparing *A Double Life* (dir. George Cukor, 1947) and *Stage Beauty* (dir. Richard Eyre, 2004), she demonstrates that, to approach these films, the question of genre is much more relevant than the issue of textual fidelity: in this case, *film noir*/thriller vs romantic comedy. Földváry suggests that film producers and consumers make their creative and receptive choices with the help of generic labels, rather than by referring to either the films' relationships to the Shakespearean text or the way they 'mirror' the Shakespearean plot. These films, more than others, have a 'double life', a Shakespearean life and a non-Shakespearean life, as is shown also by Douglas Lanier's chapter in this book. Lanier focuses on the Italian film *Il Peccato di Anna* (aka *Anna's Sin*, dir. Camillo Mastrocinque, 1952) and explores how this little-known metanarrative adaptation uses elements of *Othello* (including performance excerpts) in the service of progressive racial and gender politics (as it notably refocuses the narrative on the Desdemona figure) and how it offers 'a meditation on mid-century Italian cultural politics filtered through Shakespeare's play'. Lanier examines the film's circulation in the United States in 1954 and its rerelease in 1961, which reshaped the original message into something troublingly lurid and politically retrogressive, reminding us that 'our accounts of screen Shakespeare, particularly in the context of an international film market, need to address contexts of reception that are multiple and local'.

These 'mirror films' are one way of putting *Othello* into 'tatters', as Mariangela Tempera would say,[74] or into what Burt has coined 'Shakesbites', thus describing one of the 'effects of Shakespeare's cine-mediatization': an 'increasingly fragmented reproduction'.[75] An online platform for teachers (2010) offers to make Shakespeare 'easy' by putting his plays 'in bits'. Indeed, the website claims that, with 'Shakespeare in bits', 'The Bard hasn't been this easy to enjoy in over 400 years!'[76] The

'*Othello* title' is not available yet, but this online resource for purchase is emblematic of the new ways of 'experiencing Shakespeare' that the new media have engendered. When one moves from World Cinema to the World Wide Web, *Othello* films become 'resources', a term that is often associated with 'teaching Shakespeare' and which actually testifies to our current inability to name and address these unidentified filmic objects (UFOs) – or, should we say, unidentified digital objects (UDOs) – since they are even more 'potentially perishable commodities' than the 'world cinema' films studied by Mark Thornton Burnett.[77] The expression 'Shakespeare online *resources*' provides a facile way of encapsulating an ever-evolving, elusive Shakespearean screenscape. Ayanna Thompson's contribution to the online resource complementing this book aims to map the global-individual, vernacular-digital, hybrid, unsettled and unsettling, essentially ephemeral shapes that *Othello* can take on the computer screen. This *Othello* YouTubography or digitography, which implies new referencing codes and habits,[78] comes as a necessary complement to José Ramón Díaz Fernández's extended online film-bibliography.

What are the stakes of putting *Othello* into tatters, bites or bits? One could expect that it makes *Othello* more multicoloured or kaleidoscopic, thereby confirming the current trend towards global-hence-'post-racial' *Othello* and *re-sourcing* the vision of the play. Yet it does not seem to be the case. Ayanna Thompson's 2010 article, 'Unmooring the Moor: Researching and Teaching on YouTube' shows that YouTube *Othello* provides the means to approach and question constructions of race.[79] Stephen O'Neill has studied 'YouTube's culture of vernacular production'[80] and shown the various ways in which 'Shakespeare's texts provide a metalanguage through which race is examined'.[81] Indeed, from the very popular and many times recycled 'Othello Rap' performed by the Reduced Shakespeare Company[82] to the 'Othello Lego Movie' that represents Othello in the guise of Darth Vader,[83] from 'Shakespeare and race' online school courses[84] to the black-and-white short film *Othello Blacking Up* (2011),[85] the net too is 'ensnared' in Iago's 'net' and the seemingly unescapable questions of race raised by the play. Examining the latest trend in *Othello*-related videos – edited clips from professional productions, commentaries on *Othello* produced by theatre companies and professionally produced parodies and satires – Ayanna Thompson's contribution to the online resource suggests that *Othello* on the computer screen looks different from *Othello* on large and small screens, although online *Othello*s also contribute to the ongoing contemporary debates about the role of history in modern constructions of racial difference.

Jesús Tronch's article in this book reveals another way of exploiting Shakespeare online resources by delineating features of three *Othello* films dubbed and subtitled into Spanish: Orson Welles's (1952), Stuart Burge's (1965) and Oliver Parker's (1995). The World Wide Web here proves a new tool to study Shakespeare as translated in film adaptations by providing non-commercial subtitled versions available in video-sharing websites. Tronch's contribution explores the dialogue between professional and non-professional dubbing and subtitling ventures and examines the Spanish translation and dubbing practices, thus showing that the Web offers scholars new opportunities to read 'Shakespeare Up Close'.[86] The Web appears as a pathway both to macro and micro approaches to Shakespeare which do not make *Othello* any 'easier' but on the contrary add to the complexity of the issues raised by the play and its performance.

What these digital materials do with *Othello* recalls what the play had already undergone in Marcel Carné's 1945 *Les Enfants du paradis*, permeating the whole film with echoes beyond the actual inset performance. Lanier writes of an *Othello* that has been 'disassembled' and 'deterritorialized', becoming a 'network of themes and motifs ..., a Shakespearean body without organs'.[87] From the early silent films and the lantern slide sequences[88] to the new YouTube 'do-it-yourself' versions explored by Thompson, *Othello* seems to be a privileged field for distortion and exaggeration, and yet any little bit of these caricatures may plunge the viewers into abysms of questioning and scepticism. The popular online *Othello* rap both reveals and conceals the *Othello* trap. The processes of reduction and misrepresentation at work in the play are expressed in Iago's language of insult and slander, which reduces the story to an old black ram topping a white ewe. The treatment of the play on screen reveals that, beyond the diversity and hybridity of filmic objects and modes of mediatization of the *Othello* story, we collectively and individually become ensnared in this racial perspective. You can, like Roderigo, say 'Tush' to Iago's vision, but he seems to remain the master of the *Othello* game. Screen *Othello*s have to fight to allow viewers to hear the '*Othello* music' that tends to be drowned in Iago's noise and to affirm the power of poetry over the impact of insult.[89] We hope that this volume will contribute to shedding light on many interrelated aspects of the *Othello* films – at once narrative, aesthetic and ideological – so that Iago's ensnaring net starts to be torn or lifted.

Notes

1 S. M. Buhler, *Shakespeare in the Cinema: Ocular Proof* (Albany: State University of New York Press, 2002), 12.
2 F. Fanon, *Black Skin, White Masks*, trans. C. L. Markmann (London and Sydney: Pluto, 1986), 13.
3 L. Potter, *Othello* (Manchester: Manchester University Press, 2002), 1.
4 *Ibid.*, 1.
5 See R. Dyer, *Heavenly Bodies: Film Stars and Society* (London: BFI, Macmillan, 1987), 124.
6 See H. Quarshie, 'Second Thoughts About Othello', *International Shakespeare Association Occasional Papers* 7 (1999), 1–25.
7 See K. F. Hall, *Things of Darkness: Economies of Race and Gender in Early Modern England* (Ithaca and New York: Cornell University Press, 1995), 9.
8 See G. Taylor, *Buying Whiteness: Race, Culture, and Identity from Columbus to Hip-Hop* (New York: Palgrave, 2005), 6–58.
9 Hall, *Things of Darkness*, 9.
10 A. L. Little Jr, *Shakespeare Jungle Fever: National-Imperial Re-Visions of Race, Rape, and Sacrifice* (Stanford: Stanford University Press, 2000), 148.
11 C. Daileader, *Racism, Misogyny, and the Othello Myth: Inter-racial Couples from Shakespeare to Spike Lee* (Cambridge: Cambridge University Press, 2005), 6.
12 *Ibid.*, 7.
13 *Ibid.*, 8–9. Daileader argues that 'Othellophile narratives are less concerned with the praise or blame of their black male protagonists than with the sexual surveillance and punishment of the white women who love them. In other words, Othellophilia as a cultural construct is first and foremost *about women* – white women explicitly, as the "subjects" of representation; black women implicitly, as the abjected and/or marginalized subjects of the suppressed counter-narrative' (10).
14 See Buhler, *Shakespeare in the Cinema*, 13.
15 P. Aebischer, *Shakespeare's Violated Bodies: Stage and Screen Performance* (Cambridge: Cambridge University Press, 2004).
16 N. Taylor, 'National and Racial Stereotypes in Shakespeare Films', in R. Jackson (ed.), *The Cambridge Companion to Shakespeare on Film*, 2nd edition (Cambridge: Cambridge University Press, 2007), 275 [267–79].
17 S. O'Neill notes that in Shakespeare's time, the terminology of race was not 'invented' yet: 'Of the 16 uses of the word "race" in Shakespeare, none imply skin colour, nor is "race" ever used in reference to black characters like Othello or Aaron', *Shakespeare and YouTube. New Media Forms of the Bard* (London and New York: Bloomsbury, Arden, 2014), 128. For a more complete view on early modern race, see M. Hendricks, 'Visions of Colour: Spectacle, Spectators and the Performance of Race', in B. Hodgdon and W. B. Worthen (eds.), *A Companion to Shakespeare and Performance* (Malden: Blackwell, 2005), 511–26.

18 S. Massai, 'Subjection and Redemption in Pasolini's *Othello*', in S. Massai (ed.), *World-Wide Shakespeares: Local Appropriations in Film and Performance* (London and New York: Routledge, 2005), 95–103.

19 Many thanks to P. Holland for drawing our attention to this video.

20 The 'Sassy Gay Friend: Othello' video can be watched here: www.youtube.com/watch?v=LKttq6EUqbE (accessed 19 July 2014).

21 See D. Lanier's Lindberg 2010 lecture 'Post-racial Othello', added online in June 2012, www.youtube.com/watch?v=ScroEtGwmOQ (accessed 25 July 2014).

22 A term that interestingly derives from the Latin *denigrare*, stemming from *niger*, black.

23 See P. Chakravarti, 'Modernity, Postcoloniality and *Othello*: The Case of *Saptapadi*', in P. Aebischer, E. J. Esche and N. Wheale (eds.), *Remaking Shakespeare: Performance across Media, Genres and Cultures* (Basingstoke and New York: Palgrave Macmillan, 2003), 39 [39–55].

24 See Buhler, *Shakespeare in the Cinema*, 15.

25 J. Buchanan, *Shakespeare on Film* (Harlow: Pearson Longman, 2005), 67.

26 Aebischer, *Shakespeare's Violated Bodies*, 108.

27 Buhler, *Shakespeare in the Cinema*, 12. J. Buchanan writes that 'Shakespeare's depiction of Othello's Moorishness is intended to indicate a Muslim background. Indeed, sections of Othello's own life story as told to the Senate have parallels with that of a real Muslim-born North African of the period, Wazzan Al-Fasi', in her article 'Virgin and Ape, Venetian and Infidel: Labellings of Otherness in Oliver Parker's *Othello*', in M. T. Burnett and R. Wray (eds.), *Shakespeare, Film, Fin de Siècle* (Basingstoke: Macmillan, 2000), 180 [179–202].

28 K. S. Rothwell, *A History of Shakespeare on Screen: A Century of Film and Television*, 2nd edition (Cambridge: Cambridge University Press, 2004), 111. See also Aebischer, *Shakespeare's Violated Bodies*, 123–4.

29 See S. Hatchuel and N. Vienne-Guerrin, '"O monstrous": Claude Barma's French 1962 TV *Othello*', P. Dorval and N. Vienne-Guerrin (eds.), *Shakespeare on Screen in Francophonia*, Montpellier (France), Université Montpellier III, Institut de Recherche sur la Renaissance, l'Âge Classique et les Lumières (IRCL): 2014: www.shakscreen.org/analysis/barma_othello/.

30 See his interview in *Télérama* 627, 21–7 January 1962, 7; 17.

31 *Télérama*, 17. Our translation from the French "*Oui c'est vrai, avoue Sorano, je suis Othello*'.

32 *Télé 7 Jours*, 20–6 January 1962, 22.

33 M. T. Burnett, *Filming Shakespeare in the Global Marketplace* (Basingstoke and New York: Palgrave, 2007), 85.

34 J. R. Andreas, 'The Curse of Cush: Othello's Judaic Ancestry', in P. Kolin (ed.), *'Othello': New Critical Essays* (New York and London: Routledge, 2002), 177 [169–88].

35 Buchanan, 'Virgin and Ape', 183.

36 Burnett, *Filming Shakespeare in the Global Marketplace*, 78.

37 Buhler, *Shakespeare in the Cinema*, 29.

38 See L. S. Starks, 'The Veiled (Hot) Bed of Race and Desire: Parker's *Othello* and the Stereotype as Screen Fetish', *Post Script: Essays in Film and the Humanities* 17.1 (Fall 1997), 71–2 [64–78].

39 See R. H. Ball, *Shakespeare on Silent Film: A Strange Eventful History* (New York: Theatre Arts Books, 1968), 213; Buchanan, *Shakespeare on Film*, 55.

40 Aebischer, *Shakespeare's Violated Bodies*, 137.

41 See B. Hodgdon, 'Kiss Me Deadly; or, the Des/Demonized Spectacle', in V. M. Vaughan and K. Cartwright (eds.), *'Othello': New Perspectives* (Rutherford: Fairleigh Dickinson University Press, 1991), 222; 226 [214–55].

42 C. Rutter, 'Looking at Shakespeare's Women on Film', in R. Jackson (ed.), *The Cambridge Companion to Shakespeare on Film*, 2nd edition (Cambridge: Cambridge University Press, 2007), 258 [245–66].

43 See Aebischer, *Shakespeare's Violated Bodies*, 135.

44 Rothwell, *A History of Shakespeare on Screen*, 69.

45 A. Davies, *Filming Shakespeare's Plays: The Adaptations of Laurence Olivier, Orson Welles, Peter Brook and Akira Kurosawa* (Cambridge: Cambridge University Press, 1988), 101.

46 Rutter, 'Looking at Shakespeare's Women on Film', 258.

47 Rothwell, *A History of Shakespeare on Screen*, 226.

48 B. Hodgdon, 'Race-ing *Othello*, Re-engendering White-out, II', in R. Burt and L. E. Boose (eds.), *Shakespeare, the Movie, II: Popularizing the Plays on Film, TV, Video, and DVD* (London and New York: Routledge, 2003), 92 [89–104].

49 Lanier, 'Post-racial Othello'.

50 R. Burt, *Unspeakable Shaxxxspeares. Queer Theory and American Kiddie Culture* (Houndmills, Basingstoke and London: Macmillan 1998), 31.

51 Burnett, *Filming Shakespeare in the Global Marketplace*, 80.

52 Buchanan, 'Virgin and Ape', 191–2.

53 *Ibid.*, 186.

54 *Ibid.*, 192.

55 Buchanan, *Shakespeare on Film*, 67; 66.

56 Rutter, 'Looking at Shakespeare's Women on Film', 259.

57 Burnett, *Filming Shakespeare in the Global Marketplace*, 83.

58 Buhler, *Shakespeare in the Cinema*, 26.

59 Burnett, *Filming Shakespeare in the Global Marketplace*, 68; 85.

60 www.pbs.org/wgbh/masterpiece/othello/synopsis.html

61 Hodgdon, 'Race-ing *Othello*, Re-engendering White-out, II', 99.

62 *Ibid.*, 98–9.

63 See Buchanan, *Shakespeare on Film*, 110–11.

64 Rothwell, *A History of Shakespeare on Screen*, 260.

65 See Burnett, *Filming Shakespeare in the Global Marketplace*, 67; 70; 78.

66 Hodgdon, 'Race-ing *Othello*, Re-engendering White-out, II', 104.

67 Lanier, 'Post-racial Othello'.

68 *Ibid.*

69 See R. Burt, 'Slammin' Shakespeare in Acc(id)ents Yet Unknown: Liveness, Cinem(edi)a, and Racial Dis-Integration', *Shakespeare Quarterly*, 53.2 (2002), 201–26.

70 Potter, *Othello*, Chap. 1, 2, 3 (24–85).

71 M. Neill, 'The Look of Othello', *Shakespeare Survey*, 62 (2009), 104–22.

72 For example, in *Orson Welles, Shakespeare and Popular Culture* (New York: Columbia University Press, 1999), M. Anderegg mentions V. M. Vaughan's view that Welles 'minimized race as an issue' and P. Donaldson's view that Welles 'consistently underplays racial difference' (107–8), suggesting that the perception of race issues in the film is bound to be subjective.

73 D. M. Lanier, 'Murdering *Othello*', in D. Cartmell (ed.), *A Companion to Literature, Film, and Adaptation* (Malden and Oxford: Wiley-Blackwell, 2012), 198–215.

74 In May 2013, Mariangela Tempera organized an international conference in Ferrara entitled 'Shakespeare in tatters'.

75 Burt, 'Slammin' Shakespeare', 202.

76 See at www.mindconnex.com (accessed 25 July 2014) where 'Shakespeare in bits' is advertised as 'A new, exciting, multimedia approach to learning and teaching Shakespeare's plays – Shakespeare In Bits brings The Bard's most popular plays to life through magnificently animated re-enactment, full audio and unabridged text in one comprehensive package.' The online advertisement reads: 'Make studying Shakespeare easy and enjoyable with Shakespeare In Bits for your iPad, iPhone, Mac or PC.' For a presentation of the 'product', see: www.youtube.com/watch?v=_S5ul4xxWJw

77 M. T. Burnett, *Shakespeare and World Cinema* (Cambridge: Cambridge University Press, 2013), 233.

78 New habits such as systematically including the date of the uploading and the number of views.

79 We are echoing here A. Thompson's article, 'Unmooring the Moor, Researching and Teaching', *Shakespeare Quarterly*, 61.3 (Fall 2010), 337–56.

80 O'Neill, *Shakespeare and YouTube*, 139.

81 *Ibid.*, 158.

82 www.youtube.com/watch?v=UC-fodrvdmM (accessed 26 July 2014). Uploaded 24 July 2006; 570,192 views. The Reduced Shakespeare Company 'Othello Rap' has produced many offshoots and students' versions. A 'Lego Othello Rap' is accessible at: www.youtube.com/watch?v=P-2OTPwT22k (accessed 25 July 2014). Uploaded 17 April 2012; 192 views.

83 www.youtube.com/watch?v=Wy8Bxar-yHU (accessed 25 July 2014). Uploaded 23 March 2012; 47 views.

84 See for example: http://education-portal.com/academy/lesson/othello-racism-and-shakespeare.html#lesson

85 www.youtube.com/watch?v=qQP7J5jYrzE (accessed 25 July 2014). Uploaded 19 January 2011; 155 views. Quoted in O'Neill, *Shakespeare and YouTube*, 140 (with 93 views at the time).

86 We refer to R. McDonald, N. D. Nace and T. D. Williams (eds.), *Shakespeare Up Close. Reading Early Modern Texts* (London and New York: Bloomsbury, Arden, 2012).

87 D. M. Lanier, 'L'homme blanc et l'homme noir: *Othello* in *Les Enfants du paradis*', in N. Vienne-Guerrin and P. Dorval (eds.), *Shakespeare on Screen in Francophonia* (2010–), University Montpellier III, Institut de Recherche sur la Renaissance, l'Âge Classique et les Lumières (IRCL): 2013: http://shakscreen.org/analysis/analysis_homme_blanc (*last modified 25 March 2013*).

88 J. Buchanan, *Shakespeare on Silent Film. An Excellent Dumb Discourse* (Cambridge: Cambridge University Press, 2009).

89 See G. Wilson-Knight, *The Wheel of Fire* (Oxford: Oxford University Press, 1930), chap. 5 (109–35).

WORKS CITED

Aebischer, P., *Shakespeare's Violated Bodies: Stage and Screen Performance* (Cambridge: Cambridge University Press, 2004).

Anderegg, M., *Orson Welles, Shakespeare and Popular Culture* (New York: Columbia University Press, 1999).

Andreas, J. R., 'The Curse of Cush: Othello's Judaic Ancestry', in P. Kolin (ed.), *'Othello': New Critical Essays* (New York and London: Routledge, 2002), 169–88.

Ball, R. H., *Shakespeare on Silent Film: A Strange Eventful History* (New York: Theatre Arts Books, 1968).

Buchanan, J., 'Virgin and Ape, Venetian and Infidel: Labellings of Otherness in Oliver Parker's *Othello*', in M. T. Burnett and R. Wray (eds.), *Shakespeare, Film, Fin de Siècle* (Basingstoke: Macmillan, 2000), 179–202.

Shakespeare on Film (Harlow: Pearson Longman, 2005).

Shakespeare on Silent Film. An Excellent Dumb Discourse (Cambridge: Cambridge University Press, 2009).

Buhler, S. M., *Shakespeare in the Cinema: Ocular Proof* (Albany: State University of New York Press, 2002).

Burnett, M. T., *Filming Shakespeare in the Global Marketplace* (Basingstoke and New York: Palgrave, 2007).

Shakespeare and World Cinema (Cambridge: Cambridge University Press, 2013).

Burt, R., 'Slammin' Shakespeare in Acc(id)ents Yet Unknown: Liveness, Cinem(edi)a, and Racial Dis-Integration', *Shakespeare Quarterly*, 53.2 (2002), 201–26.

Unspeakable Shaxxxspeares. Queer Theory and American Kiddie Culture (Houndmills, Basingstoke and London: Macmillan, 1998)

Chakravarti, P., 'Modernity, Postcoloniality and *Othello*: The Case of *Saptapadi*', in P. Aebischer, E. J. Esche and N. Wheale (eds.), *Remaking Shakespeare: Performance across Media, Genres and Cultures* (Basingstoke and New York: Palgrave Macmillan, 2003), 39–55.

Daileader, C., *Racism, Misogyny, and the Othello Myth: Inter-racial Couples from Shakespeare to Spike Lee* (Cambridge: Cambridge University Press, 2005).

Davies, A., *Filming Shakespeare's Plays: The Adaptations of Laurence Olivier, Orson Welles, Peter Brook and Akira Kurosawa* (Cambridge: Cambridge University Press, 1988).

Dyer, R., *Heavenly Bodies: Film Stars and Society* (London: BFI, Macmillan, 1987).

Fanon, F., *Black Skin, White Masks*, trans. C. L. Markmann (London and Sydney: Pluto, 1986).

Hall, K. F., *Things of Darkness: Economies of Race and Gender in Early Modern England* (Ithaca and New York: Cornell University Press, 1995).

Hatchuel S. and N. Vienne-Guerrin, '"O monstrous": Claude Barma's French 1962 TV *Othello*', P. Dorval and N. Vienne-Guerrin (eds.), *Shakespeare on Screen in Francophonia*, Montpellier (France), Université Montpellier III, Institut de Recherche sur la Renaissance, l'Âge Classique et les Lumières (IRCL): 2014: www.shakscreen.org/analysis/barma_othello/.

Hendricks, M., 'Visions of Colour: Spectacle, Spectators and the Performance of Race', in B. Hodgdon and W. B. Worthen (eds.), *A Companion to Shakespeare and Performance* (Malden: Blackwell, 2005), 511–26.

Hodgdon, B., 'Kiss Me Deadly; or, the Des/Demonized Spectacle', in V. M. Vaughan and K. Cartwright (eds.), *'Othello': New Perspectives* (Rutherford: Fairleigh Dickinson University Press, 1991), 214–55.

'Race-ing *Othello*, Re-engendering White-out, II', in R. Burt and L. E. Boose (eds.), *Shakespeare, the Movie, II: Popularizing the Plays on Film, TV, Video, and DVD* (London and New York: Routledge, 2003), 89–104.

Lanier, D. M., 'L'homme blanc et l'homme noir: *Othello* in *Les Enfants du paradis*', in N. Vienne-Guerrin and P. Dorval (eds.), *Shakespeare on Screen in Francophonia* (2010–), University Montpellier III, Institut de Recherche sur la Renaissance, l'Âge Classique et les Lumières (IRCL): 2013: http://shakscreen.org/analysis/analysis_homme_blanc/ (*last modified 25 March 2013*).

'Murdering *Othello*', in D. Cartmell (ed.), *A Companion to Literature, Film, and Adaptation* (Malden and Oxford: Wiley-Blackwell, 2012), 198–215.

Lindberg 2010 lecture 'Post-racial Othello', added online in June 2012, www.youtube.com/watch?v=ScroEtGwmOQ (accessed 25 July 2014). 45 min.

Little, A. L., Jr, *Shakespeare Jungle Fever: National-Imperial Re-Visions of Race, Rape, and Sacrifice* (Stanford: Stanford University Press, 2000).

Massai, S., 'Subjection and Redemption in Pasolini's *Othello*', in S. Massai (ed.), *World-Wide Shakespeares: Local Appropriations in Film and Performance* (London and New York: Routledge, 2005), 95–103.

McDonald, R., N. D. Nace and T. D. Williams (eds.), *Shakespeare Up Close. Reading Early Modern Texts* (London and New York: Bloomsbury, Arden, 2012).

Neill, M., 'The Look of Othello', *Shakespeare Survey*, 62 (2009), 104–22.

O'Neill, S., *Shakespeare and YouTube. New Media Forms of the Bard* (London and New York: Bloomsbury, Arden, 2014).

Potter, L., *Othello* (Manchester: Manchester University Press, 2002).

Quarshie, H., 'Second Thoughts About Othello', *International Shakespeare Association Occasional Papers* 7 (1999), 1–25.

Rothwell, K. S., *A History of Shakespeare on Screen: A Century of Film and Television*, 2nd edition (Cambridge: Cambridge University Press, 2004).

Rutter, C., 'Looking at Shakespeare's Women on Film', in R. Jackson (ed.), *The Cambridge Companion to Shakespeare on Film*, 2nd edition (Cambridge: Cambridge University Press, 2007), 245–66.

Starks, L. S., 'The Veiled (Hot) Bed of Race and Desire: Parker's *Othello* and the Stereotype as Screen Fetish', *Post Script: Essays in Film and the Humanities* 17.1 (Fall 1997), 64–78.

Taylor, G., *Buying Whiteness: Race, Culture, and Identity from Columbus to Hip-Hop* (New York: Palgrave, 2005), 6–58.

Taylor, N., 'National and Racial Stereotypes in Shakespeare Films', in R. Jackson (ed.), *The Cambridge Companion to Shakespeare on Film*, 2nd edition (Cambridge: Cambridge University Press, 2007), 267–79.

Thompson, A., 'Unmooring the Moor, Researching and Teaching', *Shakespeare Quarterly*, 61.3 (Fall 2010), 337–56.

Wilson-Knight, G. *The Wheel of Fire* (Oxford: Oxford University Press, 1930).

CHAPTER 2

Othello *on screen*

Monsters, marvellous space and the power of the tale

Victoria Bladen

Othello (1602–3) explores the tragic power of storytelling. In addition to his military experience, Othello is a traveller, who wooed Desdemona with tales of exotic journeys to places where he encountered the monstrous and the marvellous: 'the cannibals that each other eat,/ The Anthropophagi, and men whose heads/ Do grow beneath their shoulders' (1.3.142–4). Roderigo, at Iago's instigation, denigrates Othello to Brabanzio by referring to him as 'an extravagant and wheeling stranger/ Of here and everywhere' (1.1.137–8).[1] The implication is that his decentredness and foreignness combine to render him inherently suspect. As John Gillies observes, Othello is a 'voyager', a figure traditionally tainted by associations with the margins, transgression and extravagance, in terms of exceeding boundaries.[2]

The peripheral places of the world, to the early modern mind, were spaces of marvel, vitality and perceived savagery, and the play taps into this rich imaginative vein. The edges of late medieval and early modern maps feature depictions of hybridity and monstrosity, of deviation and difference.[3] Even as maps progressed beyond the medieval T-O design, the habit of lining the edges with the monstrous races was common; these included the Cynocephali (the dog-headed people), the Blemmyae (headless, and with their faces in their chests, which Othello refers to), and the Sciapods, with a single large foot.[4] At the edges of maps, as the spaces of the known moved to the unknown, reality slipped into fantasy.[5]

Before the Senate, Othello conjures a tale of an exotic and colourful past, holding his audience spellbound with his narrative power. Yet as a black *other*, these are dangerous discourses to invoke, for Othello himself is a marvel from peripheral space, and thus potentially 'monstrous', both to himself and to those around him.[6] As Mark Thornton Burnett observes, Othello is 'both a presenter who locates "monstrosity" outside of himself and a self-consciously fashioned exhibit'.[7] Despite Othello's attempts to control the exotic tales he invokes, his otherness preconditions him, locating him within powerful narratives of difference. Constructions of the human in peripheral space were enmeshed in discourses based on fear of difference, and impulses to dominate. Tragically Othello, the master storyteller, is entrapped by multiple layers of narrative, not only Iago's but also the metanarratives of race and gender that create and define difference in the world of the play he inhabits, which reflect the early modern discourses the play is located within.

So how has film responded to this dimension of the play? This chapter explores how screen adaptations have dealt aesthetically and ideologically with the idea of monstrosity, examining aspects of race and gender, and considering some of the historical contexts that inform the play and which have provided inspiration for directors. I will focus on the adaptations of: Orson Welles (1952), Sergei Yutkevich (1955), Jonathan Miller for the BBC series (1981), Janet Suzman (1988), Oliver Parker (1995), Tim Blake Nelson ('O', 2001), Geoffrey Sax (2001) and Ivan Lipkies (*Huapango*, 2003).

Maps, marvels and monsters

As Ania Loomba observes, to the early modern English mind, 'lands in Southern Europe coalesce with those East or south of Europe to create a general category, "Southern", distinguished from a Northern Englishness'.[8] Venice was perceived as a gateway to the marvellous and exotic, through shipping and trade; the spatial dynamics of Venice and Cyprus, and between Europe and Asia/Africa, constitute significant dimensions of the playtext.[9] Othello's monstrous potential is enhanced as the play's setting shifts further east to Cyprus and he is cast back into his history, moving towards the site of outsiders, the space with which he is identified by others and ultimately himself.

Cartography and a sense of the spatial dynamics of *Othello* are evoked in various ways on screen. Parker's adaptation features portolan maps, with directional lines and detailed place names, together with tokens for ships. Likewise Miller's BBC production has maps, globes and navigational instruments, which evoke maritime exploration, trade and journeys to the unknown. Yutkevich's adaptation features a globe in an early scene of the film, which mesmerizes Desdemona, reiterating the play's emphasis on her fascination with Othello's traveller's tales. Suzman also evokes cartography through visual means, featuring a magnificent Renaissance-style, decorated map as a backdrop for the Senate scene.

These references are not only effective in evoking a sense of Venice, Cyprus and maritime journeys. Given the long correlation between maps and monsters, films that feature cartographic elements in their *mise-en-scène*, particularly those with an early modern aesthetic, also potentially evoke the marvellous east and latent monstrosity of space beyond the centre.

The early modern racial and spatial discourses that framed those from peripheral spaces as marvellous and monstrous, define Othello as an outsider on multiple levels. On screen, Othello's marvellous quality, his exotic difference, is often suggested through costume choices, with references to African or Middle Eastern dress, such as robes and kaftans in striking patterns, effectively conveying difference. Parker's Othello (Laurence Fishburne) wears an evocative pearl earring, which also embodies a sinister foreshadowing of Othello's reference in the final scene of the play to 'the base Indian' who 'threw a pearl away/ Richer than all his tribe' (5.2.356–7). In the Sax adaptation, John Othello (Eamonn Walker), although a contemporary London police officer, is given an exotic element when he wears a silken gown, which also becomes the damning evidence, replacing the handkerchief of the playtext, when Michael Cass (Richard Coyle) wears it.[10]

While Othello's marvelousness is fairly easily conveyed on screen, how have directors sought to convey ideas of monstrosity? In some adaptations, there are moments when peripheral or background elements of the *mise-en-scène* suggest ideas of the monstrous. In Welles's film, as Othello is reeling from Iago's (Micháel MacLiammóir) poison, he is positioned next to a strange sculptural figure with monstrous, even demonic, features (Figure 3).

Figure 3:   Othello and the lurking monster in Orson Welles's 1952 adaptation.
All rights reserved.

It echoes the monstrous Iago, with its lurking presence and evil grimace, or embodies the idea of jealousy as a monster in Othello's thoughts. Yet it also reminds us of the monstrous discourses that frame Othello.

The concept of monstrosity is bound up with notions of display and looking, as well as of warning. The link between 'monstrosity' and seeing is evident in the etymological link between 'monster' and 'demonstrate'.[11] Shakespeare would have been aware of the Latin *monstro*, to show or reveal, and *monstrum*, an unnatural thing or portent.[12] In *Othello*, looking engenders illusory monsters, and 'ocular proof' (3.3.365) ironically reiterates Othello's blindness to truth.[13] Directors' use of visual signs of monstrosity is thus fitting, emphasizing the link between monstrosity and the visual in *Othello*.

Monstrous elements are also evoked in several other productions by utilizing grotesque decoration, creating subtle evocations of monstrosity in the background. In early modern culture there are intriguing parallels between cartographic depictions of the monstrous races at the edges of the known world and the grotesque imagery of Renaissance border decoration.[14] Grotesque imagery commonly featured aspects of hybridity, fusions of the human with animal, aquatic, botanical and architectural elements.[15] The style became popular throughout Europe in all aspects of the visual arts, from Italian palazzo decoration to English page decoration (for example in the 1623 First Folio). The term 'grotesque' was sometimes used interchangeably with 'arabesque' and 'moresque' (or 'Moorish') for decorative patterns involving curving foliage patterns, derived from Islamic ornament.[16] While 'Moorish' primarily designated the grotesque style's affinity with Middle Eastern design patterns, its potential interchangeability with the grotesque also evidences a general linking of the east with otherness.

In Miller's BBC production, grotesque decoration features on the chair in the Senate room and the borders of the decorative door to the bedroom, while animal feet are on the chest in the map room. Moresque/arabesque decoration features on the wallpaper of the bedroom. Othello (Anthony Hopkins) is set against a decorative background recalling his eastern marvelousness, and potential monstrousness.

Similarly, Suzman's striking map features grotesque ornamentation, against which Othello (John Kani) is strategically positioned as he tells his tale of eastern monsters. Kani's head moves to *replace* that of the grotesque face in the strapwork above the cartouche (Figure 4), suggesting the interchangeability of the black man and hybrid decoration. Kani is visually *inserted* into the peripheral world of the marvellous and

Figure 4:   Othello becoming grotesque decoration in Janet Suzman's 1988 adaptation.

monstrous, and relocated imaginatively from Venice to the fantastical margins of the map he creates verbally, powerfully demonstrating Othello's inability to locate monstrosity outside of himself.

Othello's invocation of the monstrous races has other echoes throughout the play. Iago is obsessed with the interracial marriage of Desdemona and Othello, constructing it as an interspecies union that will produce hybrid monsters (1.1.112–15). Iago's statement that Othello and Desdemona are at 'the Sagittary' (1.1.159), possibly an inn named for the astrological sign of Sagittarius, recalls Iago's construction of Othello as a 'Barbary horse' (1.1.113) since Sagittarius was depicted as a centaur, a marvellous creature sometimes depicted at the edges of maps and decorated page borders. The centaur is also invoked by Iago in the crude description of Othello and Desdemona as 'making the beast with two backs' (1.1.118).[17] Desdemona is thus also associated with hybridity and monstrosity, through her association with Othello, a foreshadowing of Othello's ultimate perception of her as monstrous.

In Parker's film, the bedroom set design includes a humanoid candle-holder (a 'term' or 'herm') with animal feet, and a chest, also with animal feet.[18] Such imagery, in the peripheral spaces of screen compositions, invokes ideas about the construction of human identity in mental borderlands.[19] When Othello is placed next to the candelabra with his feet apart, the shot suggests a subtle affinity between the hybrid figure and the black man. The animal feet of the candelabra also function as a subtle foreshadowing of the final scene when Othello will look for Iago's cloven feet, a sign of the devil, but see nothing. 'I look down towards his feet, but that's a fable' (5.2.292): Iago's monstrosity is invisible.

Monstrosity and entrapment

Several *Othello* adaptations feature visual elements that evoke Othello's states of entrapment, his previous enslavement and his increasing psychological captivity to the narration of Iago. In Miller's BBC production caryatids feature on a chair in the bedroom, their aesthetic of entrapment providing an evocative background detail. A caryatid was originally a female figure in substitution for a column or pilaster in supporting an entablature; the term derived from a narrative about the women of Caryae, Laconia, enslaved by the Greeks as punishment for disloyalty. The male equivalent was an 'atlas', after the figure of Atlas, who Zeus condemned to supporting the heavens for eternity as punishment for his part in the revolt of the Titans.[20] Such hybrid figures became popular in early modern grotesque decoration, and these visual histories are relevant both to the conception of monstrosity in *Othello* and the aesthetic inheritance of contemporary filmmakers.

Sax creates a powerful *mise-en-scène* that resonates with the play's exploration of monstrosity when he situates a dinner, at which John Othello will unravel, in a grotto-styled room that features large atlas figures (Figure 5). Sax's atlas figures are seen behind John as he speaks bitterly of his ancestors' history as slaves. The shot suggests the connection between this labouring hybrid human-architectural decoration and the discourses of slavery and monstrosity, providing a visual analogue for the history John refers to, relevant to the race riots that are engulfing London, the context in which Sax sets his adaptation.

The grotesque aesthetic that Sax utilizes is resonant with the link between concepts of monstrosity and slavery. Marvels from the east were sources of fear as well as wonder, initiating impulses to dominate and exploit. Early modern slavery began in the late fifteenth century as

Figure 5: John Othello with an atlas figure in Geoffrey Sax's 2001 adaptation.

Columbus's idea for making the new world colony at Hispaniola economically viable.[21] The traditional location of monstrosity at the edges of the known world would have conditioned and framed the ability of early explorers and colonists to perceive indigenous populations as quasi-human and thus legitimate objects of captivity and exploitation.[22] Othello's account of his past includes reference to his time as a slave and his 'redemption' (1.3.137), his conversion to Christianity. Although Othello locates his slavery and Islamic religion in the past, Brabanzio's comment that if interracial marriage is countenanced then 'Bondslaves and pagans shall our statesmen be' (1.2.100) suggests that the stigma remains. Although in Venice Othello is a respected general, in the marvellous east he was held captive as a subhuman possession. The reference to slavery reiterates his connection with the 'monstrous', already invoked as a result of his skin colour. As John Friedman observes, the indigenous people of the New World 'replaced the races of the East in the European consciousness, assuming not only the name "Indians" but also the burden of many traditional attitudes toward "monstrous" men'.[23] Similarly, James Aubrey observes, dark skin was closely linked with early modern monster lore, thus the play's numerous references to monstrosity resonate with Othello's racial otherness.[24]

Welles utilizes a sculptural figure of an atlas in the background of a shot, which suggests notions of labour and confinement, and recalls Othello's past enslavement. It reflects on how Othello will increasingly be confined and trapped by the tales of Iago and the metanarratives that govern the construction of his identity. Welles also includes shots of black, turbaned figures behind bars, which suggest slaves subject to trade and enforced labour. It is only a passing visual suggestion yet constitutes an evocative reminder of Othello's past state and the trade in humans that is being carried on in Venice and elsewhere.

Welles features shots of ships in the harbour, which, like the images of maps, suggest the geographies of the play and also potentially recall Othello's previous state as human cargo. In Yutkevich's film, in addition to the early flashback shots of Othello (Sergey Bondarchuk) in a cage and rowing in a slave ship, later in the film, after Othello is suffering the effects of Iago's (Andrei Popov) slander, he returns to the hull of a ship, which recalls Othello's former slavery. This powerfully conflates his previous physical captivity with his now psychological entrapment.

In Parker's version, Othello's fit takes place in a torture chamber, which also features a rack, referencing his cry to Iago (Kenneth Branagh): '[t]hou hast set me on the rack' (3.3.340). Although he is not chained, he holds onto chains, thus linking his previous condition of slavery with his current subjection and mental torture.

There is a strong vein of filmic iconography across the *Othello* films that emphasizes bars, cages, nets and chains. These extend to patterns of lattice and shadow, imagery that constructs visual cages. Welles has a prominent hanging cage to contain the monstrous Iago, albeit after the damage is done. Parker also has a cage in the torture chamber. Welles and Yutkevich use the motif of fishing line racks or nets on the shore to suggest entrapment; the ship's rigging in Welles's evokes nets. As Sarah Hatchuel observes of Welles's imagery, 'metaphors of the net and the trap run through the whole film' and she highlights the connection with Iago's stated objective of using Desdemona's goodness to 'make the net/ That shall enmesh them all' (2.3.335–6).[25] Likewise James Stone identifies the 'relentless image pattern in the film: the coordinates of black and white determine a smothering grid, an inescapable prison, a fatal claustrophobia'.[26]

There are also a range of bars and grids on windows and doors across the various *Othello* films, visual motifs that resonate with concepts of enslavement and monstrosity. What is striking is that often in the construction of these visual cages, Iago too is enmeshed, another trapped monster bound by his irrational hatred. Director Blake Nelson uses gym equipment to create visual cages around Odin (Mekhi Phifer) and Hugo (Josh Hartnett) in *'O'*. The focus on visual entrapment signifies the ideological and emotional engulfment of both.

Parker's imagery of the chess board also conveys entrapment and the racial confrontations of the play, with Iago as the threatening knight between the black king and white queen. Just as Shakespeare explores the deceptive appearances of surfaces, Parker's imagery presents analogous contradictions, denoting the evil Iago as a 'white knight', traditionally a figure of heroic rescue.

Entrapment is likewise conveyed by Welles's presentation of subterranean labyrinthine spaces, with evocative shots of Desdemona amidst the enmeshing columns as victim, prey for the monster. The labyrinth was traditionally linked with monstrosity through the classical story of the Minotaur, kept by king Minos of Crete and fed with young men and women.[27] The Minotaur was a hybrid creature with the body of a man and the head of a bull, resulting from the union between a woman (Pasiphae, the wife of Minos) and a bull.[28] In Christian ideology and iconography, the labyrinth came to represent the perils of mortal life, with the monster read as a type of the Devil.[29] Welles's suggestion of Othello as the

Minotaur here layers him with additional associations of hybridity and monstrosity, adding to those of the centaur and the monstrous races.

Monstrosity is a shifting idea in the *Othello* playtext, encompassing, at different points, Othello, Iago and Desdemona.[30] The same characteristic is evident in the film adaptations. The labyrinth motif is also drawn on by Sax, through evocative images on the computer and a notepad, suggesting Iago as the monster of the labyrinth, or alternatively Daedalus, the designer of the labyrinth. We are thus invited to share in Ben Jago's (Christopher Eccleston) scheming. Blake Nelson's spiral staircase is another visual labyrinth while Lipkies in *Huapango* suggests Otilio as the monster at the heart of the labyrinth by having Julia (Lisset), at the tragic climax, climb the darkened stairs and approach Otilio in the bedroom as if she is entering the monster's lair.

The monstrous body

Just as costume choices convey Othello's marvelousness, they are equally effective in conveying monstrosity. Prominent rings around the neck and wrists may function as visual motifs of captivity; Suzman's Othello wears a prominent neck ring, which is exotic yet also suggestive of entrapment. Adaptations often depict a shift in Othello's clothing from garments connoting dignity and respect, to states of partial undress, such as unbuttoned shirts (which connote his mental unravelling) and bare chests. Othello's bare skin can connote vulnerability, sensuality and physicality, associating the character with the body (thus linking him potentially with animality, and passion over reason). This is often in stark contrast to Iago, who mostly remains buttoned up (Ian McKellen's Iago in Trevor Nunn's RSC production is the epitome of this idea; Miller's is an exception to this pattern – Iago [Bob Hoskins] appears unbuttoned and wild towards the end).

There can also be a potent racial dimension in shots when Othello has a partially or fully bare chest, which relates to the spatial-racial politics and geographical hierarchies at work in *Othello*. Western cartographical iconography, articulating the politics of geography, racialized degrees of bareness, associating personifications of particular geographical spaces with states of undress. Commonly in the frontispieces to early modern atlases, the figure of Europe is conveyed as superior in status by placement in the composition (often at the top or centre), body position (standing or throned) and clothing (full, regal clothing). Personifications of Africa and the New World are generally conveyed visually as subsidiary, usually only partially clothed and often seated or lying down; the personification of Asia is generally depicted as inferior to Europe but superior to Africa and America.[31] Even with the increase in knowledge about places and people beyond the Eurocentric 'centre', and with ethnographic representations replacing or supplementing depictions of the monstrous races, spatial and racial factors were central to constructing ideas of difference in early modern culture.[32]

Traces of this visual and ideological inheritance can come into play. In Sax's adaptation, one of the scenes contrasts Othello's bareness with Iago's clothed state, as he works his mental poison. Ben Jago's covered state corresponds with the opacity of his motives while Othello's bareness connotes his openness, his ability to be read and thus manipulated by Iago. The further racial dimension at work is apparent when such filmic imagery is placed in the context of the early modern iconographical tradition. Clothed Iago, as he looms over Othello, invokes and seems to embody something of the weight of white Eurocentric ideology that constructed Africa as inferior. Othello's internalization of racial narratives in the playtext contributes to his vulnerability and gullibility; John Othello's bareness here recalls such narratives.

Furthermore, just as the iconography of the early modern atlas frontispieces racialized body positions, those lower in the composition or near the ground connoting a lesser status and potential subservience, likewise racialized body positions can come into play in *Othello*.[33] The playtext itself enables this to some extent; the requirement for Othello to be having an epileptic fit at 4.1.41 necessitates him being either on the ground or at least seated. Proximity to the floor on screen, especially as Othello is brought psychologically low, can also function to convey an animality and lower status as his grandeur is reduced, which can resonate with the narratives of race and monstrosity that render Othello vulnerable (even where fair-skinned actors play Othello). In Miller's version, Othello looks particularly monstrous in the eyes and mouth in his reduced state on the floor. In *Huapango*, Otilio is injured in a bull-riding accident orchestrated by Santiago (Manuel Landeta) at the wedding, thus he spends most of the narrative in bed and then subsequently on the floor, emphasizing his debasement.

Directors can also suggest monstrosity through shot framing. Sax's opening shots, partial shots of Dessie Brabant (Keeley Hawes) and John Othello, visually segment and emblazon their bodies, making both visually monstrous. Later, Othello's predatory stare is menacing and monstrous, the focus on eyes resonating with the theme of sight in the playtext. Monsters can also be created visually with shadows, a technique utilized effectively by Welles, Sax and Lipkies.

In presenting filmic signs of the monstrous, the audience is invited to share Othello's gaze. We are thus drawn into the travellers' narratives that Othello himself invokes, the discourses that framed those from the 'margins' as *other*ed, marvellous and monstrous, and we are infected with Iago's poison. As such, we need to consider the filmic aspects of the third 'monster' in the play, Desdemona. Arguably more potent than the narratives of race and the lies of Iago, albeit intersecting with both, is the demon that entraps Des*demon*a – gender construction.

The gender narrative

As Bruce Boehrer observes, Shakespeare's *Othello* evidences a 'preoccupation with narrativity'.[34] Likewise Stephen Greenblatt refers to the play's 'ceaseless narrative invention'.[35] While the narratives of monstrosity and race powerfully undermine Othello's sense of self-identity, Desdemona and most of the other characters are able to transcend these negative constructions. He is 'Valiant Othello' (1.3.48), 'brave Othello' (2.1.39) and held in high regard before the tragedy unfolds. Desdemona risks the wrath of her father to marry Othello; his otherness is no obstacle to her love. However the narratives surrounding women, the negative constructions of gender which Iago effectively draws from, are arguably more potent than those of monstrosity and race. While Othello only half believes in the monsters of his traveller's tales, he is extremely quick to believe in monstrous women. His willing mind is readily able to fill the gaps of the ocular proof to complete the picture of his wife's infidelity. As Karen Newman argues, 'femininity is not opposed to blackness and monstrosity, as white is to black, but identified with the monstrous'.[36]

Othello's reference to marvellous/monstrous space in Act 1 scene 3 resonates equally with gender discourses in the playtext and its historical contexts. Othello's entrapment within the framing of the exotic involves the fraught binary of the marvellous and monstrous, and the potential for degradation as a result of elevation. As Janet Adelman observes, 'the idealization and the debasement are of course two sides of the same coin, and they are equally damaging to Othello'.[37] Likewise early modern women were commonly represented within an analogous matrix of marvellous purity and monstrous sexual infidelity. The expectation that women would be chaste, obedient and silent meant that any deviation from perfection was potentially classified as whoredom. The elevation of Desdemona paradoxically makes her vulnerable to debasement.

On screen this is played out in various ways. References to the Virgin Mary or saints are suggestive of the way in which women could be trapped within the virgin/whore binary. In Welles's film, a shot of Desdemona seems to mirror the Virgin Mary statue utilized in a shot of Othello and Iago. In Sax's adaptation, John and Dessie's apartment has framed Renaissance-style pictures of angels on the walls. In *Huapango*, Santiago has a shrine to his beloved Julia, and Otilio, after he kills her, fashions her corpse as a saint's; these aesthetics emphasize the deadly potential of masculine idealizing tendencies in constructing women, both in early modern culture and the *macho* Latino society that the film presents.

In '*O*', the spiral staircase plays a central role in the *mise-en-scène*; it embodies the marvellous/monstrous paradigm relevant to constructions of both race and femininity. Blake Nelson's metaphorical use of the spiral staircase echoes Welles's earlier use of the idea in utilizing Giovanni Condi's spiral staircase at the Palazzo Contarini dal Bovolo (1497–9). In '*O*', the vertical space is also emphasized through the film's soundtrack. Opera music (from Verdi's *Otello*, specifically Desdemona's theme song) features in the opening scene of the doves at the top of the stairwell. The opera music, ostensibly 'high' culture, reflects Desi Brable's (Julia Stiles) exalted social status at the high school, and contrasts with the later use of rap, the music of the streets, associated with Odin and blackness.

The stairwell suggests the heaven/hell polarity of Christian ideology and iconography and reflects the ideological paradigms that Othello, Desdemona and Iago are caught in. Hugo, the Iago figure, likes to hang at the top of the stairwell, near the doves and the hawk, symbolizing his aspirations and his predatory impulses.[38] He wants to fly high, to gain his father's attention, and in his twisted logic, in order to fly, he must destroy O, taking Desi with him.

Odin enjoys a high social status as the talented basketball star and favourite of the coach, Hugo's father (Martin Sheen). O, as a black marvel, is initially elevated and thus susceptible to a monstrous fall. Likewise Desi is socially constructed as universally desirable and this elevation renders her equally vulnerable. The fact that O believes he owns the ultimate prize, makes the possession fraught and fragile. As the evocative stairwell conveys, the marvellous is inherently related to the monstrous; they are twin aspects of deviation from an imagined norm. Paradoxically, ascension, being exulted above others, as a form of othering, creates a vulnerability to descent.

As feminist critics such as Dympna Callaghan, Karen Newman and others have recognized, there are strong correlations between constructions of race and gender.[39] Othello in the playtext has been a slave, owned property; in the same way, early modern women were imagined as a type of property and part of the monstrosity of infidelity for men was the loss of control over this 'property'. On screen, just as there is recurrent imagery that conveys the entrapment of Othello, directors have found various ways of visualizing the entrapment of Desdemona within the gender discourses that Othello imbibes and viciously perpetuates. In Welles, the structure of the bedroom window visualizes entrapment in gender roles. Even when Desdemona moves out from behind it, the spikes are aimed menacingly at her and Emilia (Fay Compton), making it appear as if they are in a dungeon, rather than a domestic space.

In *Huapango*, the entrapment of women within the sexist culture is emphasized with shots of Santiago's sister doing his ironing and the chauvinist treatment of Belen (Alicia Sandoval), Otilio's assistant, who is dismissed to the kitchen when she expresses concern over the gun. There is also an evocative, foreshadowing shot of Julia behind the bars of the bedroom window.

Many of the beds in *Othello* adaptations have wrought iron bedheads, enabling the visual language of entrapment to include the central site of the bed as the space of sex and death. They often create grids and visual cages that convey Desdemona's entrapment. The larger narratives of female inconstancy, which feed the need for domestic confinement and constraint of the female body, underpin this imagery. Othello, likewise, is often trapped visually within these frames, suggesting the way he is entrapped emotionally and psychologically *because* he perceives Desdemona as a possession.[40] Even in the tragic aftermath, Othello continues to conceive of her as a beautiful possession, a pearl he threw away (5.2.356), rather than an independent subject with her own right to live.

Onscreen imagery of nets echoes that of cages; examples include Desdemona's hairnet in Welles's film and the net below the basketball hoop of 'O', which evokes the shape of O's name, and the sexual 'ring' of Desi, entrapped by misogynist construction. Also in 'O', the image of a tree through fencing evokes the willow, the tree linked with Desdemona and mourning in the playtext (4.3.25–54), and thus feminine entrapment.

The cage motif is highly significant as one that connects ideas about confining monsters, resonating with both racial and gender discourses, articulating sexual anxieties (women framed by proprietary values, motivating entrapment) and racial anxieties (the suspicion of outsiders, of figures from the periphery). While Desdemona, in marrying Othello against convention, is able to transcend and challenge negative constructions of race, Othello is unable to transcend the stronger discourses of gender construction. The monstrous female proves more powerful as a tale than that of the monstrous black man. Othello is unable to perceive Desdemona outside of the discourses of possession and the reductive polarity of virgin/whore.

When Desdemona speaks openly to the Senate of her love and desire to be with Othello (1.3.179–88, 247–58), her assertiveness and frankness are characteristics for Othello to admire. Yet these attributes weigh against her later. Her so-called deception of her father is evidence of her likelihood of deceiving Othello; Brabanzio warns: 'she has deceived her father, and may thee' (1.3.292). Later, Iago reminds Othello of this: 'She did deceive her father, marrying you' (3.3.210), to which Othello agrees. Desdemona is thus trapped; in being loyal to her husband over her father, she betrays the patriarch. Thus when Othello becomes her new patriarch, she is unwittingly cast as someone likely to do the same again. Her behaviour is classified in terms of roles (challenging the patriarch), rather than individual relationships (supporting Othello). Othello's construction of female perfection includes sexual loyalty and to transgress that renders the woman monstrous. In response to Iago's poisonous vision of Desdemona's infidelity, Othello cries: 'O, monstrous, monstrous!' (3.3.431).

Othello believes he must kill monsters: unfaithful women, Turkish dogs, outsiders, himself. In Othello's last tale, he recalls that in Aleppo, 'a malignant and a turbaned Turk/ Beat a Venetian and traduced the state', in response to which he 'took by th' throat the circumcisèd dog/ And smote him thus' (5.2.362–5). In expressing hostility towards an external enemy, Othello conflates this enemy from the past with himself in the present; he becomes both aggressor and victim. Othello's tragic and flawed perception is partly due to his desire to belong to European society (and adhere to its hierarchical and generally misogynist discourses) and partly because he himself has been framed as monstrous, a former slave and non-Christian who has had to convert and prove himself a killer of outsiders, as a military hero, in order to seek acceptance.

In Miller's BBC production, there is an intriguing reference to the iconography of the penitent Magdalene in the scene of Desdemona (Penelope Wilton) before her death, which echoes Georges de La Tour's *Penitent Magdalene* (c. 1638–43). Desdemona is given the role of the Magdalene, the former prostitute, which is not applicable to Desdemona, yet suggests Othello's mental framing of his wife as promiscuous and his desire for her to confess and repent before he kills her: 'confess thee freely of thy sin' (5.2.58). Thus in Miller's version, Desdemona's final trapping before her death is via our gaze of her as a repentant whore, a misrepresentation of Desdemona's identity yet one that paradoxically embodies the saint/whore feminine paradigm that causes her death.

Othello is a site where race and gender discourses collide, both invoking ideas of deviation and monstrosity. The black outsider was perceived as deviating in terms of his appearance and also his spatial origin; he was a figure from the periphery of a mental landscape comprised of 'centres' and 'margins'. Acceptability depended on proximity to the centre. A woman was also a figure of difference, exiled from the centres of social and political power, who, from a patriarchal perspective, was potentially monstrous, needing to be controlled, possessed and dominated by fathers and husbands. Iago's crime is effective because of his ability to draw from the power of cultural metanarratives of race and gender.

Othello, by telling tales of the marvellous, unwittingly reminds us of his categorization *within* the marvellous. He is not outside the tale but always potentially within it; he himself is from the margins. He calls for 'ocular proof' (3.3.365) but mistakenly believes that what he perceives visually will be authentic and constitute an objective truth. Othello fails to understand the way that discourses shape reality, and words frame what we see, thus he is trapped by surface appearances, the illusory superficial layer to which he brings his gendered prejudices. In *Othello* the slander itself does not cause the tragedy. The tragedy results ultimately from beliefs that constructed unfaithful women as monstrous and the discourses that monsters needed to be caged, enslaved and, if unable to be controlled, killed. Race and gender in *Othello* are both subject to discourses of othering, to which Othello's invocation of marvellous/monstrous space is highly relevant.

Othello's description of Desdemona that she 'was false as water' (5.2.143) is a resonant one in the playtext and screen versions. The illusory, changeable and reflecting qualities of water, bound up with the idea of Venice, prove an apt metaphor for Othello's flawed gaze and the general perception of women as untrustworthy. Othello becomes trapped by illusions; he has internalized racial discourses that distinguish humans on the basis of surface appearances. He is susceptible to superficial narratives because he himself has been subject to them. In adopting these values, he is prepared to act on what he thinks he sees. Many films use water imagery. In Parker's, the evocative shot of Iago dropping the chess figures in the well, like voodoo dolls for his victims, anticipates the subsequent sea burial of Othello's and Desdemona's bodies. Water imagery reminds us of the illusory nature of the tales in *Othello* – tales of monsters that don't exist.

Perhaps even Iago is not a monster, merely another human being trapped by narratives that he has internalized. In Sax's film, the reflecting water evokes Venice in London and creates an illusory mirror in which John's haunting fantasies appear. The shot is apt for the layers of narratives that John is drowning in. Similarly Parker's montage of 'the tragic loading' (5.2.373) of the bed with the sea suffuses the image with the play's aquatic metaphor of falsity. Ultimately what are 'as false as water' are the prejudicial narratives surrounding race and gender that humans construct to entrap themselves.

Notes

1 T. Porter-Tsomondo, 'Stage-Managing "Otherness": The Function of Narrative in *Othello*', *Mosaic* 32.2 (1999), 4 [1–25].

2 J. Gillies, *Shakespeare and the Geography of Difference* (Cambridge: Cambridge University Press, 1994), 3, 19–20.

3 On the monstrous races generally, see J. B. Friedman, *The Monstrous Races in Medieval Art and Thought* (Syracuse, NY: Syracuse University Press, 2000). For examples, see the Psalter map (c. 1265, London) and the Hereford *mappa mundi* (c. 1300).

4 For example the Ptolemaic map in Hartmann Schedel's *Liber chronicarum* (Nuremberg, 1493) includes the monstrous races. Image: www.henry-davis. com/MAPS/LMwebpages/260.html.

5 There were strong correlations between depictions in cartography and travel literature. Accounts of the monstrous races originated in antiquity and the stories remained popular in medieval encyclopaedias and travellers' tales, such as *The Travels of Sir John Mandeville* (fourteenth century). Shakespeare's reference in *Othello* may be derived from an edition of Ptolomy's *Geography* (Basel, 1540). J. Milton French, 'Othello among the Anthropophagi', *PMLA* 49.3 (1934), 807.

6 On the interrelationship between geography and difference, see generally Gillies.

7 M. T. Burnett, *Constructing 'Monsters' in Shakespearean Drama and Early Modern Culture* (New York: Palgrave Macmillan, 2002), 101. E. C. Jacobs, and K. R. Jacobs, '"'Tis Monstrous": Dramaturgy and Irony in *Othello*', *The Upstart Crow* 9 (1989), 52–62.

8 A. Loomba, *Shakespeare, Race, and Colonialism* (Oxford: Oxford University Press, 2002), 94.

9 G. Holderness, *Shakespeare and Venice* (Farnham, UK; Burlington, VT: Ashgate, 2010).

10 A notable exception to Othello's usual exoticism in adaptations is Lipkies's *Huapango* where Otilio (Alejandro Tommasi) has no particular marvelousness about him; his difference lies only in his red-haired whiteness in contrast with the Mexican/Latino features of those around him.

11 Burnett, *Monsters*, 108. K. Newman, '"And Wash the Ethiop White": Femininity and the Monstrous in *Othello*', in J. E. Howard and M. F. O'Connor (eds.), *Shakespeare Reproduced: The Text in History and Ideology* (New York and London: Methuen, 1987), 153.

12 *The Pocket Oxford Latin Dictionary* (Oxford: Oxford University Press, 1994), art. 'monstro' and 'monstrum'. Also see Jacobs and Jacobs, '"'Tis Monstrous"', 54.

13 Burnett, *Monsters*, chapter four, particularly 112–13.

14 See the border decoration of *Les Grandes Chroniques de France*, (Burgundy, mid-fifteenth century), reproduced in T. Voronova and A. Sterligov, *Western European Illuminated Manuscripts 8th to 16th Centuries* (London: Greenwich Editions, 2003), 121.

15 The term 'grotesque' (from 'grotto', cave) was coined in the fifteenth century to describe the style of ancient Roman decoration rediscovered upon the uncovering of Nero's Domus Aurea (built AD 64–68). For a comprehensive history of the grotesque, see A. Zamperini, *Ornament and the Grotesque: Fantastical Decoration from Antiquity to Art Nouveau* (New York: Thames and Hudson, 2008).

16 The term 'moresque' is first recorded in 1611 by Randle Cotgrave, in *A Dictionarie of the French and English Tongues*, to describe: 'a rude or anticke painting, or carving, wherein the feet and tayles of beasts, &c, are intermingled with, or made to resemble, a kind of wild leaves, &c.' *Oxford English Dictionary*, 2nd edition, Online version, art. 'moresque', B.

17 Burnett, *Monsters*, 98–9, 105.

18 Figures of classical origin relevant to early modern grotesque style included 'herms', stone pillars surmounted by busts of the god Hermes, functioning originally as boundary markers (M. C. Howatson, *The Oxford Companion to Classical Literature*, 2nd edition [Oxford: Oxford University Press, 1997], 273; Zamperini, *Ornament and the Grotesque*, 289), and 'terms', humanoid or zoomorphic busts, armless, surmounting square pillars, related to the god Terminus: *OED*, art. 'term', V, 15; Howatson, *Oxford Companion*, 553.

19 On links between *Othello*'s theme of vision and the grotesque see generally Patricia Dorval, 'Shakespeare on Screen: Threshold Aesthetics in Oliver Parker's *Othello*', *Early Modern Literary Studies* 6.1 (2000), 1–15.

20 Howatson, *Oxford Companion*, 76.

21 F. Bellec, *Unknown Lands: The Log Books of the Great Explorers* (Melbourne, Australia: Hardie Grant Books, 2002), 62, 110, 112; Newman, "And Wash the Ethiop White", 148.

22 The correlation between peripheral monstrosity and racial exploitation is apparent in a page from a Franco-Portuguese atlas (c. 1583, The Hague, Koninklijke Bibliotheek) where the grotesque border decoration suggests marvellous wonders to be found elsewhere, while also ominously resonating with the depiction of slave labour on the African continent; the image is reproduced in Bellec, inside and back cover.

23 Friedman, *Monstrous Races*, 4.

24 J. R. Aubrey, 'Race and the Spectacle of the Monstrous in *Othello*', *Clio* 22.3 (1993), 222 [221–38]; Newman, "And Wash the Ethiop White", 149.
25 S. Hatchuel, *Shakespeare from Stage to Screen* (Cambridge: Cambridge University Press, 2004), 21.
26 J. W. Stone, 'Black and White as Technique in Orson Welles's *Othello*', *Literature/Film Quarterly* 30.3 (2002), 189.
27 Howatson, *Oxford Companion*, 312.
28 *Ibid.*, 367.
29 See C. Wright, *The Maze and the Warrior: Symbols in Architecture, Theology and Music* (Cambridge, MA and London: Harvard University Press, 2001).
30 References to monstrosity: 1.3.386, 2.1.13, 2.3.200, 3.3.111–2, 3.3.170, 3.4.156–7, 3.4.158, 3.3.382, 3.3.431, 4.1.59, 4.1.60–1, 5.2.196.
31 Examples include: the frontispiece to an atlas by Abraham Ortelius, *Theatrum Orbis Terrarum* (1570) (http://kunstpedia.com/articles/the-decorative-cartographic-title-page-part-one.html); the 1606 title page engraved by Jodocus Hondius for the edition of Gerard Mercator's atlas reproduced in R. Shirley, *Courtiers and Cannibals, Angels and Amazons: The Art of the Decorative Cartographic Titlepage* (Houten, The Netherlands: Hes & De Graaf Publishers, 2009), 91; and the title page to *Civitates Orbis Terrarum*, vol. v (1596–7) by George Braun and Frans Hogenberg (Shirley, 57).
32 Also see Gillies, *Geography*, chapter three and 98.
33 See Abraham Ortelius's *Theatrum Orbis Terrarum* (1570), where Europe is placed at the top of the continental hierarchy, with the others below and the new continent America on the ground.
34 B. Boehrer, 'Othello's Monsters: Kenneth Burke, Deleuze and Guattari, and the Impulse to Narrative in Shakespeare', *Journal X* 3.2 (1999), 120 [119–38].
35 S. Greenblatt, *Renaissance Self-Fashioning: From More to Shakespeare* (Chicago: University of Chicago Press, 1980), 235.
36 Newman, "And Wash the Ethiop White", 145, 156. Burnett, *Monsters*, 117.
37 J. Adelman, 'Iago's Alter Ego: Race as Projection in *Othello*', *Shakespeare Quarterly* 48.2 (1997), 129.
38 S. Criniti, 'Othello: A Hawk among Birds', *Literature/Film Quarterly* 32.2 (2004), 115–21.
39 D. Callaghan, *Shakespeare without Women: Representing Gender and Race on the Renaissance Stage* (London and New York: Routledge, 2000).
40 Newman, "And Wash the Ethiop White", 150.

WORKS CITED

Adelman, J., 'Iago's Alter Ego: Race as Projection in *Othello*', *Shakespeare Quarterly* 48.2 (1997), 125–44.
Aubrey, J. R., 'Race and the Spectacle of the Monstrous in *Othello*', *Clio* 22.3 (1993), 221–38.
Bellec, F., *Unknown Lands: The Log Books of the Great Explorers* (Melbourne, Australia: Hardie Grant Books, 2002).

Boehrer, B., 'Othello's Monsters: Kenneth Burke, Deleuze and Guattari, and the Impulse to Narrative in Shakespeare', *Journal X* 3.2 (1999), 119–38.

Burnett, M. T., *Constructing 'Monsters' in Shakespearean Drama and Early Modern Culture* (New York: Palgrave Macmillan, 2002).

Callaghan, D., *Shakespeare without Women: Representing Gender and Race on the Renaissance Stage* (London and New York: Routledge, 2000).

Criniti, S., 'Othello: A Hawk among Birds', *Literature/Film Quarterly* 32.2 (2004), 115–21.

Dorval, P., 'Shakespeare on Screen: Threshold Aesthetics in Oliver Parker's *Othello*', *Early Modern Literary Studies* 6.1 (2000), 1–15.

Friedman, J. B., *The Monstrous Races in Medieval Art and Thought* (Syracuse, NY: Syracuse University Press, 2000).

Gillies, J., *Shakespeare and the Geography of Difference* (Cambridge: Cambridge University Press, 1994).

Greenblatt, S., *Renaissance Self-Fashioning: From More to Shakespeare* (Chicago: University of Chicago Press, 1980).

Hatchuel, S., *Shakespeare from Stage to Screen* (Cambridge: Cambridge University Press, 2004).

Holderness, G., *Shakespeare and Venice* (Farnham, UK; Burlington, VT: Ashgate, 2010).

Howatson, M. C., *The Oxford Companion to Classical Literature*, 2nd edition (Oxford: Oxford University Press, 1997).

Jacobs, E. C. and K. R. Jacobs, '"Tis Monstrous": Dramaturgy and Irony in *Othello*', *The Upstart Crow* 9 (1989), 52–62.

Loomba, A., *Shakespeare, Race, and Colonialism* (Oxford: Oxford University Press, 2002).

Milton French, J., 'Othello among the Anthropophagi', *PMLA* 49.3 (1934), 807–9.

Newman K., '"And Wash the Ethiop White": Femininity and the Monstrous in *Othello*', in J. E. Howard and M. F. O'Connor (eds.), *Shakespeare Reproduced: The Text in History and Ideology* (New York and London: Methuen, 1987), 143–62.

Porter-Tsomondo, T., 'Stage-Managing "Otherness": The Function of Narrative in *Othello*', *Mosaic* 32.2 (1999), 1–25.

Shirley, R., *Courtiers and Cannibals, Angels and Amazons: The Art of the Decorative Cartographic Titlepage* (Houten, The Netherlands: Hes & De Graaf Publishers, 2009).

Stone, J. W., 'Black and White as Technique in Orson Welles's *Othello*', *Literature/Film Quarterly* 30.3 (2002), 189–93.

Voronova, T. and A. Sterligov, *Western European Illuminated Manuscripts 8th to 16th Centuries* (London: Greenwich Editions, 2003).

Wright, C., *The Maze and the Warrior: Symbols in Architecture, Theology and Music* (Cambridge, MA and London: Harvard University Press, 2001).

Zamperini, A., *Ornament and the Grotesque: Fantastical Decoration from Antiquity to Art Nouveau* (New York: Thames and Hudson, 2008).

CHAPTER 3

Rethinking blackness
The case of Olivier's Othello

Peter Holland

No one turns to a movie's taglines for a judicious evaluation of the film. Their purpose is marketing and hype. But the one currently used to sell the DVD of Stuart Burge's *Othello* (1965) is particularly striking (see Figure 6) – indeed, the point of my chapter is, quite simply, that it is also troubling and one that demands we engage with it: 'The greatest Othello ever by the greatest actor of our time.' Part of what is troubling is that the second half is, for many of us, quite simply true. We can argue for hours about the relative merits of Gielgud versus Olivier but I don't need to in this chapter. We can argue about whether the semantic field for *actor* means the word is here implicitly constricted to parameters defined as *stage* actor as part of a cultural hierarchy that still cannot see the movies as adequately valid as an art form and can still only see the theatre as the space in which the highest aesthetic value is attached to the actor's work. But I won't do that either.

The current DVD cover is dominated by two words in the same typeface and capitals, occupying the same width of image: 'OLIVIER OTHELLO'. This is more than the actor's name above the title, that argument over the billing that still, for me, is bound up with the joke in *Shakespeare in Love* about Marlowe's death: 'A quarrel about the bill'; 'The bill! Oh, vanity, vanity!' 'Not the billing, the bill!'[1] There is, instead, an offering of equivalence in which the very minuteness of 'Laurence', placed inside the 'O' of 'Olivier' and the equally tiny 'AS' perched between the two lines cumulatively suggest less that it is Olivier *as* Othello than, in the time-honoured phrase, that Olivier *is* Othello; equivalence is all. The actor's supreme achievement is to be the character.

Well, perhaps, but this is also a performance that angered some at the time of its release and more now. At the Prague World Shakespeare Congress in 2011, Djanet Sears showed a montage of clips of Olivier from the film, mashing it up with a new soundtrack of Al Jolson, in *The Jazz Singer* (1927, remade in 1980 with Olivier as the Jolson character's father),

Figure 6:   Cover of the 2007 DVD edition of Stuart Burge's 1965 *Othello*.

the epitome of the blacked-up white man as entertainer. Funny, yes. Fair? That's the question, a question that will become frequently reformulated in this chapter.

Olivier's is a performance that no longer seems to attract critical interest outside of work on *Othello*'s stage history and not much even then. Studies of Shakespeare on film simply ignore it or have forgotten about it. Its moment seems to have passed and 'the greatest Othello ever' is apparently of no interest to those of us working in Shakespeare film studies and barely even to those working on the history of *Othello* in performance. Something is wrong in that, something that suggests a revisiting is required.

Let me clarify three matters to start with. Firstly, I saw Olivier's Othello on stage – twice: it opened on 23 April 1964 at the National Theatre (then playing at the Old Vic), directed by John Dexter, to mark Shakespeare's 400th birthday. I was a young teenager of 13. It was astonishing and I have never quite recovered.

Secondly, common consent has it that the film is, *qua* film, something of a disaster. It was filmed in three or four weeks by the simple expedient of William Kellner rethinking Jocelyn Herbert's sets for the National Theatre production into sets that would fit a sound stage, and there was no time to do any substantial rethinking of the performances to move them from stage to screen. Though the DVD's description of it as 'An actual performance of the National Theatre' is wrong, it is not too far from the truth. Limited in ways that, in others' control, might be an aesthetic of constriction, the film just seems tame in its parameters. There are, for instance, no exterior shots, no effects, no non-diegetic sound, no under-scoring, no music at all. Long speeches were filmed on three cameras simultaneously and edited from the three shots so that the performance did not need to be interrupted.[2] It was emphatically a record of a stage performance, even if not an 'actual' one, and there are really remarkably few moments at which the camera work or editing or anything else distinctly connected with film technique is even adequate, let alone remarkable. Compare it to Welles's *Othello* and the gulf is painfully immense. Olivier regretted later that more was not done: 'somehow I was lacking in confidence and full vitality; perhaps, subconsciously, I was being gnawed by the question: "Why aren't we making a full-blown Shakespeare film of this?" Certainly I regret that now.'[3]

Thirdly, Olivier's performance was not of course the last occasion on which a white actor blacked up to play the role but the notion was already profoundly in question. I would argue, however, it was the last time on which a white actor playing the role was accorded significant accolades (including, incidentally, and usually forgotten, an Academy Award nom-ination for Olivier – he lost out to Lee Marvin in *Cat Ballou* – and there were nominations for all three other leading actors: Maggie Smith for Desdemona and Joyce Redman for Emilia, both as Best Supporting Actresses, and Frank Finlay as Best Supporting Actor for his Iago). There were significant blacked-up performances over the next two decades – Donald Sinden for Ronald Eyre (RSC, 1979), Paul Scofield for Peter Hall (National Theatre, 1980), Anthony Hopkins for the BBC TV Shakespeare (1981) in a performance that Hopkins might rather forget – but nothing that remotely attracted the praise that Olivier's performance did. And let me emphasize now that, while the reviewers' chorus was by no means unanimous and the objections were interesting and ones I shall pursue, the bulk of response was marked by something close to ecstatic awe.

I carefully referred to the film in my opening phrases as 'Stuart Burge's *Othello*'. Burge was primarily a television director at this time and was, I suspect, chosen because he had filmed the Chichester *Uncle Vanya* with Redgrave and with Olivier as Astrov, shown on television in November 1963. As Burge put it, he was 'the only person around . . . who knew about quick TV . . . Olivier was in a hurry, and I was probably the only person who could have done it, as he wanted, in three weeks'.[4] An honourable worker, Burge's experience of transferring stage to television screen was significant, but putting Chekhov on television and Shakespeare on the cinema screen are wildly different tasks and something fundamental will emerge implicitly here about scale and measure and control. His only Shakespeare experience prior to this was a 1959 television *Julius Caesar* with Eric Porter as Brutus. Whatever might be explored here about a TV/cinema gap, Burge's *Othello* is no better on TV than on cinema screen, and no worse either.

And nor is Olivier's Othello. Yet what seems to me to need considering, not least because film studies conspicuously tend to underplay investigation of film acting except, primarily, as part of star studies, is exactly what Olivier was doing and, more significantly, how we might deal with the sheer bravura, the unquestionable over-the-top-ness of so much of the performance, a performance of near hysteria in its excesses and a performance whose engagement with race is always nerve-wrackingly teetering on the edge of racism. Which side of the edge it falls on is recurrently part of my concern. Kenneth Tynan, not writing about race but about the performance's histrionics, was worried by a run-through he watched. In his notes he commented,

> L.O. must make it clear earlier on that this is a new interpretation. That is, make Othello obviously egocentric. Otherwise audiences will think not that this is an egocentric OTHELLO but that this is an egocentric PERFORMANCE.[5]

But I want first to resist the notion that Olivier's performance is unremittingly excessive, to suggest indeed that, irritated though he was by Tynan's usurping of a directorial authority, he took the comments to heart. Take, for instance, Othello's encounter with Brabanzio in the second scene. The sequence is initially constructed primarily from a camera angle aligned with Othello, on the right of the stage-space, seen here implicitly, as throughout the film, effectively as part of a proscenium arch view. It is, as always, clear where the theatre audience would have been. On Brabanzio's 'Damned as thou art' (1.2.64), a cut to Brabanzio's point-of-view shows Othello ever so slightly furrowing his brow by a millimetre, a reaction which registers strongly and persuasively the pain of Brabanzio's assumption that the Moor is inevitably damned. After returning to a close-up of Brabanzio, it cuts back to the same Othello shot on 'the sooty bosom/ Of such a thing as thou' (1.2.71–72) and again a tiny movement in Othello's look, here fractionally dropping his eye contact with Brabanzio as we read him responding to the raced insult with a kind of inevitability of 'here we go again' – the same kind of reaction that speaks to the continual awareness of the likelihood of such comments as that moment in Olivier's Shylock in the court scene when the use of the word 'alien' (4.1.344) makes him slump. But what in *The Merchant of Venice* is a big moment is here a point delicately made, a minuteness that is both thoroughly filmic – for it would not make its mark on stage except in a very small house – and of an exactness that is strongly realist.

If Olivier up to this moment in the performance has been laying out his stall in terms of the make-up, the walk, the lowering of the pitch of his voice and the recurrent chuckle (Pauline Kael calls it a 'happy, thick, self-satisfied laugh'[6]) – all markers of a raced performance, all signs that this Othello performance is a white man playing black, demanding that we see and hear the blackness of his performance – then these small responses speak of an unraced realism, a way of showing response which is not somatically located in racial identity, let alone caricature, even if the cause of the response is exactly in the recognition of the extent to which Brabanzio cannot see other than the raced body, in the inevitable damnation and the sooty bosom of the dehumanized 'thing' (1.2.72). In a performance in a production, Trevor Nunn's (RSC, 1989), defiantly at an opposite pole of realism from the staginess of John Dexter's, Willard White achieves nothing as subtle and powerful as this, a mark, if of nothing else, of the gap between White's abilities/talents as an actor and Olivier's.

There is here a fascinating tension. The scene has played strongly in terms of our viewing the raced body and, now, of our seeing in it a parodic form of its own realism. Precisely insofar as this Othello is so visibly blacked, so much a product of technique, so emphatically defined through what the actor has done to his body and voice, and through his choices to signify marked raced identity, we are placed in a position like Brabanzio's, seeing in Othello what Brabanzio sees as the other but, presumably, now feeling unsure whether this is a representation within the conventions of realism utilized by the production or preceding it, whether the implied, visible racism can be turned to meaning within *Othello* or only within the mechanics of the production. The former might be interesting, the latter only troubling.

Olivier's theatre work often depended on physical transformation. His Shylock, for instance, began from a set of false teeth that pushed the jaw differently, with the upper lip forward. Everything else came from that. But that decision was seen as a raced marker. As usual, Olivier watched people: 'soon I became aware that the so-called Jewish nose was to be seen more frequently on Gentile faces than on Jewish ones ... Then suddenly

I saw what it was, it was the mouth that was different. Larger, more sensitive, much more mobile.'[7] I watch Olivier's Shylock and I cannot see the mouth as Jewish. What on earth would a Jewish mouth be like, given that there is no cultural homogeneity among Jews? Olivier's assumption underpinning his characterization is disturbing, though his Shylock does not pose quite the same problems or to the same degree as his Othello.

The physicalization of his Othello is, in part, a change in Olivier's physical size. Not tall and comparatively slim, Olivier has a bulk in his presence as Othello, achieved in part by the flowing robes but most especially an uprightness that stretches the shoulders wide and pushes the belly forward and the buttocks back. We might see that stance as a racial imitation. We might do the same with that walk, a consequence, Olivier says, of a comment by Alfred Lunt on his Oedipus, decades earlier: 'the more intense you got, the more rigidly did your big toes stand straight up in the air!'[8] The walk was an attempt, Olivier offers, to avoid that by keeping

> each foot flat to the ground as it trod the floor ... I then tried to relax the foot, without placing the heel down first but putting my whole weight on each foot in turn as it touched the ground, thus introducing those swaying hips so generously commented upon, and regarded as the keystone of an elaborate characterization that even went to the lengths of studying the gait of the barefooted races!'[9]

Olivier may be telling the truth but there is also the account of his being in the wings watching Sammy Davis Jr performing at the Prince of Wales Theatre in London night after night. The brushing of Iago's cheek with the red rose in 1.2 was 'modelled ... on the way Davis played with the microphone' and Davis took credit for helping Olivier with what Holden calls 'sundry bodily rhythms and movements'.[10] But it is the deliberate creation of negritude that is most overwhelming. Olivier was proud of his achieved blackness:

> Black all over my body, Max Factor 2880, then a lighter brown, then Negro Number 2, a stronger brown. Brown on black to give a rich mahogany. Then the great trick: that glorious half yard of chiffon with which I polished myself all over until I shone. Pancake make-up looks powdery and, when you sweat, it is apt to break out in little rivulets if you aren't careful, but if you use this wonderful bit of chiffon, it gleams a smooth ebony. [Note the change in wood here from *mahogany* to *ebony*]. The lips blueberry, the tight curled wig, the white of the eyes, whiter than ever, and the black, black sheen that covered my flesh and bones.'[11]

Immediately after playing Othello, Olivier played the Mahdi in the movie *Khartoum* (dir. Basil Dearden and Eliot Elisofon, 1966) and discovered his mistake in the Othello make-up:

> I put white greasepaint along the lower edge of each eye to increase its size, as I had done for both the play and the film of *Othello*.
> 'Oh no, oh no, don't do that, black is what you want,' they all said.
> 'Won't it make my eyes look tiny?'
> But they were right. I kicked myself for not having discovered this before. Black on the edge and quite a lot of black round the eye is far more effective; it made me look much more African.[12]

Note the doubleness here: the eye looks both large *and* more African.

The make-up is always a problem for the white actor playing Othello. In Paul Hiffernan's 1770 plan for a Shakespeare temple, his choice of plays to be represented excluded *Othello* on the grounds that 'the blacking screens, and renders incommunicable to spectators, all impassioned working of the countenance'.[13] In Isaac Jackman's farce *All the World's a Stage* (1777), there is a delicious account of country-house theatricals as the stage-struck daughter Kitty describes rehearsing *Othello* with one of her servants, Cymon:

> He had black'd all his face with soot and goose dripping; and he did look so charmingly frightful! . . . when Cymon kissed me in bed, he blacked my left cheek so abominably, that when I came down to breakfast in the morning, the family were all frightened out of their wits.[14]

I am emphasizing Olivier's concern with the make-up technique here, a long way from soot and goose dripping, because it plainly mattered greatly to Olivier. On stage it worked. Othello was still a role for a white actor, even shortly after Paul Robeson had played it again, this time in Stratford in 1959–60. But on screen two things happen. The first is that film realism makes Olivier's make-up and hence the performance resonate with the African Americans in D. W. Griffith's *Birth of a Nation* (1915) where, notoriously, the pro-Klan narrative has the variously vicious or indolent African Americans played by white actors if the role is substantial, especially Gus, the 'renegade Negro', played by the white actor Walter Long. Much more than the blackface of Jolson (and remember that, ironically, Olivier would play the Jewish cantor father of the Jolson figure in the 1980 remake of *The Jazz Singer*), where the gap between the onstage blackface and the offstage Jewish identity is always being marked, the Griffith model is doubly racist in its denial of African American roles to African American actors.

But the second problem is that the frequent failure of colour reconciliation in the film means that Olivier's make-up blackness keeps changing colour, not least on different days of filming, so that the colour is marked by a new difference, an internal inconsistency that moves from shades of mahogany to an ebony with a blue tinge that is no skin colour known to humanity. And then there is that wig, of course. If you look, for example, at photographs of other Othellos it is striking how few of them wear a wig at all. Try Verdi's Otello: even in the many films of performances by the greatest of our time, Plácido Domingo, you'll see how often Domingo wears his own hair. Even when he does wear a wig on stage, the wig is usually not raced as either black African or Moor. The exception, significantly, is in Franco Zeffirelli's 1986 film of *Otello* where the requirements of the conventions of film realism require that the image is transformed into one of a coherent raced identity.

A parenthesis: why is a white actor playing Othello now culturally unacceptable,[15] but no one seems ever to query a white singer playing Otello? There was no significant complaining about Domingo's Otello in Zeffirelli's film, only about the cuts to the opera. Possibility one: opera-goers are unregenerated imperialists. Possibility two: the paucity of black opera singers, especially Verdian tenors, poses a casting problem for a popular opera. Possibility three: opera-goers are able to see the performative gap caused by an inherently structural non-realism more readily than those watching Shakespeare, as if singing the text of Boito's libretto in Verdi's music is necessarily remote from *verismo* in a way that Shakespeare's blank verse is not. And, if this is right, what does this say about the nature of realism in our cultural constrictions of Shakespeare as verse drama?

Second parenthesis on operatic *Ot[h]ellos*: one clip of Domingo as Otello shows what happens when the make-up is not as complete as Olivier's. In a performance, available on YouTube, of the Act 2 duet with Piero Cappuccilli as Iago, Domingo's shirt is open to the waist to reveal that the body make-up stopped an inch or so *above* where the waistband of his trousers now is.[16]

Olivier was not the only principal in the cast on stage with body make-up. Maggie Smith shared the role of Desdemona with Billie Whitelaw who remembered:

> To make my own skin look 'as white as alabaster' as the bard says, I had alabaster make-up all over my body. Once, as I knelt down at his feet, I put my hand on his knee. He glared down at me: there was a white mark on his black knee! Some of my white alabaster had come off on his beautiful shiny black make-up.[17]

The famous photo of Olivier leaving a trace of his make-up on the nightdress of Desdemona has its reverse image. The woman performs her whiteness as completely as Olivier worked to perform blackness. Maggie Smith seems, to my eye, to be using similar body make-up in at least some sequences of the film.

Olivier's purpose in the body make-up is crucial to his presentation of the otherness of the body. Again and again the camera sees his legs, those calves that are below the robes, even in the Senate scene, though it rarely shows his bare feet. The heavy anklets and bracelets that speak of a slave's shackles now transformed into body jewellery draw attention to the limbs – and, of course, one bracelet marks how the ornament both conceals and becomes the weapon, its flicked-out blade threatening Iago in Act 3 and killing Othello in Act 5, a move that, as so often for Olivier, opens the palm, drawing focus to the hand. The robes reveal as well as conceal, inviting our gaze at the black body, a gaze that is sexualized and hence voyeuristic, a kind of narcissism in the display asking for our look.

Olivier's is, quite simply, the sexiest Othello I know. Even more than in Oliver Parker's 1995 film where both Laurence Fishburne and Irène Jacob are offered as sexy bodies in a vision of the play that depends on its exploration of the pornographizing imagination, the ability to project the sexualized encounter of bodies, Olivier's sensuousness is both there and oddly troubling – precisely because it cannot but be the performance of a sexual body that is not the actor's. Though Parker is in some respects more interested in provoking the audience's fantasies of a naked Fishburne than a naked Jacob, or, that is, also, of each actor more than of each character, Olivier's Othello is unremittingly sensuous, sinuous and marked in his otherness through each and every move. Even at a moment like the exiting of the Senate, Olivier contrives – and my verb choice here is very deliberate – to make us see the body in movement as alien to the codes of Venetian aristocratic behaviour: where the rest of the senators bow to the Duke, Othello touches forehead, lips and chest, before ending with that inverted hand, bent at the wrist to show the open palm, which is an Olivier trade-mark in all his Shakespeare work, as his weight shifts onto the back leg in a single sequence that speaks of respect offered by someone of a cultural otherness. Then his body twists sideways to kiss the duke's hand in thanks for 'your son-in-law is far more fair than black' (1.3.289) before he bends to pick up the hem of the Duke's robe, flick it rather magnificently into mid-air where it is caught by the appropriate attendant. As Kael neatly comments, '[a]s a lord, this Othello is a bit vulgar, too ingratiating, a boaster, an arrogant man'.[18]

This, in effect, is a mark of a continued enslavement, in that laugh that seeks so hard to please, to be included, to be subservient, early in that scene. But there is something else: that delivery of 'Anthropophagi' (1.3.143) that, as Kenneth Tynan noted of the stage performance, is spoken 'as if to say: "That, in case you didn't know, is the scholarly term for these creatures"'. And, Tynan continues, 'He also manages to convey his sardonic awareness that this is just the kind of story that Europeans would expect Africans to tell . . . Throughout the speech, he is at once the Duke's servant and the white man's master'.[19] As Olivier commented, his view 'had to look out from a black man's world. Not one of repression, for Othello would have felt superior to the white man'.[20]

The unsympathetic reading of the sexiness is that Olivier has given in to the white fantasy of black male sexuality, the way western responses to the black body are unable not to think of the black penis (the only part of Olivier's body that was not made-up). The sympathetic reading is that Olivier deliberately conjures up that white fantasy in order to quiz its truthfulness and consider the ways in which it has been the determinant of much of the white world's response to blackness. I like the way Pauline Kael sums up this Othello as 'grand and barbaric and, yes, a little lewd'[21] – that last word pinpoints exactly what is so disturbing: this isn't Parker's exploration of sex in the bedroom, in the imagination of who is doing what to whom behind the net curtains that conceal and reveal the bed; this is a sexuality in every moment of the character's being. This never stops being sexy and a little bit dirty, not a grand passion but one that is unafraid of lust, of those 'rites' or 'rights' for which Desdemona loves him (1.3.256): it may be 'rites' in Quarto (Q) and Folio (F) but of course a homophone with 'rights' and the audience has no means of giving one or other priority. It is no accident that the Othello who enters to quell the disturbance in Cyprus here, roused from his bed with his wife, is holding a large, curved scimitar, the most blatant of phallic symbols, a steel erection that is deliberately so unlike the Venetian rapiers, a sign of a penis that is not like theirs either. No accident either that, when this Othello announces that 'All my fond love thus do I blow to heaven' (3.3.450), the hands gesture not at his heart, our conventional seat of love, but point down at the base of his belly towards his crotch. This fond love is rampantly (I use the word deliberately) sexual.

This emphasis on the black body is balanced also by the emphasis on a particular kind of moorishness that is deliberately set against the black African identity of that body (wig and all, for there is nothing about the wig that allows for an Arab raced identity) and its usual robes. The

helmet for the arrival at Cyprus and the scimitar, for instance, speak of a
culture that is Arab, Moorish, Islamic. To swear 'by yon marble heaven',
to create 'the due reverence of a sacred vow' (3.3.463–4), Othello kneels
as if on an imaginary prayer mat, moving in ways even more familiar to
us now than they were to Western society fifty years ago, making a vow
that, in its assumption that Islam can be twisted into a religion
of obsessive revenge, is even more likely to seem right now than it did
then, and yet which also combines realism and parody in the swaying
torso. From the start, this Othello has worn a large crucifix round his
neck – indeed, a number of different ones in different scenes, crosses that
he fingers and kisses, signs that he is, as Tynan describes it, 'a fully
"assimilated" Moor'.[22] As he swears revenge, as Tynan describes it,
'he tears the crucifix from his neck and flings it into the air. Othello's a
Moor again'.[23]

The equivalence here of Islam and a kind of dangerous paganism is
now complexly resonant and politically unacceptable. I don't think
Olivier and John Dexter, the stage production's director, did know and
I don't see how they could be expected to have known in 1964 quite how
this representation of a religious other, as well as a raced other, would
read. No one at this point would have demonstrated Jewishness in *The
Merchant of Venice* in a quite comparable way. That they were ignorant is
a sign of historical shift. Post-9/11, signs of Islam are read differently and,
as I watched the film again, the overlaying of black Africa and Moorish
Africa seemed a blurring of othernesses, a definition, as it were, that all
that is non-white is dangerous, able to be lumped together, incapable of
differentiation. It is magnified still further by the extent to which
reviewers spoke – though Olivier did not – of a West Indian influence
on the performance, without, apparently, noticing the irrelevance of
such a referent: wherever in Africa this Othello might come from, he
is not from the West Indies. John Simon, for instance, wrote of Olivier
'giv[ing] us a handsome jet-black Jamaican . . . with a melismatic Calypso
accent'.[24]

How easily, for instance, how glibly Tynan manages to move from
that description of Othello's reversion to his pre-conversion identity to
this account of Othello's scene after eavesdropping on Cassio and Iago
discussing Bianca and the handkerchief:

> he circles the stage, a caged jungle king *in extremis*, with Iago immobile at
> the centre. Dexter to Finlay: 'Think of yourself as a ring-master. Just give
> him an occasional flick of the whip – like "Hey, that's not your way" – to
> keep him in order'.[25]

Moor to jungle king to circus animal, a trajectory that denies Othello
anything but animality and that sees the lines between one of the world's
great cultures, tribal Africa, and a prowling leopard to be easily permeable.
My choice of animal comes from Olivier himself whose walk as Othello
was 'like a soft, black leopard . . . lithe, dignified and sensual'.[26]

And here comes the most difficult manoeuvre in renegotiating our
position over this performance: is there a significant gap between what
I am describing as defining this production's representation of the other,
the range of meanings blackness is permitted to have and the kinds of
meanings available in the early modern period? And, if so, is there a need
to differentiate between a number of possible historicizations of early
modern constructions of race: that of the early 1960s and the kinds of
constructions so brilliantly and complexly recuperated since then? What
the work of, say, Kim Hall, Margo Hendricks and Ania Loomba has
taught us so excitingly and effectively is precisely about the forms in which
it was possible for an early modern audience to conceptualize blackness,[27]
and I find it striking how completely Olivier's Othello lends itself to
precisely that form of conceptualization. In other words, Olivier, all
unknowingly, creates precisely some of the forms of early modern
constructions of blackness.

Of course the other looming presence over the production is F. R.
Leavis's analysis of the role in the 1937 essay 'Diabolic Intellect and the
Noble Hero'[28] – extracts from Leavis's essay were included in the theatre
programme, as well as from W. H. Auden's piece on Iago as practical
joker.[29] Leavis's argument is that what marks out the action is not Iago's
intellect but 'Othello's readiness to respond', that Othello is 'simple-
minded . . . egotistic' with 'a habit of self-approving self-dramatization'
and a 'nobility' that is 'the disguise of an obtuse and brutal egotism' so that
'[s]elf-pride becomes stupidity, ferocious stupidity, an insane and self-
deceiving passion' and 'Othello's noble lack of self-knowledge is shown
as humiliating and disastrous' and 'there is no tragic self-discovery' and so
on.[30] As Anthony Quayle said to Olivier, comparing Othello to Titus
Andronicus, 'Othello's another part that's entirely composed of moaning,
bellowing and screaming against fate'.[31] Leavis's essay is a controlling
determinant on everything Olivier was doing. But it is also aligned with
the role that Quayle described to Olivier years before Olivier would play it.

A further parenthesis: as Barbara Hodgdon brilliantly showed, Leavis
had his revenge later for what he saw as the abuse of his ideas on stage.
In 1972, in a lecture in Belfast on 'Reading Out Poetry', Leavis considered
the word 'interpret', defining it as 'what the great Shakespearean actor, say

Sir Laurence Olivier, does to Shakespeare'. That doesn't sound too bad, except that Leavis continues: 'even if one can imagine [the actor] intelligent, he will, in his accomplished and trained conceit, ignore the poetry, having decided upon his own interpretation. He will see only opportunities for elocutionary impressiveness'.[32] As Hodgdon shows, Leavis's vehement antihistrionism attaches to Olivier, not necessarily as Othello, precisely those qualities that Leavis himself attaches to and attacks in Othello whose '"dangerous" habit of self-dramatization enables him to "enjoy a magnificent death in his own private theatre, which is also for the actor the only theatre"'.[33]

For Leavis, the actor's stupidity and limited, self-regarding performance can be separated from the character's similarly limited and self-regarding performance. I continue to be unsure that that is always possible when watching Olivier as Othello, to be unsure whether the construction of the character is not also an assumption from the particular general to the raced generality. But Leavis's original article provokes a very different issue. The central problem here becomes then whether the two crucial assumptions, 'Othello is black' and 'Othello is ferociously stupid', are interdependent. Is the former that which creates the latter? Is Othello stupid *because* black? For some, that must be true. Whether or not it is true for Olivier is irrelevant. The language Olivier uses about his performance does not seem to me to see the two as causatively linked. But it cannot help but be possible to read them as inseparable and the race as determining. Is it then impossible to play a character who risks being both black and stupid and stupid because black? And there are other kind of linkages that are present, invoked in the comments around the performance that are equally offered and provocative. On the one hand, there is Olivier defensively saying that Othello 'is a savage man – not on account of his colour; I don't mean that';[34] on the other, Dexter telling the cast before the first read-through that Othello 'is a pompous, word-spinning, arrogant black general'[35] – and I worry at what kind of cultural work the word 'black' is doing in that list of adjectives.

Pauline Kael wrote of the film, 'What Negro actor at this stage in the world's history could dare bring to the role the effrontery that Olivier does?' and she has often been misunderstood to be saying that, as Ace Pilkington put it, 'Olivier could play a Negro better than a Negro could'.[36] That is not her point. Instead, she is arguing that Olivier's effrontery, that bravura style that always characterized his work, that excess that at times in this performance replicates the worst of nineteenth-century barnstorming, depends on a tradition of theatre artistry that no black actor of the 1960s had. Hence Zeffirelli's comment on seeing the theatre performance:

I was told that this was the last flourish of the romantic tradition of acting. It's nothing of the sort. It's an anthology of everything that has been discovered about acting in the last three centuries. It's grand and majestic, but it's also modern and realistic. I would call it a lesson for us all.[37]

It is also, I would argue, the closest we will ever get to the ambiguities and problematics of early modern representations and constructions of Othello. Its realism is also its indebtedness to caricature, the stereotypicality that was most firmly described and attacked by Bosley Crowther, the *New York Times* reviewer of the film in 1966, but which I would want to value highly precisely for those reasons that Crowther attacks it:

> he hits one – the sensitive American, anyhow – with the by-now outrageous impression of a theatrical Negro stereotype. He does not look like a Negro (if that's what he's aiming to make the Moor) – not even a West Indian chieftain, which some of the London critics likened him to. He looks like a Rastus or an end man in an American minstrel show.[38]

Its offensiveness is, then, part of its point, its magnificence as a statement of record of a white conception of blackness. Not to find it offensive is to mistake its achievement. To remain unsure whether the offence is contained within the structures of an intention that is not racist is central to the demands it makes of us. Its success lies precisely in our not knowing any longer quite what to make of it.

Notes

1 See M. Norman and T. Stoppard, *Shakespeare in Love* at www.moviescript sandscreenplays.com/BenandMatt/shakespeareinlove.txt, accessed 3 June 2014.
2 See R. Manvell, *Shakespeare and the Film* (New York: Praeger Publishers, 1971), 118.
3 L. Olivier, *On Acting* (London: Weidenfeld and Nicolson, 1986), 198.
4 A. Holden, *Laurence Olivier* (New York: Atheneum, 1988), 388.
5 Quoted in R. Lewis, *The Real Life of Laurence Olivier* (London: Century Books, 1996), 222.
6 P. Kael, *5001 Nights at the Movies* (London: Elm Tree Books, 1983), 438.
7 Olivier, *On Acting*, 112.
8 Olivier, *Confessions of an Actor* (London: Weidenfeld and Nicholson, 1982), 211.
9 *Ibid.*, 212.
10 Holden, *Laurence Olivier*, 381.
11 Quoted in *ibid.*, 101–2.
12 Quoted in *ibid.*, 198.
13 P. Hiffernan, *Dramatic Genius* (London, 1770), 6.

14 I. Jackman, *All the World's a Stage* (London, 1777), 28. My thanks to Michael Caines for the reference.

15 The only major statement by an actor against the model of a black actor playing Othello is by Hugh Quarshie in 'Second Thoughts About Othello', *International Shakespeare Association Occasional Papers* 7 (1999), 1–25.

16 'Otello and Jago – Cappuccilli & Domingo – 20 atto Otello', YouTube www. youtube.com/watch?v=hBItqvQfcHU, accessed 3 June 2014.

17 Whitelaw, quoted in D. Callaghan, '"Othello was a white man": Properties of Race on Shakespeare's Stage', in T. Hawkes (ed.), *Alternative Shakespeares 2* (London: Routledge, 1996), 203.

18 Kael, *5001 Nights*, 438.

19 K. Tynan (ed.), *Othello: The National Theatre Production* (New York: Stein and Day, 1967), 6.

20 Olivier, *On Acting*, 98–9.

21 Kael, *5001 Nights*, 438.

22 Tynan, *Othello*, 6.

23 *Ibid.*, 9.

24 J. Simon, 'Pearl Throwing Free Style', in C. W. Eckert (ed.), *Focus on Shakespearean Films* (Englewood Cliffs: Prentice-Hall, 1972), 155.

25 Tynan, *Othello*, 10.

26 Olivier, *On Acting*, 99.

27 See, for example, K. Hall, *Things of Darkness* (Ithaca: Cornell University Press, 1962); M. Hendricks and P. Parker (eds.), *Women, 'Race', and Writing* (London: Routledge, 1994); A. Loomba, *Shakespeare, Race, and Colonialism* (Oxford: Oxford University Press, 2002).

28 F. R. Leavis, 'Diabolic Intellect and the Noble Hero', *Scrutiny* 6 (1937), 259–83, reprinted in *The Common Pursuit* (London: Chatto and Windus, 1952).

29 W. H. Auden, 'The Joker in the Pack', *The Dyer's Hand and Other Essays* (New York: Random House, 1962), 246–72.

30 I deliberately quote from the extracts reprinted in Tynan, *Othello*, 97–8.

31 Quoted in Olivier, *On Acting*, 75.

32 F. R. Leavis, 'Reading Out Poetry', in G. Singh (ed.), *Valuation in Criticism and Other Essays* (Cambridge: Cambridge University Press, 1986), 260, 263, quoted in Barbara Hodgdon, 'The Critic, the Poor Player, Prince Hamlet and the Lady in the Dark', in R. McDonald (ed.), *Shakespeare Reread* (Ithaca: Cornell University Press, 1994), 259.

33 Hodgdon, 'The Critic', 263, quoting Leavis, 'Reading Out Poetry', 266.

34 Quoted in J. Hankey (ed.), *Othello* (Bristol: Bristol Classical Press, 1987), 109.

35 Tynan, *Othello*, 4.

36 P. Kael, *Kiss Kiss Bang Bang* (Boston: Little, Brown, 1968), 173–4; Ace Pilkington, 'Othello's Stature: Three Filmed Versions of the Moor', *Encyclia* 68 (1991), 304.

37 Quoted in Tynan, *Othello*, 11.

38 B. Crowther, 'Minstrel Show "Othello": Radical Makeup Marks Olivier's Interpretation', *New York Times*, 2 February 1966.

WORKS CITED

Auden, W. H., 'The Joker in the Pack', *The Dyer's Hand and Other Essays* (New York: Random House, 1962), 246–72.

Callaghan, D., '"Othello was a white man": Properties of Race on Shakespeare's Stage', in Terence Hawkes (ed.), *Alternative Shakespeares 2* (London: Routledge, 1996), 193–215.

Crowther, B., 'Minstrel Show "Othello": Radical Makeup Marks Olivier's Interpretation', *New York Times*, 2 February 1966.

Hall, K., *Things of Darkness* (Ithaca: Cornell University Press, 1962).

Hankey, J., ed., *Othello* (Bristol: Bristol Classical Press, 1987).

Hendricks, M. and P. Parker, eds., *Women, 'Race', and Writing* (London: Routledge, 1994).

Hiffernan, P., *Dramatic Genius* (London, 1770).

Hodgdon, B., 'The Critic, the Poor Player, Prince Hamlet and the Lady in the Dark', in R. McDonald (ed.), *Shakespeare Reread* (Ithaca: Cornell University Press, 1994), 259–93.

Holden, A., *Laurence Olivier* (New York: Atheneum, 1988).

Jackman, I., *All the World's a Stage* (London, 1777).

Kael, P., *5001 Nights at the Movies* (London: Elm Tree Books, 1983).

Kiss Kiss Bang Bang (Boston: Little, Brown, 1968).

Leavis F. R., 'Diabolic Intellect and the Noble Hero', *Scrutiny* 6 (1937), 259–83, reprinted in *The Common Pursuit* (London: Chatto and Windus, 1952).

'Reading Out Poetry', in G. Singh (ed.), *Valuation in Criticism and Other Essays* (Cambridge: Cambridge University Press, 1986), 253–75.

Lewis R., *The Real Life of Laurence Olivier* (London: Century Books, 1996).

Loomba A., *Shakespeare, Race, and Colonialism* (Oxford: Oxford University Press, 2002).

Manvell R., *Shakespeare and the Film* (New York: Praeger Publishers, 1971).

Norman, M. and T. Stoppard, *Shakespeare in Love* at www.moviescriptsandscreenplays.com/BenandMatt/shakespeareinlove.txt, accessed 3 June 2014.

Olivier L., *Confessions of an Actor* (London: Weidenfeld and Nicholson, 1982).

On Acting (London: Weidenfeld and Nicolson, 1986).

'Otello and Jago – Cappuccilli & Domingo – 20 atto Otello', YouTube www.youtube.com/watch?v=hBItqvQfcHU, accessed 3 June 2014.

Pilkington A., 'Othello's Stature: Three Filmed Versions of the Moor', *Encyclia* 68 (1991), 301–14.

Quarshie H., 'Second Thoughts About Othello', *International Shakespeare Association Occasional Papers* 7 (1999), 1–25.

Simon J., 'Pearl Throwing Free Style', in C. W. Eckert (ed.), *Focus on Shakespearean Films* (Englewood Cliffs: Prentice-Hall, 1972), 154–7.

Tynan K., ed., *Othello: The National Theatre Production* (New York: Stein and Day, 1967).

CHAPTER 4

Othello *retold*
Orson Welles's Filming Othello

Sébastien Lefait

Filming Othello (Federal Republic of Germany, 1978) is often deemed a minor Orson Welles film because of its essay form, which translates on screen into a series of static shots of the director talking directly to the camera. An understandable consequence is that, despite Welles's claims that the essay film is 'a new kind of movie' and 'not a documentary at all',[1] *Filming Othello* is almost never analysed as a film.[2] Although its duration (83 minutes) classifies it as a feature rather than as a making of, *Filming Othello* is mostly treated as the valuable commentary of one of Holly-wood's greatest directors on one of his masterpieces. The film's framework, however, is more complex than it may appear at first. Besides the talking-head shots in which the filmmaker comments on his work, *Filming Othello* includes footage from a conversation between Welles and actors from *Othello* (1952) at a dinner party, extracts from a talk Welles had with a movie theatre audience after a showing and shots of Welles speaking lines from the play in front of the camera. In addition, several neglected elements suggest the film could be revalued if it were studied as a filmic work *per se* rather than as a cinematic by-product.[3]

The first element concerns Welles's selection and sometimes manipula-tion of sequences from his 1952 adaptation of *Othello* for inclusion in his film. Indeed, the director re-edited some of the sequences from his former movie before inserting them in *Filming Othello*.[4] Such changes are barely noticeable, except to punctilious analysts of both works. This apparently anecdotal facet of the movie forbids one to read it merely as a commentary on his previous film or as an *Othello potpourri*. It suggests that Welles used the opportunity of shooting *Filming Othello* as a one-off chance to modify his former film and to rerelease it in an updated version. From this viewpoint, there is reason to consider *Filming Othello* not only as a perspective on Welles's version of the play but also as a reconstruction of his former film.

The second telling anecdote about *Filming Othello* concerns one of the sequences inserted by Welles between scenes from his earlier adaptation. The inclusion implies that Welles's temptation to remake *Othello* may not have been circumscribed to the director's self-quotations, however distorted they may be. In an interview given to Lawrence French about his collaboration with Welles for *Filming Othello*, American film director and cinematographer Gary Graver insisted on a detail in the film's editing that goes completely unnoticed at first. Graver revealed that, for the sequence when Welles, Hilton Edwards and Micheál MacLiammóir who respectively played Othello, Brabanzio and Iago in *Othello*, discuss the meaning of Shakespeare's play over lunch, some of the reverse shots on Welles were added years after the conversation took place.[5] This revelation is significant on many grounds. The temporal discrepancy mentioned by Graver directly relates to the principle on which *Filming Othello* is based: the clear separation between the 1952 film's visual treatment of the play and Welles's oral rendition, captured in 1978, of a text that includes extracts from Shakespeare's play. Only *Filming Othello*'s opening contradicts the disjunction tenet. It replays the beginning of *Othello* and then reveals, by showing a movieola (a film-editing machine), that Welles utilizes footage from his 1952 film in order to edit it together with pictures shot in 1978. This suggests the essay film continues the 1952 Shakespearean adaptation. Welles's use of a new soundtrack over pictures from his 1952 opus, however, soon contradicts the continuity effect.

Moreover, Graver's revelation that Welles doctored the footage does not merely indicate that the director wanted to secure total control over his film. It also implies that even the documentary sequences featured in it may have been scripted. This places *Filming Othello* in the same category as other films of Welles's late period dealing with the power of cinematic deceit (*F for Fake*, 1973) or with the impossibility of completing a film in the contemporary cinematic context (*The Other Side of the Wind*, unfinished, shot between 1969 and 1976). Even more importantly, Graver's observation that '[in *Filming Othello*] a guy's talking in Paris, and two years later Orson is answering him back in Beverly Hills'[6] sounds like a half-hearted exposure of the director's propensity to play God, aided by the magical powers of cinema. The disclosure that Welles exacted his control over *Filming Othello* without taking care of the level of objectivity supposedly attached to the documentary genre also informs the film's overall architecture. Moreover, it brings out the nature of the trick used to construct it: the dissociation of words from the corresponding images that, complete with clever editing techniques, is one of the main sources of cinematic creation, as well as a key ingredient in faking reality through film.

Based on those initial observations, my argument is that the anecdote reported by Gary Graver fundamentally calls for a reinterpretation of *Filming Othello*, because of the link it elicits between the essay film and Shakespeare's play. The editing technique used by Welles finds its grounding in Shakespeare's *Othello*. The very dissociation on which the film is based is an angle on the play's juxtaposing of moments when Iago pours poison into Othello's ear and moments when Othello is made to watch scenes without being able to hear the corresponding text. Act 3 scene 3 and Act 4 scene 1 exemplify this dichotomy. In the play, as I shall clarify later, the result of this dissociation is an almost perfect form of dramatic illusion. The presence of this component in Shakespeare's work and in the essay film is a strong incentive to consider *Filming Othello* not only as a perspective on Welles's version of *Othello* but also as a morphological reading of the play itself. As Welles himself suggests in the essay film's concluding words, Shakespeare's work could have given a different *Othello*. Considered from this angle, I propose to demonstrate how *Filming Othello* is Welles's re-adaptation of Shakespeare's play. To this effect, I will first show that, as Anthony Brennan suggests in the chapter of his *Shakespeare's Dramatic Structures* entitled 'Iago, the strategist of separation', separating visual perception from oral perception is the core of Iago's deception strategy.[7] I will then study how Welles treats this Shakespearean exercise in the illusionary power of drama, first in *Othello* then in *Filming Othello*.

Shakespeare's Othello

According to Ana Maria Manzanas Calvo and Jesùs Benito, Iago becomes such a 'strategist of separation' by distorting Othello's perception of himself and of the world surrounding him.[8] This technique is at its most effective in the play's pair of complementary scenes, Act 3 scene 3 and Act 4 scene 1. In those scenes, Iago's art as an agent of chaos and as a demoniacal creator of the 'version of reality'[9] that he thrusts upon Othello reaches a climax when he applies the separation principle to Othello's perception of events to transform Desdemona into a whore to the Moor's eyes.

In Act 3 scene 3, Iago manages to make Othello believe that Desdemona is having an affair with Cassio. This is clearly underlined on line 445, when Othello clenches Iago's success by declaring he now 'see[s] 'tis true' (3.3.449) that Desdemona is cheating on him. At the beginning of the scene, Iago's tactics may seem to consist merely of the well-known art of innuendo. He uses insinuatory comments to distort Othello's perception of Desdemona's conversation with Cassio (3.3.1–32). This verbal venom gains its efficiency from being used *after* Desdemona and Cassio have left the stage. Othello does not have the possibility of checking whether Iago's description of the encounter between Othello's wife and her supposed lover is accurate or not. Additionally, as Iago declares he suspects foul play, he effects another disconnection, this time at an extradiegetic level. Throughout the play, Shakespeare places the audience in an overinformed position compared to Othello.[10] The spectators have seen and heard the allegedly incriminatory conversation between Cassio and Desdemona and they know that Iago's plan is to make Othello believe they are emotionally involved with each other. Through this information discrepancy, the spectators are led to focus on the reasons for Othello's misinterpretation of events. They become aware that disconnecting Othello's sensual perceptions from each other plays an essential part in Iago's manoeuvring.

Then, as Othello challenges Iago to provide 'the ocular proof' (3.3.365) of Desdemona's guilt moments after the Moor has asserted that he wants to see before he doubts, Iago's strategy takes a decisive turn. Comforted by the observation that Othello is likely to treat a monster planted in his brain as something he actually saw, Iago proceeds to the purely verbal creation of images, which Othello promptly mistakes for true. The device gradually leads the Moor to suspend his disbelief, to such an extent that he treats Iago's tale of Cassio's dream (3.3.415–30) as if he had really been there to attend the scene. To make this product of his imagination more realistic than the rest of his double talk, Iago adds reported speech and probably a few illustrative gestures. In depriving Othello from visual perception and providing him with a well-honed hypotyposis, Iago thus manages to make him visualize pictures that do not exist. He thus convinces Othello, despite ironic comments that 'this was but his dream' (3.3.432), that he actually saw something. At the end of this scene, Othello no longer doubts that Desdemona has been unfaithful and he first acts on this conviction by making Iago his lieutenant (3.3.481).

After spotting those chinks in Othello's armour in this temptation scene, Iago sets out, in Act 4 scene 1, to deceive the Moor by resorting to a similar pattern. He prevents him from getting a full grasp on situations by isolating his visual perceptions and subsequently takes advantage of the Moor's vivid imagination to poison his ear with verbally created pictures that superimpose on what he has seen. As the scene develops towards the crucial moment when Iago gives Othello a misleading ocular proof of

Desdemona's guilt by making him focus on her handkerchief in Cassio's hand, it appears that Iago's separation principle is still at work. The handkerchief, however concrete and visual it may be, is used to 'prove' a blatant falsehood, at least from the spectator's point of view. As a visual object, it helps convince Othello. Iago's poisonous innuendo, however, dictates its significance.

The scene's climactic moment, in which Othello 'overhear[s] and misconstrue[s] an actual conversation'[11] between Iago and Cassio without hearing their words, amplifies the same principle. In this parody of an eavesdropping scene, Othello sees Iago and Cassio without hearing them. For Othello, having seen the 'fleers' and the 'gibes' on Cassio's face is almost the same as having heard them even if he did not. This is because Iago told him, before the pantomime, what sort of dialogue he should create in his mind's ear. By placing the lines before the dumb show, Iago acts as a narrative instance and as a stage producer who organizes elements belonging to his reality. Using a prop and a few people, he makes them appear, in one of the many 'undeclared playlets'[12] he organizes throughout the play, as the mere retelling of the tale he has made up.

By driving Othello to gaze awry on his surroundings, Iago plants a warped vision of reality into his head. This 'monstrous world' (3.3.382), which Iago regards as 'a kind of absurd theatrical spectacle',[13] is a specular image of the fake universe of drama, a pale imitation of God's creation that refers theatrical practice to its religious or ethical stakes. If it is true that each of Shakespeare's plays examines a specific aspect of the construction of a theatrical illusion,[14] *Othello* derives its specificity from its study of theatre as an analytical operation followed by a synthetic one. While initially disconnected from their usual name and meaning, visual elements are then connected to new ones, springing from the playwright's language, during the theatrical performance. I will now argue that, in his adaptation of the play, Welles introduces a specific perspective on this dramatic principle.

Welles's Othello

Presenting Iago as a dissociating force, hence as a playwright figure, is one of the guiding principles of Welles's 1952 adaptation of *Othello*. Before taking a detailed look at *Filming Othello*, in which Welles separates words from pictures in a more radical way, it is necessary to analyse his initial treatment of this key component in the play's reflexivity. If *Filming Othello* is a re-adaptation of Shakespeare's play, be it an abstract one, one can reasonably think the reason for Welles's urge to make another version lies in the incompleteness of the original one, or in its lack of relevance twenty five years later.

In his 1952 version of *Othello*, Orson Welles may play only one role, the eponymous one, but he does so, as is customary for him, in a schizophrenic way. The actor/stage producer/film director is famous for his need to exert comprehensive control over his works. This aspect of the artist is well summarized in the recent film *Me and Orson Welles* by Richard Linklater (2008), in particular through an argument between the director and his set designer for his 1937 production of *Julius Caesar* for the Mercury Theatre in New York. The argument leads Welles to assert violently that the show is his and that there is consequently no need for the name of the set designer to be credited in the programme. Besides insisting on Welles's urging desire to be the Shakespeare of American culture, this – probably invented – episode brings forward the widespread notion that he only reluctantly employed collaborators for works he considered the products of his sole mind. Moreover, it is common knowledge among film scholars that manipulating the sound-track in postproduction was Welles's favourite way of ensuring total artistic supremacy. About *Macbeth* (1948), Mary Pat Klimek remarks that 'Welles's sound manipulation in the opening scenes ... asserts his control over the soundtrack'.[15] In *The Magnificent Ambersons* (1942), Welles compensates for the fact he does not play any of the visible characters by narrating the story in voice-over. He also brings all the characters back under his creative aegis when, in a willingly unusual credit sequence, he reads a list of the major contributors to the film. In this sequence, Welles's voice gives unity to a montage of symbolic illustrations (e.g., a movie camera when Stanley Cortez is mentioned as the photographer). It is followed by a succession of cameo shots when the names of the cast as the main *dramatis personae* are spoken, leading up to Welles's concluding words: 'I wrote the script and directed it. My name is Orson Welles. This is a Mercury production.' In visual terms, the narrative is rounded up through the inclusion, at the moment those final sentences are spoken, of a close-up of a microphone that hangs from a boom.

Because the microphone is a visual reference to orality, this signature affects, at least symbolically, the images depicted on-screen. The oral mark is an explicit way for Welles to demonstrate that the voice, rather than a sheer creative tool, is also an instrument of power, and that the cinematic apparatus magnifies this quality.

In *Othello*, Welles resorts to similar tricks. For instance, as Michael Anderegg remarks, the director often substitutes 'one actor's voice for another', and even speaks himself for both Othello and Roderigo.[16] He also emphasizes his presence as the main source of cinematic magic through a voice-over presentation of the plot. The dyer's hand, however, is present in the film in a more distanced, and even reflexive manner, since this treatment of voice-over is consistent with Iago's disjunction of verbal elements from visual ones in the play. Additionally, a prologue in which not a single word is spoken precedes the voice-over presentation of the setting and of the main characters. The famous opening sequence has a choral function, which it fulfils visually. It shows the funeral procession of Othello and Desdemona, and provides a sense of narrative wholeness, by framing the film, at both of its ends, with visions of its ending. Strangely enough, however, Welles's poetic presence is not the only one to be felt throughout the scene. The dissociation of the events from the sounds they produce is created by adding a music whose notes are also characterized by extreme variations. This effect has been described as 'dissonance' by Youssef Ishaghpour, who treats the notion as 'the meaning and substance of the film', while considering that it also informs its construction.[17] The music, however, as the only element in the soundtrack, does not only draw attention to the omnipresence of Welles's editing intervention. It also fosters a visual treatment of the scene that makes Iago's supervising presence in it hard to miss. Iago attends the funeral from inside a cage hanging in mid-air above the abstract movements of the procession below. While Welles usually leaves his marks on his film's most prominent moments, with a natural preference for beginnings and endings, *Othello* evinces an evolution in his use of this technique. In keeping with the contents of the adapted play, Iago, a manipulative presence throughout *Othello*, is now on Welles's side, sharing his supervising look over what seems to be their joint work.

As a result, both creative forces are present in the film, as muted gods, through the prologue that circumscribes the narrative. What precedes and follows their manipulative actions thus constitutes a voiceless gaze. Conversely, one can describe their manoeuvring throughout the unravelling of the plot as verbal. Complementarily, it is a form of postproduction: in Iago's production as in Welles's, the sounds are inserted in such a way as not to match the corresponding images, as they would do in real life.[18] Rather, they come before, after, or over the pictures on display. The sight/sound division principle implemented in the film, therefore, directly reflects Iago's strategy. This diegetic feature even filters up to infect the narrative regime of the film in the climactic moments of Iago's deceit. In Welles's treatment of Act 4 scene 1, Othello is made to attend a silent conversation between Bianca and Cassio, the oral contents of which have been given to him beforehand by Iago. In this sequence, the dissociation principle operates at the cinematic level. To present in a realistic way what is usually left a matter of convention on stage – that the spectators can hear Bianca and Cassio's conversation as well as Othello's asides while the latter is deprived of verbal information – Welles intervenes on the soundtrack. The conversation occurs outside and Othello watches it, trying to hear what Bianca and Cassio are saying from a nearby building, through a rectangular opening in a wall. As the soundtrack clearly emphasizes, the noise of the waves and wind outside the building is so loud that it makes the conversation barely audible for the audience. The dialogue turns into a booming succession of disconnected words for Othello. Welles magnifies, in postproduction, this discrepancy between what the spectators hear and what Othello does not – or not as clearly – perceive. He does so through a distinct contrast between the extreme loudness of the outside passages in the sequence and the near silence of those located inside – a silence that is synonymous with underinformation. This treatment makes the on and off presence of the noise of the waves an unrealistic sound used for the sake of narrative coherence. It is, therefore, the extradiegetic equivalent of Iago's disconnection of sight and sound and a manipulative stratagem directed at the spectators.

In this scene, Iago's clever management of space subtends the separation principle thanks to which he poisons Othello's mind. Throughout the film, this facet of his scheming translates into a subtle handling of editing and of camera angles. Welles's swift editing and constant use of high, low or tilted camera angles give an impression of discontinuity and collage. As a result, the jerky pace at which the pictures appear and disappear contrasts with the fluidity of the dialogues, or with Welles's uninterrupted voice-over commentary in the introductory sequence placed after the credits. In a similar vein, the incessant variations in camera angles introduce multiple perspectives on the events of the plot. By displacing the narrative subject of the gaze, they establish a clashing relationship between a fractured visual regime and a more even and steady oral flux. Visual perception becomes hectic to such an extent that it sometimes seems random. On the contrary, verbal information, because it is distilled in a continuous way, seems to be under control, emanating as it does from a controlling presence.

The discontinuity that defines the film's 'scopic regime'[19] is a necessary complement of Othello's inflexible soundtrack in that it strengthens the manipulative power of the voice. The baroque locations chosen to shoot the film are characterized by vertical and horizontal dislocation, an impression that is magnified by Welles's shooting style. In Venice and in Cyprus, numerous alleys and corridors, stairways and cellars, walls and loopholes create a multilayered, mazelike environment. This architecture makes it easier to see without being seen, or, to fit Othello's predicament in Act 4 scene 1, without hearing. Consequently, the characters evolve in spaces that are suited to Iago's surveillance practices and tricks. As a result, the net he casts over them to 'enmesh them all' (2.3.336) seems made of a material that he only can see through. Iago's mastery over the site of the film enables him to move spiderlike from frame to frame. It is also a form of visual dominance allowing him to deprive Othello of visual information then bombard him with scenes to watch, while simultaneously muting the dialogues they feature.

Besides, the editing and camera angles exalt the discrepant nature of the shooting location's geography. As a result, Iago seems constantly assisted by the director in his schemes. This impression prevails in the many scenes that exploit depth of field to make characters emerge from the background into hearing range. This association between Iago and the director, which is obtained by emphasizing the similarity of their directing techniques, follows an ascending pattern throughout the movie. For instance, the high angles featured in the film become more and more radical: they no longer merely render Iago's supervising presence, but point to a superior, directorial point of view. This leads Welles to include bird's-eye shots that refer to the perspective from Iago's overhanging cage seen in the prologue, but also to the supervision of the artist over his work.

In *Othello*, therefore, Welles brings himself close to Iago by implementing a dissociation principle similar to the ensign's, yet assisted by the cinematic instrument. In *Filming Othello*, given the film's design, the same principle is applied in a more radical and abstract way. The filiation between the play and Welles's 1952 adaptation even makes it possible to consider that, in *Filming Othello*, Welles fulfils his lifelong dream of playing more than one part in the same film in a delayed way, by casting himself as Iago. He does so, however, by impersonating the character's supervising, invisible and controlling presence rather than by playing the part in front of the camera.

Filming Othello

If Shakespeare's play actually deals with the shift of perspective on reality that makes dramatic illusion possible, *Filming Othello* can be said to be in keeping with this reflexive quality, only at a further remove. As the conversation between Orson Welles, Hilton Edwards and Micheál MacLiammóir suggests, the director's purpose in making *Filming Othello* was to provide a new perspective on his film. The discussion concerns the character of Iago and revolves around the various interpretations to which the supposed malignancy of the character has led. Welles and MacLiammóir alternatively provide their reading of the role, the former saying that he treated the character as impotent and the latter claiming that Iago is the mystery of the play. Hilton Edwards, for his part, arbitrates the exchange by providing a scholarly point of view encompassing several possible angles. After politely gratifying Welles's vision of Iago with the reply that there is nothing in the script to contradict his theory, Edwards provides his own analysis. Iago, he claims, is 'evil for its own sake, the way we see a cat catching a mouse, or a cat playing with a rabbit'.[20] In his reply, Welles leads the other two to consider that evil is a relative notion, on which one can cast different perspectives. He remarks that the cat catching the mouse looks evil to us, but it does not look evil to either one of the animals.

In *Filming Othello*, Welles acts as director and main actor of a film he seems to be editing in real time, sitting as he is behind his movieola. He thus induces a relative viewing of his film. Thanks to the instrument, Welles is at the focal point of the various perspectives on *Othello*, which he organizes and manipulates. The impression that *Filming Othello* is made of bits and pieces speedily put together, therefore, is only a smokescreen and the same kind of magic trick Welles more openly uses in *F for Fake*. The offhand quality of the film is an illusion barely concealing that, in this film, Welles is pulling all the strings, at last. Consequently, by selecting what the spectators will watch, Welles becomes like Iago in the play and in his 1952 adaptation: he closes the spectator's eyes on whole sequences from his former film and makes them watch other sequences he supposedly extracted from the original work. In so doing, he forces a falsifying perspective on his film. This angle is similar to the one Iago uses on Othello to make him misinterpret what he sees: for both masters of the gaze, commenting on pictures deprived of their soundtrack is an essential element in warping visual perception. From this angle, Welles's choice of titles makes full sense. The main point is not to explain what filming *Othello* was like, as in an ordinary 'making-of' documentary, but to show the artist filming his own film again. In his essay film, Welles is capturing his *Othello* so the spectators see it from a different angle, acting to distort the meaning of his original work and provide a new one. His remark that he wishes he could have done the film over again in his concluding comments should therefore be heard as tongue-in-cheek: in *Filming Othello*, he creates for himself the possibility of doing so.

Additionally, investigating the so far untrodden paths of Shakespearean adaptation thanks to the essay film leads Welles to deconstructing more traditional ways of dealing with Shakespeare on film, ways Welles's own prize-winning *Othello*, among others, has made canonical. Tellingly, the replayed prologue at the beginning of *Filming Othello* lasts just long enough for its mesmerizing quality to settle in. After less than two minutes of footage, however, the camera tilts down into the dark surface of a wall in the Cyprus location, which is followed by an anticlimactic shot, a close-up on the running movieola. Nevertheless, the tragic music of the prologue continues playing for a few seconds before the reel stops unwinding. The soundtrack has been disconnected from the original movie and applied to the new one. After this basic sign that the 1952 *Othello* has been disjoined so some of its components can be reorganized and completed with new ones, Welles includes a less obtrusive indication of the same fact in the next shot. The face of the 1978 Orson Welles appears in frames from the reel that has now stopped running, a clear sign the director has attached the soundtrack to a new film.

The pictorial cliché of the artist at work who is present in his own production, however, is more than a stylistic effect. In fact, as Welles starts telling the 'round unvarnished tale' of how he seduced spectators around the world thanks to his expertise in cinematic narrative, it gradually appears how close his live rendition of artistic creation is to Iago's course of action in the play. In *Othello*, the ensign creates theatrical fiction in real time for the Moor's eyes and ears. By subtly dealing with commentary, innuendo and the imaginative power of words, he induces Othello to misperceive events. Similarly, Welles soon disconnects his former film from its soundtrack to attach voice-over comments devised to modify the spectators' perception of his 1952 film.

By casting a fresh look on his former work, Welles imposes an angle on it, in ways that sometimes make revisioning verge on revisionism. About ten minutes into the film, Welles mentions Laurence Olivier's *Othello*, to claim he chose a different perspective on the play. To contrast his film with Olivier's, he uses a quote by 'the critic, Jack J. Jorgens who wrote a book on Shakespeare on Film', immediately confessing his inability to remember Jorgens's exact words. Welles's admission of forgetting is more of a problem than his jocular tone makes it sound. In fact, memorial approximation percolates from the way Welles blends quotes into his own prose until there is no knowing who said – or wrote – what about which one of the two films.[21] In Welles's presentation of Olivier's filmic version, it seems to have come before Welles's own adaptation. Olivier's film (directed by Stuart Burge), however, stemmed from his theatrical production at the National Theatre in 1964 and was released in 1965, more than ten years after Welles's film. Whether this ambiguity is conscious or not, it reveals the main motivation for making *Filming Othello*: to provide Welles with the benefit of hindsight and allow him to have the final say in the field of *Othello* adaptations. Directing *Filming Othello* thus appears as a necessity, resulting from the need to supplement a limited interpretation of *Othello*, or even to correct a misreading of the play. Because of those mixed up references to critical readings of his own film and Olivier's, Welles's commentary also evinces the urge for his visionary rendition of the play to be the latest contribution in the collective progress towards the perfect Shakespeare film. It serves to recontextualize the 1952 film, to make it relevant to times and conditions different from those of its release. At the end of *Filming Othello*, the scene of Welles's talk with the audience after a showing fulfils a similar purpose. Even though the sequence creates the illusion of a conversation about the film, it is a pretext for lengthy speeches by the artist about how to receive and perceive his film.

Throughout *Filming Othello*, therefore, Welles makes his own film appear different from what it was upon its release. The time lag between making or viewing the film and its ready-made interpretation by its author allows for the pasting over of commentaries that affect its place in collective memory. At other times in *Filming Othello*, Welles uses the same technique in even subtler ways, by using editing to bridge temporal gaps in order to give pictures and sounds the look of real events. In such cases, the spectator's look on reality becomes warped by the artist's authoritative comments. Welles uses this manipulative strategy to make the general perspective on his films his sole preserve. The best instance of this technique is the scene of the lunch with Hilton Edwards and Micheál MacLiammóir. As Youssef Ishaghpour has noted, the sequence is full of editing glitches, because 'Welles carefully remade the shots of himself, in 35mm, with a beautiful still-life array of fruit baskets and bottles in front of him'.[22] That he just 'remade' them, however, is a lenient way of putting it. Adding shots afterwards, along with the lines spoken in those shots, is an editing technique mostly used to create a conversation that never took place. While there is no doubt that the conversation featured in *Filming Othello* really took place, as proved by Welles's appearance in three shots with the other two near the end of the sequence, one can reasonably think the original conversation did not happen exactly as it is rendered in the film. This is all the more likely as the sequence elicits little care for verisimilitude. The background wall behind Welles is different from the one behind the other two characters and the continuous flow of the exchange, as well as the accuracy of each view on the play, further contribute to creating a sense of artificiality.

To justify this editorial intervention, invoking the need to provide a well-polished final product is not sufficient, above all because *Filming Othello* is all but polished in form. More consistently, this way of interfering with reality, even more so as it seems gratuitous, allows Welles to mimic Iago's behaviour in the play. The sequence barely hides that someone has tampered with it. What precedes it introduces this reading, as it shows Welles at his movieola, about to play the sequence he has just finished editing for the spectators. Before doing so, however, he lingers a moment on close-up shots of Hilton Edwards, to praise him as 'a great director' and as 'the best of teachers'. In the sequence that follows, he nevertheless treats his mentor as a mere character. He does so by rearranging bits and pieces from Hilton Edwards's illuminating comments to fit his own replies that, although they sound spontaneous, have been well prepared for. The whole sequence, in the end, leads up to Orson Welles, the only character in it to control its final meaning.

Welles also indulges in another type of manipulation, to which he easily admits in the first half-hour of his film, when he declares that his camera in *Othello* plays variations on Iago's snare. Implicitly, the director thus confesses to using the cinematic apparatus to entrap his spectators, in ways that still apply in *Filming Othello*. In this film, however, the visual snare is merely extradiegetic, while it used to appear as a motif infecting the shots in the 1952 *Othello*. This entails that Iago's remote presence in *Filming Othello* is exclusively translated in terms of a scopic regime that is articulated in a complex way with a manipulative soundtrack. This impression becomes more and more substantial shortly before the end of the film's first hour, after the lunch sequence. First, Welles shows pictures from his original film that seem randomly put together and are therefore hard to connect with each other. To provide consistency, he gives the kind of voice-over soliloquy that features nowadays on DVDs under the category 'director's commentary'. Or at least, that could be the case if the commentary were about his film. Welles's words, however, apply to the play and his construction of the meaning of *Othello* is in keeping with the reconstruction he offers of his film. As a consequence, *Filming Othello* seems to be subtended by a new angle on Shakespeare's work. The pictures, because they are disconnected from one another, appear to illustrate the interpretation provided by Welles's voice-over commentary of his 1952 film. The spectators are placed in the same position as Othello in Act 4 scene 1. They are made to see what they see through the prism of an interpretation that is artificially added to their visual perception. The object of the alteration, however, is now a mediated moment of visual perception, rather than the unmediated perception of reality that is altered by the fictionalizing action of drama. In the next sequence, Welles appears in a close-up and starts reciting lines from the 'ocular proof' scene (3.3). The pictures from his film have disappeared because he has disconnected them, once again, from the words of the play. Because of this separation, Shakespeare's words, awkwardly introduced as they are by Welles's 'Now I'm gonna quote from' presentation, are placed on the same level as his other voice-over speeches in the film. They act as comments on his former *Othello* and point to the fact that visual evidence has become cinematic. Present-day Iagos are now to be found, like Welles, behind such tools for manufacturing ocular proof as the omnipresent movieola, editing the round, unvarnished pictures caught by reality-capturing devices and commenting on them to turn them into fiction.

According to Michael Anderegg, *Filming Othello* 'almost creates, or at least evokes, another film *Othello* in place of the one Welles actually made'.[23] Consequently, the essay film poses as a late addition to the 'textual puzzle that surrounds *Othello*', and confirms 'the provisional, unfinished, never-to-be-fixed state of so much of Welles's work'.[24] To complement Anderegg's textual analogy, through which he constructs Welles's *Othello* as 'yet another variation of a text [Shakespeare's play] which has always been unstable and unfixed',[25] I thus propose to consider *Filming Othello* not only as an outgrowth to Welles's 1952 adaptation but also as a *corrigendum*. The essay film, indeed, presents Welles's marginal comments on his former work, most of which suggest that the 1952 film needs to be amended. It invites spectators and analysts to watch *Othello* again and to consider its links with the play from a new angle. As a whole, rather than just in the newly edited sequences of *Othello* it includes, *Filming Othello* is an alternative version of Welles's 1952 film. It can therefore be treated as a re-adaptation of the play, one in which the deforming perspective of Iago has left the diegetic world, to be adopted by Welles. A new reading of the visual implications of Shakespeare's *Othello* seems to make the essay film necessary. Based on this interpretation, Welles implements an innovative adaptation system, after reshuffling the rules of cinematic adaptation with his former Shakespearean films. In *Filming Othello*, Welles acts as an avatar of Iago, placing himself outside the film in which he appeared years before and setting out to deconstruct it to dictate how to watch it. Consequently, Iago's decon-struction principle becomes part of a new adaptation strategy. Welles tears apart his former film in order to reveal the underlying bedrock for an innovative adaptation of the play. This adaptation is a structural one, as it were. Welles extracts the pattern of Iago's manipulation from the source work and gives this pattern pre-eminence by leaving the plot of *Othello* behind. A necessary consequence of this adaptation technique is that the new version erects itself on the remnants of the older one, which Welles submits to an analytical process. As a result, the new adaptation comes with a discourse on adaptation strategies. As a corrective on the old-fashioned way of making Shakespearean films, one whose credentials are heightened by the fact it is provided by the very author of such adapta-tions, *Filming Othello* promotes a reading of the play pared down to its essence and structures itself in accordance with this reading. This essence concerns the scopic regime of drama: *Othello* deals with the way theatre produces illusions by making the spectators gaze awry on reality. It is also, however, more universal than this mere illustration of Shakespearean reflexivity, as it is concerned with manipulating the senses and draws conclusions that apply beyond the precinct of the theatre. For Welles, Iago's forcing of perspectives on the real can no longer be treated as the epitome of dramatic illusion, not only because the cinematic apparatus now provides tools that are more efficient for creating such illusion, but also because film has changed the way reality is perceived. The scopic regime on which Iago and Shakespeare based their illusion has evolved, at least partly. This alteration makes Welles's treatment of it in his 1952 *Othello* irrelevant in some respects and prompts him to dislocate his film and to re-adapt the play. In the new version, Iago's manipulation of visual perception is treated as the art of tampering with film material. This perspective shows that an up-to-date discourse on deceit should not ignore either the prosthetic eyes and ears that equip humanity or the display and sound systems on which perception currently feeds. What is preserved, therefore, is the aesthetics of the play – in the double sense of how it is perceived and of how it analyses perception. This achievement comes at the cost of a recontextualization that concerns, rather than the plot or its meaning, the scopic regimes of reality and fiction. Consequently, *Filming Othello* is an anti-*director's cut* version. The film proclaims, in praise of Shakespearean adaptation, the need for *Othello* to be remade over and over, as the evolution of watching patterns gives new significance to the play's anatomy of how our senses dysfunction, sometimes at our expense, but also for the benefit of fictional alchemy.

Notes

1 M. W. Estrin (ed.), *Orson Welles: Interviews* (Jackson, MS: University Press of Mississippi, 2002), 207.

2 The film is available for viewing on YouTube at www.youtube.com/watch? v=fvqeQt8aLnU

3 To this, one should add the possibility that *Filming Othello*'s many missing sequences, if they had ever been found, would have changed its overall significance.

4 Y. Ishaghpour, *Orson Welles cinéaste, une caméra visible, vol. 3 (Les films de la période nomade)* (Paris: Éditions de la Différence, 2001), 801. In the chapter of his *Orson Welles, Shakespeare, and Popular Culture* on what he calls 'The Texts of *Othello*', Michael Anderegg also notices that *Filming Othello* includes 'several newly edited sequences from the original film'. M. Anderegg, *Orson Welles, Shakespeare, and Popular Culture* (New York: Columbia University Press, 1999), 98.

5 The full text of the interview is available in L. French, *A Complete Transcription of Welles's Last Finished Film:* Filming Othello *and an Interview with Cinematographer Gary Graver by Lawrence French*. Available at: www.wellesnet.com/ filming_othello.htm. Accessed 9 May 2014. In a similar vein, Anderegg remarks that *Filming Othello* employs 'editing strategies that work at cross-purposes to documentary "truth"' (Anderegg, *Orson Welles*, 100).

6 All references to Graver's interview are excerpted from L. French, *A Complete Transcription*.

7 A. Brennan, *Shakespeare's Dramatic Structures* (London: Routledge & Kegan Paul, 1986), 142–59.

8 A. M. Manzanas Calvo and J. Benito, '*Othello* and the Textual Construction of the Self' in M. F. García-Bermejo Giner, P. S. Garcia et al. (eds.), *Multidisciplinary Studies in Language and Literature: English, American and Canadian: in Memoriam Gudelia Rodríguez Sánchez* (Salamanca: Ediciones Universidad de Salamanca, 2008), 204–5.

9 Brennan, *Shakespeare's Dramatic Structures*, 144.

10 *Ibid.*, 142–3.

11 *Ibid.*, 155.

12 *Ibid.*, 143.

13 *Ibid.*, 148.

14 This idea is frequently expressed in the works of Shakespeare specialists. See for instance B. Escolme, *Talking to the Audience: Shakespeare, Performance, Self* (Abingdon and New York: Routledge, 2005), 18.

15 M. P. Klimek, 'Imagining the Sounds of Shakespeare' in R. Altman (ed.), *Sound Theory, Sound Practice* (New York: Routledge, 1992), 212.

16 Anderegg, *Orson Welles*, 115–16.

17 Ishaghpour, *Orson Welles cinéaste*, 85.

18 For a comprehensive list of the elements in Welles's *Othello* that emphasize the disconnection of sounds from pictures, see Anderegg, *Orson Welles*, 114–16. Anderegg convincingly ascribes such mismatching to Welles's artistic intentions, and shows that, in the film, 'synchronization, in effect, comes to stand for calm

and stasis', whereas fragmentation is an expression of chaos (116). My opinion is that this latter view naturally places the film's dislocated editing on Iago's side.

19 As D. G. Denery II recalls, 'Christian Metz ... introduced the expression "scopic regime" to name dominant and structuring relations between observer, image and object'. D. G. Denery II, *Seeing and Being Seen in the Later Medieval World: Optics, Theology, and Religious Life* (Cambridge University Press, 2005), 9. The reference is to C. Metz, *The Imaginary Signifier: Psychoanalysis and the Cinema.* Trans. Celia Britton (Bloomington, IN: Indiana University Press, 1982), 61–3.

20 All references to the text of *Filming Othello* are excerpted from L. French, *A Complete Transcription.*

21 Michael Anderegg similarly notices Welles's tendency to present Jorgens's interpretations as his own when he comments on his artistic use of the camera in *Othello* (Anderegg, *Orson Welles*, 101).

22 Ishaghpour, *Orson Welles cinéaste*, 803.

23 Anderegg, *Orson Welles*, 100.

24 *Ibid.*, 99.

25 *Ibid.*, 120.

WORKS CITED

Anderegg, M. *Orson Welles, Shakespeare, and Popular Culture* (New York: Columbia University Press, 1999).

Brennan, A., *Shakespeare's Dramatic Structures* (London: Routledge & Kegan Paul, 1986).

Denery II, D. G., *Seeing and Being Seen in the Later Medieval World: Optics, Theology, and Religious Life* (Cambridge University Press, 2005).

Escolme, B., *Talking to the Audience: Shakespeare, Performance, Self* (Abingdon and New York: Routledge, 2005).

Estrin, M. W. (ed.), *Orson Welles: Interviews* (Jackson, MS: University Press of Mississippi, 2002).

French, L., *A Complete Transcription of Welles's Last Finished Film:* Filming Othello *and an Interview with Cinematographer Gary Graver by Lawrence French.* Online. Available at: www.wellesnet.com/filming_othello.htm. Accessed 9 May 2014.

Ishaghpour, Y., *Orson Welles cinéaste, une caméra visible, vol. 3 (Les films de la période nomade)* (Paris: Éditions de la Différence, 2001).

Klimek, M. P., 'Imagining the Sounds of Shakespeare' in Altman R. (ed.), *Sound Theory, Sound Practice* (New York: Routledge, 1992), 204–16.

Manzanas Calvo, A. M. and J. Benito, '*Othello* and the Textual Construction of the Self' in García-Bermejo Giner M. F., Garcia P. S. et. al. (eds.), *Multidisciplinary Studies in Language and Literature: English, American and Canadian: in Memoriam Gudelia Rodríguez Sánchez* (Salamanca: Ediciones Universidad de Salamanca, 2008), 197–208.

Metz, C., *The Imaginary Signifier: Psychoanalysis and the Cinema.* Trans. Celia Britton (Bloomington, IN: Indiana University Press, 1982).

CHAPTER 5

'Institutionally racist'
Sax's Othello *and tethered presentism*

Peter J. Smith

Pre-scription

What follows started life as a conference paper presented at the University of Montpellier III on 22 June 2012. It is an experiment in what I am calling 'tethered presentism', a critical approach which takes place within the context of current and concrete events, a presentism tethered to a particular time: *now* or, in the case of what follows, *then* (22 June 2012). I offer a reading of Geoffrey Sax's film version of *Othello* in the light of contemporary legal cases and the Euro 2012 football tournament. Although that tournament has now finished and the various trials mentioned have progressed, I have not sought to update the paper as it was given. The reader will find, in a postscript, a description of the position at the time of writing (30 June 2014) but this too, in due course, will be superseded. Tethered presentism must of necessity acknowledge its own transitoriness, the compensation for which is a demonstration of the topicality of particular readings and the integration of critical practice and immediately pressing sociopolitical concerns.

Euro 2012 and contemporary racism

I have been following the saga of Roy Hodgson's England team selection for Euro 2012. In October 2011, Chelsea played Queen's Park Rangers. During the course of that match, the Chelsea centre half, John Terry, was alleged to have racially abused QPR's Anton Ferdinand. Instead of bringing him to trial and resolving his case one way or the other, Westminster Magistrates' Court agreed to delay Terry's trial to allow him to play in the European Championship (he will face trial in July). Whether such an indulgence would have been granted to anyone less famous on the grounds that their professional commitments clashed with their trial dates is a moot point – but let that pass.

Hodgson selected Terry for the England squad and, for what he described as 'football reasons', he chose to exclude Rio Ferdinand, Anton's elder brother. This has given rise to the suspicion that Rio Ferdinand, who has played no fewer than 81 times for his country, was excluded because to have an alleged racist abuser and the victim's brother in the same squad would have been bad for morale (this in spite of the fact that Ferdinand is on record as saying that he would be prepared to play alongside Terry). In other words, it appears that Rio Ferdinand has been excluded from the national team because his brother was the alleged victim of a racial insult. Hodgson has admitted, 'I can't turn round to you and say it didn't occur to me. I'm a football person. I work in football, day in, day out. I don't live on the planet Mars. So you can't expect me to say I didn't give that a thought'.[1] Hodgson went on to argue that a player of Ferdinand's experience ought only to play in the first eleven but since he wasn't wanted in the starting team, there was no point taking him (this in spite of the fact that Ferdinand is on record as saying he'd be happy to start out on the substitutes' bench). Jamie Moralee, an adviser to Ferdinand has described Hodgson's decision as 'nothing short of disgraceful' and criticized the England manager for showing Ferdinand 'a total lack of respect'. Hodgson has responded by maintaining that Ferdinand's exclusion was for 'football reasons' only and 'I'll have to live with the fact – no doubt in this tournament and maybe for years ahead – that people have said other things'.[2]

This flurry of internecine argument over racist accusations came just ten days after the BBC broadcast of a *Panorama* programme (2 June 2012) which documented the deep-seated racist hatefulness of football fans in Poland and the Ukraine, the two countries that are jointly hosting Euro 2012. The documentary included footage of white supremacists chanting anti-Semitic insults and making monkey noises at black players, raising arms in Nazi salutes to a chorus of '*Sieg Heil*' and, perhaps most shockingly, physically attacking a small group of Asian fans who were not segregated because they were supporting the same team. During the programme, the footage was shown to Sol Campbell, a black footballer and a veteran of Tottenham, Arsenal and Newcastle, as well as former England captain, who branded the behaviour 'absolutely disgusting' and advised black and Asian English fans to stay at home 'and watch the whole thing on TV. You could end up coming back in a coffin'. Campbell has also vowed to return all of his 73 England caps if it is ever proven that Hodgson's exclusion of Ferdinand were for anything other than 'football reasons'.

On 18 June 2012 *The Guardian* reported that Croatia's head coach, Slaven Bilic, criticized Croatia's fans for making monkey noises and throwing a banana onto the pitch during Croatia's game against Italy on 14 June. The Czech Republic defender Theodor Gebre Selassie attracted the racist chants of Russian fans during the match on 8 June. Selassie did not file a report stating, 'It was nothing extreme. I've experienced much worse'.[3]

But the Euro tournament is by no means the only seat of contemporary racism. The rise of the Golden Dawn party in Greece, whose official spokesman, Ilias Kasidiaris, is currently on the run having assaulted two female left-wing politicians on a live TV broadcast, and who missed a court appearance scheduled for 11 June on charges of assault and possession of a weapon, is the latest spectacular demonstration of the link between austerity economics and reactionary politics. The recent emergence of Jean-Marie Le Pen's daughter, Marine, and granddaughter, Marion Maréchal-Le Pen, who came to power for the far right in the French legislative elections on 17 June 2012, is another instance uncomfortably closer to home. In the UK while the Kick Racism Out of Football campaign is able to demonstrate some success in comparison to the bad old days of the 1970s and '80s, the emergence of Islamophobic groups and the English Defence League signals that the UK is by no means home and dry – wherever that 'home' happens to be.

What I want to argue is that the Andrew Davies / Geoffrey Sax adaptation of *Othello*, first broadcast over a decade ago (2001) has, due to the shape of current events, taken on a fresh and contemporary resonance. On 31 May 2012, *The Guardian* reported that the newly re-elected mayor of London, Boris Johnson, had announced a review of the progress of various recommendations made in the Race and Faith inquiry report published in July 2010 and commissioned by Johnson in 2008: 'It's important that we look at where we are now ... the progress made and how we are getting on'.[4] Bernard Hogan-Howe, Metropolitan Police Commissioner, remarked that he had intended such changes to have been implemented by 2013 but that, given the high number of recent complaints, he was spurred to accelerate the process: 'I think it's vital that we always challenge ourselves but clearly in these complaints if any of them are true and for that to be tested, there are things there we need to sort out. And so for that reason I think it's vitally important that we make sure that racists know they've got no home in the Met, and I've tried to make that as clear as possible verbally.'[5]

Yet, *Face the Facts* on BBC Radio Four reported on 4 June 2012 that in spite of the former Home Secretary Jack Straw's undertaking to implement the Macpherson Report's recommendation to increase 'recruitment, retention and promotion' of black and minority policemen, in 2010, while 165 signed up, 204 left. (The Macpherson Report resulted from a review of procedures in response to the murder of Stephen Lawrence – see later discussion.) Charles Critchlow of the National Black Police Association remarked on the programme that the Police have 'a problem when it comes to dealing with race issues'. The programme cited the case of West Yorkshire policeman Kashif Ahmed who, in spite of being a Muslim, was commanded to fetch his superior officers a bacon butty.

The most spectacular of these recent instances is that of Alex MacFarlane whose case is to be heard on 29 June 2012 – just over a week away. MacFarlane arrested 21-year-old Mauro Demetrio on suspicion of driving while under the influence of drugs though no subsequent action was ever taken against him. While being arrested, Demetrio managed to switch his mobile phone on and the subsequent conversation was recorded.[6] The policeman can clearly be heard telling Demetrio, 'The problem with you is you will always be a nigger, yeah?' In spite of this apparently watertight evidence, the Crown Prosecution Service initially declined to prosecute MacFarlane. They reversed their decision only after pressure from the Independent Police Complaints Commission following the review of complaints about racism from the Met.

Just as Tim Blake Nelson's basketball spin-off, *'O'* (also 2001) was intensified by its proximity to the Columbine shootings – indeed the film's release was postponed by eighteen months in a vain attempt to distance it from the agony of the Columbine massacre – so the issues surrounding the conspicuous racist treatment of various footballers as well as the MacFarlane case intensify the current concerns about racism in the police. Sax's *Othello* offers an example of, at best, a weirdly prophetic insight or, at worst, a despondently accurate portrayal into the deep-seatedness of 'institutional racism' and the longevity of such corrupt systems which reside at the heart of our law-enforcing mechanisms. I would like to think that we *have* come a long way from the days of Millwall F. C. and Leeds United fans with their publicly proclaimed racism but if this is indeed the case, shouldn't Sax's film be looking jaded by now?

The murder of Stephen Lawrence

Writing in 1817, William Hazlitt suggested that *Othello* is set apart from the other three major tragedies by virtue of its very ordinariness:

The moral it conveys has a closer application to the concerns of human life than that of almost any other of Shakespear's plays. 'It comes directly home to the bosoms and business of men.' The pathos in *Lear* is indeed more dreadful and overpowering: but it is less natural, and less of every day's occurrence. We have not the same degree of sympathy with the passions described in *Macbeth*. The interest in *Hamlet* is more remote and reflex. That of *Othello* is at once equally profound and affecting.[7]

It is the present and quotidian nature of *Othello* that makes it so powerful. For Hazlitt the play's intensity lies in the capacity of the reader to empathize with the sufferings of the play's protagonist. Distanced from the regal madness of Lear by his obsessive and reiterated eminence – 'they cannot touch me for coining ... [I am] every inch a king' (20. 83–104) – the audience registers his insanity less as a portrait of senile infirmity than an elemental image of the apocalypse: 'Is this the promised end?', asks Kent (24.258).[8] Similarly the historically isolated brutalism – not to mention the strange, folkloric supernaturalism – of ancient Scotland, insulates the audience from the tragic vision of *Macbeth*. Finally *Hamlet*'s ponderous psychology renders its hero's pensive interiority too 'remote' for audience pity. The play's challenges are intellectually and philosophically rarefied; it is, therefore, unrivalled but, by the same token, inaccessible.

Othello, on the other hand, is a play striking in its everydayness; as Barbara Everett points out, '*Othello* is Shakespeare's only tragedy set entirely in the present.'[9] The play is contemporary in time, space and occurrence: it is merely about infidelity (or rather suspected infidelity), about jealousy, about petty rivalry (one soldier is promoted over the head of another), and about the ubiquity and tyranny of desire. *Othello*, for Hazlitt, is steeped in the problems of 'every day's occurrence', set amid the commonplace, the customary and the plain, what Wordsworth refers to as 'earth's diurnal course'.[10] *Othello*'s ordinariness is a feature of the play remarked upon by successive generations of critics. A. C. Bradley called it 'a drama of modern life' and over a quarter of a century later, George Wilson Knight shared this sense of the play as being peopled with recognizable characters, each complete with his or her own idiosyncrasies: 'In *Othello* we are faced with the vividly particular rather than the vague and universal ... The persons tend to appear as warmly human, concrete'.[11] Again, the play is judged unusual alongside the metaphysical dimensions of the other tragedies: '*Othello* is a story of intrigue rather than a visionary statement'.[12] *Othello* is characterized as a play that is remarkable for its straightforwardness, unusual in its usualness.

Moreover this historically rooted critical commonplace about the play's ordinariness remains current. In her 2012 essay on the play, Jeanette

Roberts Shumaker contends that '*Othello* may be Shakespeare's most relevant and accessible tragedy'.[13] As recently as 2005, Emma Smith writes of 'the ongoing fact of the play's unsettling relevance'.[14] While 'relevance' is a word that we unhesitatingly strike through in our undergraduates' essays, might it not be an appropriate term here? Surely the topicality of Sax's film derives immediately from the *relevance* of the play which, in turn, derives from the ordinariness of its scenarios. It is not a play about epic or dynastic struggles; it is a play about the blandness and recognizableness of human jealousy and self-interest.

But Sax's film's up-to-dateness is vouchsafed by its conversation with a current criminal case. In an interview of 2001, the play's adapter, Andrew Davies, was asked, 'Are the racial politics in your adaptation especially topical in Britain?' to which he responded, 'Yes, there's a famous case here called the Stephen Lawrence case . . . It's still quite a hot issue'.[15] Davies is referring to one of the most notorious and protractedly unsolved murder cases of recent times.

On 22 April 1993, a black 18-year-old, Stephen Lawrence, was approached by a racist gang at a bus stop in South London where he was attacked and stabbed to death. The very next day the police received an anonymous phone call identifying the perpetrators as Neil Acourt and David Norris. They were arrested and subsequently released. In April 1995 Stephen's family began a private prosecution against Acourt, Norris, as well as Jamie Acourt (Neil's brother), Gary Dobson and Luke Knight. One year later, this case collapsed. In February 1997, all five suspects appeared at a coroner's investigation and all five exercised their right to remain silent but the jury, without identifying any perpetrators, returned a verdict of 'unlawful killing'.

On 31 July, following the Home Secretary, Jack Straw, announced the formation of a judicial investigation under Sir William Macpherson which was denounced by the Police Complaints Authority. The Macpherson Report was eventually published on 24 February 1999 and found the Metropolitan Police Force to be riddled with 'pernicious and institutionalised racism' which it defined as being 'the collective failure of an organisation to provide an appropriate and professional service to people because of their colour, culture or ethnic origins'.[16] The report went on to single out Sir Paul Condon, the Met's Commissioner, as culpable. Amid allegations of police incompetence and racism, Macpherson's report called for an increase in the recruitment of officers from ethnic minorities.

More controversially, Macpherson proposed the scrapping of the so-called double jeopardy rule which prohibited second prosecution for the same crime. In 2003 this recommendation was accepted and a new law passed which stipulated that should 'compelling' new evidence come to light, a person could stand trial for a crime of which they had previously been found innocent. In May 2011 Gary Dobson's acquittal was quashed and he, together with David Norris who had never been charged with the stabbing, stood trial in November 2011. In January 2012, *nineteen* years after the crime took place, Norris and Dobson were convicted of murder and sentenced to life with a minimum of fourteen and fifteen years respectively.

On 31 May 2012 the Met denied that it had sought to shield Lawrence's murderers and maintained that it had passed all relevant material on to the Macpherson enquiry. Accusations have been levelled at Ray Adams, former Met commander who left the Met to work for NDS, a security company owned by Rupert Murdoch, as well as John Davidson who worked on the initial, flawed investigation into the murder. Adams was accused of taking bribes from and fraternizing with criminals, including a subsequently convicted murderer, Kenneth Noye. The Lawrence family lawyers asserted that one of Noye's accomplices was Clifford Norris, father of the accused, David. In addition, it was alleged that Davidson was also an associate of Clifford Norris and deliberately hampered the murder enquiry in an attempt to clear David. While internal investigations gave the Met clean bills of health, the Lawrence family was unsatisfied and called for an independent enquiry. On 1 June 2012, the Home Secretary, Teresa May, upheld this request to which Mrs Lawrence responded: 'it will be conducted by someone independent of both the police and the IPCC, organisations in which I have little faith and confidence'.[17]

The Sax *Othello* was a co-production between London Weekend Television and Masterpiece Theatre based in Boston. When it was shown in the States on PBS in January 2002, the ITV documentary, *The Murder of Stephen Lawrence*, was screened by the same channel in the same month. In the light of Davies's interview, and the proximity of the screenings of *Othello* and the Lawrence documentary, there is an ineluctable connection between Davies's adaptation and the insidious racism at the heart of the Met. What is appalling is that the adaptation is preternaturally prophetic of the condition of the Met at the present time.

The Davies/Sax film

Davies's adaptation appropriates and updates Shakespeare's play, setting it in the Metropolitan Police Force. While the film follows the contours of

Shakespeare's *Othello*, its ending lacks the play's poetic justice. Jago (the film's Iago character played by Christopher Eccleston) not only goes unpunished but is elevated to a position of authority from whence he can continue to promote racist policies. The film opens with a police raid on the council flat of black tenant Billy Coates (played by Morgan Johnson) and on the riots following his hospitalization. The sequence is oddly prophetic of the riots that began on 6 August 2011 following the shooting of Mark Duggan in his car. For four days the Met failed to contain youths who rampaged, looted and burned London as well as sparking similar riots in Bristol, Manchester, Liverpool and Birmingham. This led to much hand-wringing by David Cameron who spoke at the time of 'broken Britain' and dysfunctional families. Magistrates' courts ran an extended schedule in order swiftly to enforce order. Many of the sentences handed down were Draconian and have led to a large number of appeals.

Sax's film repeatedly cuts between the scenes of riot and a high-level banquet at which Bill Patterson's Sinclair Carver (the Met's Commissioner) announces with a statement straight out of the factual Macpherson Report, his new policy 'to recruit and promote black and Asian officers in the Metropolitan Police'. We cut to John Othello (Eamonn Walker), the only black policeman amid a sea of white faces. His dining neighbour, applauding the announcement while scowling at him makes clear the hypocrisy of the Force.

There follows a meeting between Ben Jago and Carver in the gents' – a nod perhaps to Richard Loncraine's 1995 *Richard III* which has Richard (Ian McKellen) soliloquizing his Machiavellian schemes while urinating, before catching us watching him in the mirror. The black-and-white tiled floor of the toilet in Sax's film – which will reappear in the Wellesian bathhouse when Jago tells Othello that Cass's bodily fluids have been found on Othello's dressing gown – is also an allusion to the chessboard upon which Kenneth Branagh's Iago stands a black king, a white queen and a white knight while pondering his options in Oliver Parker's 1995 film version of the play.

'So, where are all these black officers, you're gonna bring on?', Jago asks the Commissioner facetiously. 'Good point', he responds, 'If I could find any whose brains were as big as their dicks, I'd be a happy man, eh? Well it's the truth, isn't it? ... They're just not up to snuff.' The sexually well-endowed black man stereotype reappears later in the film. As Jago tells Othello to watch his wife in the company of her bodyguard, Michael Cass (the Cassio figure played by Richard Coyle), he alludes to Cass's prolific sexual history, describing him wryly as 'quite a swordsman'. Othello responds by gesturing to his own crotch as though to suggest that Dessie's sexual needs are being well served. Of course, we have just heard from PC Alan Roderick (Del Synnott) that Coates was attacked by PCs Adey, Stiller and Gaunt after he provoked them by waving his penis at them and asking Adey, 'Hey Bitch, you come to suck me?' There is something disturbing and unresolved about the suggestion that masculine sexual performance is racially distinct, particularly in the light of Cass's clumsy lunge at Dessie (Keeley Hawes) following their shared birthday bottle of champagne. It is as though Cass's whiteness is directly linked here to his inability to perform sexually.

The sexual suspicions of Shakespeare's Iago – that 'it is thought abroad that 'twixt my sheets/ He has done my office' (1.3.369–70) – are not articulated in Sax's film where Jago and Lulu (the Emilia figure, played by Rachael Stirling) have only recently met. The motivation here, by contrast – made explicit in the concluding moments when in answer to Othello's question, 'Why?', Jago hurls at him 'Because you took what was mine' – is over promotion to the position of Police Commissioner. Nonetheless, the film's suggestion of racially distinct sexual practice is made explicit by the juxtaposition of Othello and Dessie's lovemaking (another allusion to the Parker film) and the fully clothed Jago roughly bringing Lulu to climax by shoving his hand between her legs. She offers to reciprocate but he tells her 'it's not necessary'. We see Lulu and Jago later, post-coitally, she wearing his jacket and he in her pink dressing gown (see Figure 7).

Just as Cleopatra emasculates Antony by dressing him in her 'tires and mantles' and putting on 'his sword Philippan' (2.5.22–3), so Jago is symbolically effeminized by being dressed in Lulu's tiny dressing gown, which contrasts with the grandly voluminous gold silk of Othello's robe so central

Figure 7:   Jago in Lulu's dressing gown in Geoffrey Sax's 2001 adaptation.

to Othello and Dessie's lovemaking. This robe functions in the adaptation as a substitute for the handkerchief (in the play) where it becomes the forensic rather than merely ocular proof of her apparent infidelity.

Stuart Hampton-Reeves writes that the adaptation makes much of the Othello/ Jago relationship 'by making sure that Jago's racism was tinged with homoeroticism'.[18] We do see him kneading Othello's bare shoulders in the bathhouse but the declarations of love which bookend the film – Jago's 'It was about love. Don't talk to me about race, politics, stuff like that' – are not to be trusted. Jago, in a pair of parallel moments, demonstrates himself to be as much the victim of his ambitions as their architect. Having arranged for Commissioner Carver's racist jibes to be recorded by a journalist hidden in the toilet, Jago goes round to Carver's house to console him. As he embraces the commissioner, the camera circles round and we see Jago raising his eyes to us as a foreboding bell tolls his iniquity (one of the film's less subtle techniques). The moment is echoed when, hearing of Othello's promotion over his own head, Jago has to bite back his fury – to which he subsequently gives vent in an appallingly racist rant – and feign delight on Othello's behalf. His response is an ingenious combination of police-speak (he do the police in stereotyped voices) and apparently harmless-because-affable racism: 'Let's be'avin' you, you clever, big, black bastard'. This time, as the camera circles behind Othello and fixes on Jago's expression we see not the controlling Machiavellian but a distorted grimace of jealousy and hate. Jago does not look at the camera, unable at this point, to share his intelligence with us.

There follows the most explicitly racist section of the film, an updated equivalent of Iago's soliloquy which ends the play's first Act: 'I hate the Moor' (1.3.368). As the camera follows him down a crowded corridor in the police station (though as with onstage soliloquy only the audience/viewer hears him), Jago explodes with racist insults (see Figure 8): 'You stupid

Figure 8:   Jago's racist rant in Geoffrey Sax's 2001 adaptation.

patronising ape' and, as he mimes the outstretched hands of a blacked-up minstrel, 'How very darkie Sunday-school: "That's Ben Jago's job. I'm just a token, handsome nigger."'

Jago's fulminating rage is exhausted and we next see him straightening his tie and remarking to camera how the outburst has surprised even him. Although, from now on, we'll not see this unleashed side of Jago again, the sequence demonstrates the root and the degree of his professional and racist jealousy. We are miles away from Dr Johnson's description of Iago as being 'cool [in his] malignity, silent in his resentment, subtle in his designs, and studious at once of his interest and his vengeance'.[19] Coleridge's reworking of Johnson's verdict, 'motiveless malignity', in his notes on Iago's "Thus do I ever make my fool my purse" soliloquy (1.3.365) is also inapt here.[20]

Jago displays an adroit capacity to affect empathy with those around him. As he wheedles the facts of Billy Coates's murder out of the callow PC Roderick, he embraces him. Again we see a close-up of Jago's face as he tells Roderick, 'I know son, I've been there'. So intense is the empathy that Jago's cheeks are streaked with tears as the young policeman admits he is an accessory to murder.

After Roderick is ostracized by his colleagues for undertaking to testify against the arresting officers, Jago offers him a glass of whisky and tells him, 'You do the right thing and everybody shits on you . . . I understand; I've been there'. The 'I've been there' phrase exactly reappears in response to Othello's confiding in Jago of his love for Dessie, 'I never thought I could feel so much for another person'. Jago responds, 'Oh yeah John. I know what you're talking about. I've been there'. As Shakespeare's Iago puts it, 'I must show out a flag and sign of love,/ Which is indeed but sign' (1.1.157–8).

Perhaps the most disturbing instance of this empathic capacity occurs following Othello's outburst in a restaurant to which Cass has come in order to scotch the rumours of his and Dessie's affair. Othello goes for him and the two are only separated by Jago whose restraint of Othello rapidly turns into a man hug. Having sat down, Jago turns to the viewer over his shoulder: 'So, what do you think? I know, I feel it too. I'm almost sorry I started this. Too late now. It's up and running. It's beyond my control.' This fatalistic pronouncement belies the strength of Jago's motivation and there is an ingenious double take since we know, here, he is lying to *us*.

Following the failure of Roderick to testify at the Old Bailey – it seems Jago has managed to get him to take his own life with a combination of pills and alcohol – the case against Adey and the other policemen collapses and Othello realizes that he has broken the promise he made to the rioters to deliver justice. We see the (factual) newsreader Jon Snow announce the collapse of the case (interestingly we also see Snow reading the news in Ralph Fiennes's 2011 film version of *Coriolanus*). Obsessed by his professional failure and his marital problems, Othello appears on a TV chat show and, when challenged about racism, fails adequately to respond. From here Othello's fortunes spiral downward. Convinced by Jago that Cass's semen has been found on his gold robe, he (to the tolling bell again) enters the flat to confront and stifle Dessie.

Lulu, just like Emilia, intuits that Jago has been telling lies and confronts him. It is here that Jago explains his vindictive *raison d'être*: 'Because you took what was mine.' There is none of the remaining bewilderment as there is at the end of Shakespeare's play: 'Demand me nothing. What you know, you know./ From this time forth I never will speak word' (5.2.309–10).

Following Othello's suicide, we see the Prime Minister (John Harding) remarking upon the need for a 'safe pair of hands' and Jago appears in the ceremonial uniform of the Commissioner of Police and, as he offers his trite self-justification – 'It was about love. Don't talk to me about race, politics, stuff like that' – the screen whites out. So the future direction of the Met is to be restored to the 'safe pair of hands' which belongs to another white racist. Jago has replaced Carver and the failure of Othello will perhaps make such 'daring' appointments of black officers more unlikely in the future. Defeatist? Apathetic? Reactionary? Glumly realistic?

Tethered presentism

Stephen Greenblatt and Catherine Gallagher suggest a causal link between the rise of the New Historicism and the increasing enfranchisement of hitherto disempowered social groups. The emerging prominence of this critical approach during the 1960s and '70s, they write,

> reflected in its initial period the recent inclusion of groups that in many colleges and universities had hitherto been marginalized, half hidden, or even entirely excluded from the professional study of literature: Jews, African Americans, Hispanics, Asian Americans, and, most significantly from the point of view of the critical ferment, women.[21]

Critical practice, that is, is inflected by and responsive to the relative positions of gender, social and racial groups; in as much as the function of philosophy (or in our case, lit. crit.) is not to describe the world but to change it, we might easily go as far as to say that critical practice is, at every level, ideologically, perhaps even, politically tethered to the lived realities of these gender, social and racial groups. As Thomas Cartelli and Katherine Rowe put it, 'contemporary performances of *Othello* are haunted less by the play's theatrical or cinematic history than they are by the crises in racial relations we see staged daily'.[22] The consequence of this must be that critical practice (which necessarily includes interpretation, performance and, as here, adaptation) has an ethical responsibility.

This reasonably well-established principle has been given a new incarnation recently in the approach known as 'presentism', which Ewan Fernie has characterized as 'a strategy of interpreting texts in relation to current affairs which challenges the dominant fashion of reading Shakespeare historically'.[23] And he adds, 'The times are thrown into a process of dialectical self-questioning which might result in an alternative future'.[24] Fernie notes that the promotion of 'such responsibility to the present above the historicist obligation to the past' is 'a *deceptively simple* manoeuvre [but one which] constitutes a major methodological departure'.[25]

Offering a reading of Geoffrey Sax's film version of *Othello* within the context of current racial tensions (high-profile like those of Euro 2012 footballers or low-profile like those of all the arrested individuals who don't have the opportunity to turn on recording devices) is hardly a sophisticated thing to do but it may, nonetheless, remind us in a timely way of the stubborn inertia of prejudice. Stephen Lawrence's murder waited almost two decades for justice to be done and Sax's film seems as up to date now as it did when it was first broadcast over a decade ago. Given the importance of the issues it raises, perhaps there is much virtue in that deceptive simplicity.

Postscript

John Terry was found not guilty of a racially aggravated public order offence at Westminster Magistrates' Court on 13 July 2012. The next day, *The Guardian* reported: 'Duwayne Brooks, a close friend of the murdered teenager, Stephen Lawrence, tweeted: "Fucking bullshit. How can John Terry be found not guilty? You fucking black cunt is now free to be used by everybody."' Following Terry's acquittal, the Football Association launched its own hearing and, on 28 September

2012, found Terry guilty, banning him for four matches and fining him £220,000. On the eve of the hearing, Terry announced his retirement from international football.

Euro 2012: Following the elimination of England from the tournament, having lost to Italy on penalties on 24 June, Richard Williams, writing in *The Guardian* two days later, discussed the extent to which Wayne Rooney's disappointing performance belied the high hopes he had excited. The language of *Othello* lurks curiously just below the surface: 'there is a feeling that England have taken care of their most naturally gifted player not wisely but too well'.

Alex MacFarlane was charged with a racially aggravated public order offence and was tried in October 2012. The jury were unable to reach a verdict and he was subsequently retried. Again, the jury failed to reach a verdict and Judge Michael Gledhill QC decided that MacFarlane had suffered a 'momentary loss of judgement' and ordered that a formal not guilty verdict be returned. The judge went on to pronounce that a third trial was 'not in the public's interest'.

On 6 March 2014 *The Guardian* reported that Home Secretary, Theresa May, had ordered a public inquiry into undercover policing after Mark Ellison QC found that police had planted 'a spy into the Lawrence family camp'. *The Guardian* quoted Neville Lawrence (Stephen's father): 'What the home secretary has announced today is 21 years overdue. Mark Ellison's report has simply corroborated what I have known for the past 21 years and our long fight for truth and justice continues.'

Notes

1 *The Guardian*, 10 June 2012. Stuart Hampton-Reeves and Adam Hansen have been generous with their literary criticism and I thank both of them.
2 *The Observer*, 9 June 2012.
3 *The Guardian*, 13 June 2012.
4 *The Guardian*, 31 May 2012.
5 *The Guardian*, 31 May 2012.
6 See www.youtube.com/watch?v=4IKqUUnm6XA. Accessed 10 June 2012.
7 J. Bate, ed. *The Romantics on Shakespeare* (Harmondsworth: Penguin, 1992), 489. Hazlitt's quotation is a version of Francis Bacon's description of his *Essays*: 'they come home to men's business and bosoms.'
8 These quotations are from *The History of King Lear* rather than *The Tragedy*.
9 B. Everett, *Young Hamlet: Essays on Shakespeare's Tragedies* (Oxford University Press, 1989), 40.

10 W. Wordsworth, 'A slumber did my spirit seal', in J. Butler and K. Green (eds.), *Lyrical Ballads and Other Poems, 1797–1800* (Ithaca and London: Cornell University Press, 1992), 164.

11 A. C. Bradley, *Shakespearean Tragedy: Lectures on* Hamlet, Othello, King Lear, Macbeth (London: Macmillan, 1956 [1904]), 180. G. Wilson Knight, *The Wheel of Fire* (London: Methuen, 1962 [1930]), 97. N. B. Allen is even more forthright on the rounded humanity of Shakespeare's characters: 'Iago, Othello, Desdemona, Emilia, and Cassio are so lifelike, so convincing that . . . we suffer with them – in the study as well as in the theatre' ('The Two Parts of *Othello*', *Shakespeare Survey* 21 (1968), 24.

12 Wilson Knight, *The Wheel of Fire*, 97.

13 J. R. Shumaker, '*Othello*', in William Baker and Kenneth Womack (eds.), *The Facts on File Companion to Shakespeare*, 5 vols. (New York: Facts on File, 2012), IV, 1508.

14 E. Smith, *William Shakespeare's Othello* (Horndon, Devon: Northcote, 2005), 29.

15 See www.pbs.org/wgbh/masterpiece/othello/ei_davies.html. Accessed 6 June 2012.

16 See www.gov.uk/government/uploads/system/uploads/attachment_data/file/277111/4262.pdf. Accessed 30 June 2014.

17 *The Guardian*, 1 June 2012.

18 S. Hampton-Reeves, *Othello: The Shakespeare Handbooks* (Houndmills, Hampshire: Palgrave Macmillan, 2010), 138.

19 Quoted in Shumaker, '*Othello*', 1539.

20 S. T. Coleridge, in R. A. Foakes (ed.), *Lectures 1808–1819 On Literature, The Collected Works of Samuel Taylor Coleridge*, 15 vols. (Princeton: Princeton University Press, 1987), II, 315.

21 Quoted in E. Fernie, 'Shakespeare and the Prospect of Presentism', *Shakespeare Survey* 58 (2005), 169–84, 172.

22 T. Cartelli and K. Rowe, *New Wave Shakespeare On Screen* (Cambridge: Polity, 2006), 123.

23 Fernie, 'Shakespeare and the Prospect of Presentism', 169.

24 *Ibid.*

25 Fernie, 'Shakespeare and the Prospect of Presentism', 174, my emphasis.

WORKS CITED

Allen, N. B., 'The Two Parts of *Othello*', *Shakespeare Survey* 21 (1968), 13–29.

Bate, J., ed., *The Romantics on Shakespeare* (Harmondsworth: Penguin, 1992).

Bradley, A. C., *Shakespearean Tragedy: Lectures on* Hamlet, Othello, King Lear, Macbeth (London: Macmillan, 1956 [1904]).

Cartelli, T. and K. Rowe, *New Wave Shakespeare On Screen* (Cambridge: Polity, 2006).

Coleridge, S. T., in R. A. Foakes (ed.), *Lectures 1808–1819 On Literature, The Collected Works of Samuel Taylor Coleridge*, 15 vols., (Princeton: Princeton University Press, 1987).

Everett, B., *Young Hamlet: Essays on Shakespeare's Tragedies* (Oxford University Press, 1989).

Fernie, E., 'Shakespeare and the Prospect of Presentism', *Shakespeare Survey* 58 (2005), 169–84.

Hampton-Reeves, S., *Othello: The Shakespeare Handbooks* (Houndmills, Hampshire: Palgrave Macmillan, 2010).

Shumaker, J. R., *'Othello'*, in William Baker and Kenneth Womack (eds.), *The Facts on File Companion to Shakespeare*, 5 vols. (New York: Facts on File, 2012), IV, 1508–52.

Smith, E., *William Shakespeare's Othello* (Horndon, Devon: Northcote, 2005).

Wilson Knight, G., *The Wheel of Fire* (London: Methuen, 1962 [1930]).

Wordsworth, W., *Lyrical Ballads and Other Poems, 1797–1800*, J. Butler and K. Green, eds. (Ithaca and London: Cornell University Press, 1992).

CHAPTER 6

Intertextuality in Tim Blake Nelson's 'O'

Ronan Ludot-Vlasak

'O' is a free adaptation of *Othello* written by Brad Kaaya and directed by Tim Blake Nelson which relocates Shakespeare's tragedy in a South Carolinian prep school. Odin (Mekhi Phifer), who is the only African American student at Palmetto Grove Academy, is a basketball champion and also happens to be dating the dean's daughter, Desi (Julia Stiles). One of his teammates, Hugo (Josh Hartnett), resents Odin's success, all the more so as his father (Duke Goulding, played by Martin Sheen) is the basketball coach and claims he loves Odin 'like his own son'. In order to take his revenge, Hugo manipulates Odin, his teammate Michael/Mike (Andrew Keegan), his girlfriend Emily (Rain Phoenix) and Roger (a rich overweight student obsessed with Desi, played by Elden Henson), but his plot takes an unexpected turn. Roger is supposed to murder Mike, but does not have the courage to go through with it and only wounds him. Hugo kills them both, while Odin strangles Desi in her bedroom. When Hugo's plan is exposed by Emily, he shoots her in front of Odin who then points the gun at his own chest and pulls the trigger. Hugo is eventually arrested by the police and taken into custody. Although the film was made in 1999, Miramax postponed its release until 2001 because of the Columbine shootings.

'O' received mixed reviews. While the actors' performances were often praised,[1] some critics considered that the plot was hardly plausible and that the 'conflicts ha[d] been laid out in fairly simplistic terms',[2] or that the film's treatment of race and gender relations was inadequate.[3] My aim in this essay is not to assess the quality of the film – let alone discuss its fidelity to Shakespeare's tragedy – but to address the question of adaptation in relation to intertextuality. If one is to follow Thomas Leitch's categories, Nelson's adaptation is a form of updating, i.e. a strategy which consists in 'transpos[ing] the setting of a canonical classic to the present in order to show its universality while guaranteeing its relevance to the more immediate concerns of the target audience'.[4] Although I do not disagree with this assertion, I will argue that the relations between the film and Shakespeare's works do not merely boil down to the migration and updating of a plot in a different social and cultural context, but involve complex transcultural and intertextual transactions.

By articulating intertextuality and adaptation, I do not only intend to follow Robert Stam, who convincingly argues that 'one way to look at adaptation is to see it as a matter of a source ... hypotext's being transformed by a complex series of operations ... The source text forms a dense informational network, a series of verbal cues that the adapting film text can then take up, amplify, ignore, subvert or transform.'[5] I will envisage this adaptation *as* an adaptation, i.e. as an 'inherently palimpsestuous work, haunted at all times by [its] adapted text',[6] yet my argument will not be limited to the presence of *Othello* in *'O'*. Exploring Shakespearean intertextuality in the film does not only consist in identifying and commenting on references to the source text. In what follows, I will also focus on explicit references to *Macbeth*, on the implicit circulation in the film of images from other plays as well as on the use of Verdi's operatic adaptation of *Othello*. Another element to be taken into account is that intertextual references may not only be rendered verbally. Although one must obviously overcome the simplistic vision according to which literature is verbal and cinema visual – such a critical stance is even more debatable when it comes to the adaptation of a theatre play – some images of the tragedy are displaced and thus materialized on screen. I will attempt to shed light on these shifts from the verbal to the visual. More generally, my contention will be that *'O'* relocates the social and ideological environment of the play while also recuperating, literalizing and revisiting Shakespearean motifs and images. One of the aims of this article is precisely to explore their circulation in the film and the new forms of meaning and reading they generate.

Daniel Vitkus argues that the 'O' in *Othello* is 'an archetypal image, developing several hieroglyphic meanings' of the hero's initial and that 'its circular shape implies a "turning" or a "conversion"' – a pattern which structures the plot of the film.[7] The letter 'O' also works as a multifaceted symbol in *'O'* and involves a complex network of echoes and associations displacing some motifs of the play. It first recalls the basketball hoop, which is emblematic of Odin's glory and fall. The young hero is no longer the bravest of all soldiers, but an outstanding high school basketball player who is likely to be recruited by a leading university team. The basketball court is turned into a postmodern avatar of Shakespeare's wooden O:[8] an almost empty space on which O(din) displays his athletic prowess in front of an enthusiastic, if not mesmerized, audience – one of the effects of this public performance of masculinity being that it tends to naturalize and legitimize gender difference. The 'O' thus points to Odin's and Hugo's dreams of success, which are represented onscreen by the staircase at the beginning of the film: not only does the low vantage point chosen by the director create a sense of verticality and upward movement, but it is also associated with Odin's name since it makes the staircase look like an 'O' while showing the oriel window, which is O-shaped as well (see Figure 9).

Furthermore, the oval 'O' recalls the shape of an eye: this shot enables the viewer to discover a place no one but Hugo – except for Roger and Odin, on one occasion – have access to. The landing on the top floor of the building is indeed the place where Hugo likes to isolate himself and where he hides the hawk – the name and the living mascot of the team – which he steals. More generally, by intertwining the ideas of gazing, knowledge and deception, 'O' emphasizes a motif which informs the play: Othello's desire for an 'ocular proof' of Desdemona's guilt. Indeed, gazing is central to the dynamics of the film: Hugo observes Mike and his girlfriend before he gives him the scarf Odin offered Desi, Odin spies on Desi on several occasions or eavesdrops on Hugo and Mike's conversation about her without realizing that Hugo is manipulating him. Last, the title addresses gender-related issues, as it simultaneously recalls the fake engagement ring Odin gives Desi as a token of their eternal love, as well as sexuality and Desi's body.[9]

One scene encapsulates these different aspects (success, gazing and gender/sexuality). During a slam-dunk contest, Odin, who is on drugs, dunks the ball so hard that he destroys the backboard. Mark Thornton Burnett is right to observe the link between race and eye-witnessing in this scene. If one bears in mind that O sees Desi and Michael together for the first time 'through a library window' – glass here 'functions . . . as the barrier that frustrates the move to white membership and cultural integration' –, the destruction of the basketball hoop may be seen 'as an attempt

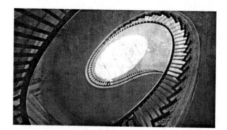

Figure 9:   The O-shaped staircase and the oriel window in Tim Blake
Nelson's 2001 'O'. All rights reserved.

to regain visual clarity and dismantle illusion'.[10] In Barbara Hodgdon's words, O also 'rapes' the backboard, shattering its glass backing before holding the hoop high over his head'.[11] He turns his head and glares at Desi and Mike who are sitting together and fail to make sense of his infuriated gaze. This violence recalls the scene in which the young man overpowers and eventually rapes Desi on the night they decide to have sex, but it also foreshadows the plot's most violent ending; the circular shape of the letter 'O', around which the poster of the film revolves, points to the very structure of the script and to Hugo's strategy: 'Everything comes full circle' the poster says (see Figure 10).

Not only are Hugo's motivations made more explicit than in Shakespeare, but some images which are associated with his monstrous plan materialize on screen. In order to justify his enterprise, Iago explains to Roderigo that Othello made Cassio his lieutenant instead of him and that he suspects the Moor has 'done [his] office' ''twixt [his] sheets' (1.3.369–70), but apart from these two arguments, no other explanation is given to the spectator. As the villain answers Othello in the final scene, 'Demand me nothing. What you know, you know.' (5.2.309). While discussing Iago's famous 'I am not what I am.' (1.1.65) in relation to narrative self-fashioning and improvisation, Stephen Greenblatt argues that the line

> goes beyond social feigning: not only does Iago mask himself in society as the honest ancient, but in private he tries out a bewildering succession of brief narratives that critics have attempted, with notorious results, to translate into motives. These inner narratives – shared, that is, only with the audience – continually promise to disclose what lies behind the public deception, to illuminate what Iago calls 'the native act and figure' of his heart, and continually fail to do so; or rather, they reveal that his heart is

Figure 10:   Poster for Tim Blake Nelson's 2001 *'O'*.

precisely a series of acts and figures, each referring to something else, something just out of our grasp.[12]

Although Iago engenders his monstrous plan in front of the audience, he is already starting to plot against his master when the play begins. On the contrary, the first two scenes of the film emphasize Hugo's frustration and prepare the viewer for the action to come. One of the effects of such a choice is to give credibility to his motivations; he wishes he could be in Odin's place, but this form of resentment also reveals his desire to arouse his father's admiration – a character who does not exist in the tragedy and to whom there is no reference. The first game of the film is a case in point: in order to win the game, the coach's strategy consists in using Hugo and another player as decoys – which means that they are not to touch the ball at any time – whereas Odin and Mike will score. Despite their lack of psychological and compositional subtlety, such scenes which revolve around Hugo's sense of being utterly neglected by his father or his desperate attempts to attract his attention aim at providing a plausible explanation for his acts – making them easier to 'grasp', to reuse Greenblatt's words. The presence of a father figure also anchors the film in a patriarchal system in which proving one's manhood is 'largely a homosocial enactment' prompting 'American men [to] define their masculinity, not as much in relation to women, but in relation to each other'.[13] Significantly, Hugo's mother is hardly to be seen and remains almost completely silent.

As Hugo's motivations are thus more visible than Iago's, some images associated with the villain's plan also materialize in Nelson and Kaaya's adaptation. Apart from the black and white contrast, one form of imagery which structures the whole play is poison. Not only does Iago reveal to the audience that his resentment and frustration are 'like a poisonous mineral, gnaw[ing his] inwards' (2.1.284), but he also compares his own revenge plan to a 'pestilence' he intends to pour into his master's ear (2.3.330). Othello himself considers that his feeling of jealousy 'comes o'er [his] memory/ As doth the raven o'er the infectious house,/ Boding to all!' (4.1.20–2).[14] When Brabanzio discovers in Act I that his daughter married Othello, he is convinced that the latter has 'abused her delicate youth with drugs or minerals' (1.2.75), which Desdemona clearly refutes. Once Othello has decided that his wife must die, he first intends to poison her:

> OTHELLO: Get me some poison, Iago, this night. I'll not expostulate with her, lest her body and beauty unprovide my mind again. This night, Iago.
> IAGO: Do it not with poison. Strangle her in her bed, even the bed she hath contaminated. (4.1.194–8).

In the first two examples, poison remains a simile pointing to the way both Iago and Othello are devoured by their own obsessions and, in the last two examples, it never materializes onstage: it turns out that Othello did not use any 'mineral' to woo Desdemona and, in Act 4, he gives up his plan to poison her.

On the contrary, the poison imagery is literalized in Nelson's film. Hugo, who is far from being as talented as Mike or Odin, is addicted to steroids supplied to him by his drug dealer. Odin himself starts taking drugs after Hugo plants the seeds of doubt in him: the latter offers him cocaine one evening and on the following day, just before the slam-dunk contest, he gives him pills which boost his aggressiveness whereas Odin thinks he only bought doping substances. While Iago delights in seeing that 'The Moor already changes with [his verbal] poison' (3.3.329), poison in the film is both verbal and physical, Odin's behaviour being altered by the drugs he starts taking. This literalization of the poison imagery also anchors the film in the social and ideological context in which it is relocated.

Nelson and Kaaya's decision to set Shakespeare's tragedy in a contemporary American prep school opens up new forms of meaning and interpretations. Othello's ethos is shaped by military values. As he explains to the Duke in Act 1, he conquered Desdemona's heart by speaking 'of most disastrous chances' or 'Of moving accidents by flood and field' (1.3.133–4). Shakespeare's character is a model of honour and bravery, which he proved on the battlefield, but he wooed her by relating his 'pilgrimage . . ./ Whereof by parcels she had something heard' (1.3.152–3). In *'O'*, the values and exploits which enable an individual to reach glory are no longer military. Those who achieve fame are those who display physical strength and Odin's scoring a basket one second before the end of the game – thus giving his team an unexpected victory – is an avatar of Othello's 'hair-breadth scapes' (1.3.135). While Desdemona 'devour[s] up [Othello's] discourse' (1.3.149), what seduces Desi and makes Odin an object of desire is not his relating his exploits, but the very performance of his sporting achievements on the basketball court. To use Greenblatt's terminology, self-fashioning is no longer narrative. Indeed, Odin is hardly a talented orator. As he tells Desi at the beginning of the film, 'The first time I talked to you, I thought I was gonna faint.'[15]

Furthermore, the battlefield on which Othello fought for Venice is relocated within the social arena – Roger Ebert aptly argues that the film shows that 'high school sports have become like a kind of warfare'.[16] Characters no longer fight for the good of the community, but to reach individual fame or conquer the heart of their beloved. Central to the representation of these individualistic drives is the motif of verticality – hinted at for instance by the staircase previously mentioned, or by Odin jumping as he dunks the ball. This is where the image of the hawk comes into play. This motif is both verbal and visual: Hugo wishes he were a hawk, but the bird is also the mascot of the basketball team.

When the film was released, some critics were puzzled by the hawk imagery. According to Elvis Mitchell in the *New York Times*, 'after a languorous first 40 minutes that gives time to nothing except Hugo's fixation on hawks, the picture vaults into a violent climax'.[17] David Ansen is even more critical: 'Director Nelson has talent when his pretensions don't get the better of him (what's with all the hawk metaphors?).'[18] In what follows, I would like to respond to these statements by exploring this imagery in the light of Shakespeare's references to hawking. This first requires a detour into the world of medieval and Renaissance literature and arts, in which the figure of the hawk was deeply linked with hunting.

Without reviving the legend of Shakespeare's having been prosecuted for poaching, the accuracy and variety of the terminology the playwright uses in his dramatic works testify to his knowledge – at least theoretical – of hunting. While his plays contain over fifty references to hawking, Kyd's, Greene's, Marlowe's and Fletcher's are almost devoid of them.[19] Hawking images in Shakespeare may first refer to gender relations, especially in comedies – for instance when Kate is compared to a haggard by Petruccio in *The Taming of the Shrew* (4.2.174). Their use in his historical plays also raises social, political and moral issues. Indeed, hunting constituted one of the main preoccupations of both medieval and early Renaissance nobility. It was a highly codified form of entertainment which was believed to be fit for the aristocracy and to teach a nobleman how to behave according to his social rank. The role of hunting – and especially hawking – as social representation is emphasized in the three parts of *Henry VI*. This is the case for instance in *2 Henry VI* (2.1) when Queen Margaret enters 'with her hawk on her fist', this scene enabling the playwright to characterize the protagonists according to their social rank, a pattern which is all the more striking as social contrasts and clashes are central to the dynamics of the scene.[20]

Yet in these plays, Shakespeare also departs from traditional uses of hawking in art and literature in order to explore its moral and political implications. The three plays point out the discrepancy between these hunting scenes, and the savagery later unleashed in *3 Henry VI* – plots, murders and fights are often depicted in hunting terms – enables

Shakespeare to show the moral degradation of the aristocracy, who progressively lose what distinguishes them from both the commons and the animal realm. In 2.1 of *2 Henry VI* – a scene in which the king and several noblemen go hawking – the dramatic interest of hawking rapidly shifts from the social dimension of the activity to its political implications. Gloucester's hawk's having flown much higher than the others – and especially the king's – is immediately interpreted by Suffolk as a sign of the Duke's disproportionate ambition. In Walter J. Ong's terms, hawking becomes a metaphor of power as 'overness'.[21]

This image of the soaring hawk as a symbol of power informs *'O'*, but raises different issues due to the contemporary context in which it is relocated. At the beginning of the film, Hugo says in voice-over (do we have access to his inner thoughts or is he addressing the viewer, so taking up a recurrent pattern in Shakespeare's tragedies?): 'I always wanted to live like a hawk. I know you're not supposed to be jealous of anything, but to take flight, to soar above everything and everyone. Now that's living.' The captain's name may also hint at Norse mythology, Odin being the God of war, victory and the dead. Yet in O's case, the film relates the twilight of a semi-god who lives in a world where glory is never long-lasting. Furthermore, the association in the film between Odin's name, hawking and blinding – O is a character who cannot see or interpret signs properly – may indirectly call to mind Richard Fleischer's *The Vikings* (1958) in which Einar (Kirk Douglas) is wounded by Erik's (Tony Curtis) hawk, which takes one of his eyes, and the Viking prince dies shouting the name of Odin.

Burnett points out that the birds in the opening scene suggest that Hugo 'is akin to a dark hawk, while O resembles a white dove'; the image of the hawk thus seems to challenge 'conventional signifiers of race' – although O then 'mov[es] back to type'.[22] The end of the first basketball game is relevant to this mirror effect between the two characters: Odin is being carried in triumph by his teammates while Hugo is watching the scene from a distance. These two shots are followed by a close-up of the hawk and we see once again Odin carried by his friends while Hugo remains at a distance. If the hawk stands for Hugo's wildest dreams, the character that is the most clearly associated with the animal and soars above everything is Odin, the best player of the school and probably of the whole championship. In not-so-subtle a way, Hugo's dream of becoming a hawk is clearly emblematic of his desire to take Odin's place, both on the basketball court and in his father's heart, and thus pertains to the public and private spheres.

Yet the connotations attached to the hawk evolve throughout the film.
The ending is particularly telling in this respect. When Hugo is arrested
and about to be taken into custody by the police, he repeats his first words
in voice-over (as the circular shape of the 'O' in *Othello* hints at,[23] we were
warned that 'everything comes full circle'), but adds two short sentences:
'I always wanted to live like a hawk. I know you're not supposed to be
jealous of anything, but to take flight, to soar above everything and
everyone. Now that's living. The hawk is no good around normal birds.
It can't fit in.' The image of absolute power is turned into a symbol of
marginality and used here in reference to Odin. As Hugo adds, 'Odin is a
hawk. He soars above us. He can fly.' Although the last two sentences
might be seen as an awkward and clichéd metaphor referring to the young
man's being dead and flying with angels – and to a Valhalla of sorts
recalling the Norse legacy of O's name – the hawk imagery also alludes
to his social and racial marginality. Ultimately, since hawks are often
blinded when they are tamed, this motif points to Odin's being incapable
of seeing that he is the object of Hugo's manipulation.

Moreover, the hawk imagery stands in sharp contrast to the doves which
live on top of the staircase. As a common symbol of purity and peace, the
white birds seem to echo Desdemona's 'whiter skin ... than snow,/ And
smooth as monumental alabaster' (5.2.4–5). In such a reading, the doves
may apply both to Desi and Odin. Yet the contrast between the doves'
white plumage and the dark hawk is also a visual contrast which is relevant
to the racial issues informing the film – the contrast between Desdemona's
and Odin's skins as well as the social and racial gap between Odin and
the rest of the school – all the more so since the hawk remains alone
whereas the doves are clustered together on the window sill.

The black-white binarism thus permeates the use of birds as visual
motifs in *'O'* and may be read according to the film's ambivalent racial
politics explored by Celia R. Daileader. While the film testifies to the
filmmaker's desire 'to "sell" early modern ideology to liberal-minded,
multicultural, anti-sexist, post-modern audiences' and to make the plot
more plausible (especially by expanding the time-frame of the play), 'the
murder scene is still incredible' to her. Indeed, she argues that the 'racist
premise' of the film (and of the play) is that 'if a white teenager strangled
his girlfriend on the mere *suspicion* that she was "two-timing" him, he
would be dismissed as a psychopath: here we are supposed to take him
for a tragic hero'. Furthermore, the sex scene of the film proves to be
particularly ambiguous as 'the rape sub-text to *Othello* is ... graphically
literalised' although 'it's not clear why'.[24] In other terms, it seems that the

film recycles – but may also simultaneously reactivate – some clichéd fears and fantasies about African Americans' sexuality. It is probably no coincidence that it is set in a southern state. Yet the image of the hawk as outcast is also relevant to Hugo's situation, since he is now to be a pariah. The film operates, then, a paradoxical movement: while the social, racial and cultural gap between Odin and his schoolmates is emphasized throughout the film – except when the team wins a game thanks to Odin – the hawk also blurs the line between the hero and the villain, the latter turning his victim into an idealized double with whom he identifies.

This desire for Hugo to be Odin may be read as a free interpretation of Iago's famous 'Were I the Moor I would not be Iago' (1.1.57) and may shed light on the interpretive choices made by the director and the scriptwriter. In his Arden edition of the play, M. R. Ridley argues that 'Shakespeare seems to have deliberately given Iago a trick of speech by which he makes remarks which appear at first hearing well-turned and significant, and on examination turn out to mean very little'.[25] It might also reveal Iago's ambition and social frustration. In Greenblatt's words, Iago's 'ability to imagine his non-existence' is more complex than it seems:

> Is the 'I' in both halves of the line the same? Does it designate a hard, impacted self-interest prior to social identity, or are there two distinct, even opposing selves? Were I the Moor, I would not be Iago, because the 'I' always loves itself and the creature I know as Iago hates the Moor he serves or, alternately, because as the Moor I would be other than I am now, free of the tormenting appetite and revulsion that characterize the servant's relation to his master and that constitute my identity as Iago.[26]

If one reads the line from the perspective of the film's interpretive stance, the reading which clearly prevails is the one which emphasizes Iago's desire to be in the Moor's place. This interpretation may also impact our reading of the following line ('In following him I follow but myself', 1.1.58) as well as the last words of his speech ('I am not what I am', 1.1.65). When he utters these words, he both insists on the fact that he is a deceiver, and parodies a famous biblical passage (Exodus 3.14) and thus defines himself as a devilish character who is the exact antithesis of the divine. But read in the light of the film, it may also hint at Iago's dissatisfaction with his own identity.

My point is not to say that this reading is more relevant than others, but to show that the adaptation of the play is not a mere transposition of the tragedy in an American high school, but requires a certain number of interpretive choices and that intertextuality is a process which may work both ways. If it is possible to read the film in relation to the play (yet in such a case, the risk is to have an essentialist vision according to which the

work '"contains" an extractable "essence", a kind of "heart of the arti-
choke" hidden "underneath" the surface details of style'),[27] it is also
possible to read the play in the light of the film and to see how intertextual
references as well as the displacement and circulation of images may
generate or favour new readings.

Another form of displacement consists in disconnecting motifs associated with the Shakespearean characters and relocating them in the film.
The willow song was removed from the script, but not the image of the
tree, which is displaced and haunts 'O'. The motel where Odin and Desi's
tryst turns into a rape is called the Willow Motel,[28] and later in the film,
the viewer discovers in a three-second shot an oak tree covered with
Spanish moss which looks like a weeping willow. At this point in the plot,
Hugo starts to make Odin doubt Desi's fidelity and his manipulative game
is proving efficient. Not only is the shot of the tree an Americanized hint at
Shakespeare's play – Spanish moss is emblematic of the Deep South –
which a viewer who has read the tragedy may easily recognize, but it also
foreshadows the bloody denouement of the film, all the more so as this
shot represents the tree at sunset. Significantly, the last scene of the film, in
which Hugo sits in the back of a police car, is preceded by a shot showing
the viewer another oak tree draped with Spanish moss. The music which is
played is the Ave Maria sung by Desdemona in Verdi's *Otello*. Although it
is a way to allow 'Desi's previously silenced perspective to enter the film's
concluding polyphony and to offset its dissonances',[29] the aria no longer
points to Desdemona's distress and feeling that she is about to die, but to
all the characters who died in the film – and especially Odin – as well as to
Hugo himself.[30]

This shift from a verbal to a visual motif – which is yet haunted by the
text – as well as this strategy of dissemination enabled Nelson and Kaaya to
root the image of the willow in the dynamics of the plot, but this process
also impacts the characterization of Desi. This reconfiguration turns her
into a much less obedient and submissive character than Desdemona. The
latter married the Moor without asking her father's consent, yet she is
referred to as 'A maiden never bold,/ Of spirit so still and quiet that her
motion/ Blushed at herself' (1.3.94–6). When she confronts her father in
the same scene, she reminds him that, although her primary loyalty is now
to her husband, he is 'the lord of duty' (1.3.183). Later in the play, whereas
Othello humiliates his wife in public, she still assures him of her loyalty
and warns Emilia at the end of Act 4 that they 'must not now displease
him' (4.3.16). During the first half of the film, Desi refuses to submit to
patriarchal authority. When her father questions her about her relationship

with Odin, she confronts him and answers: 'Dad, it's none of your business.' Later in the film, when Odin orders her to give him the scarf Emily has stolen from her, she also refuses to search for the object any longer and retorts in a determined tone of voice: 'I said we'd talk about it later.' Yet her submissive attitude after the rape clearly undermines this form of gendered self-assertion and suggests the presence in the film of patriarchal patterns involving the control of women's bodies through male violence and female submission and silence.

In a reader/viewer-oriented approach, these intertextual traces do not have the same meaning for a viewer who is familiar with the play as opposed to one who has never read it. Moreover, the question of intertextuality in the film is not limited to Kaaya and Nelson's re-creation of *Othello*. As adaptations may be regarded as 'multilaminated' works 'directly and openly connected to recognizable other works' and more specifically as 'palimpsests through our memory of other works that resonate through repetition with variation',[31] one may analyse *'O'* in relation to other cinematic adaptations of the play. For instance, the railings and gates throughout the film hint at the visual motif of the cage in Orson Welles's adaptation. Besides, intertextuality is not limited to Shakespeare. Martin Sheen's part as Duke Goulding may be read in relation to his impersonation of the American president in the TV series *The West Wing* (NBC, 1999–2006). All these possible echoes create a complex intertextual network which depends on who watches the film.

In *'O'*, this question of intertextuality is raised in a Shakespearean *mise-en-abyme*. In the only scene which takes place in a classroom, the students and the teacher comment on a quotation written on the blackboard: 'How tender 'tis to love the babe that milks me.' It is one of Lady Macbeth's famous lines, which she delivers when she urges her husband to murder his king (1.7.47–59). The two characters are interrupted by their teacher, who asks them if they know any of Shakespeare's works, a question Hugo ironically answers by saying: 'I thought he was a movie writer.' The episode lends itself to a metatextual reading for several reasons. First, the quotation is relevant to the plot that is to unfold. According to the teacher, Lady Macbeth uses this image in order to persuade her husband to do her 'dirty work'. In Burnett's words, this interpretation 'offers inadvertent encouragement to Hugo's misogynist reflections' and 'the gloss panders to constructions of female scheming, but implicit too is the idea of sexual excess', which is visible for instance in the use of 'dirty'.[32] Significantly, it is during this scene that Hugo informs Odin that he saw Mike with the scarf he offered Desi and convinces him to kill her and Mike shortly after – Lady Macbeth's clearly challenging her husband's masculinity when he is about to give up his murderous plan may also suggest that Desi's alleged affair with Mike jeopardizes O's masculine ethos. Second, it may be seen as an intertextual joke aimed at the viewers who know the play, while simultaneously hinting at the fact that 'O' is not *Othello*.[33] It may also show the ability for a film adaptation to contribute to Shakespearean studies. Ultimately, the process of displacement, relocation and/or dissemination at work in such an adaptation may thus shift the question of meaning in adaptation from the source text to the reader/viewer's response.

Notes

1 See D. Ansen, 'Final Score: O, What a Pity', www.newsweek.com/final-score-owhat-pity-152007, 9 September 2001, last accessed 24 June 2014; P. Tatara, 'Review: *"O"* overdone, but powerful', http://edition.cnn.com/2001/SHOW BIZ/Movies/08/31/review.o/index.html, 31 August 2001, last accessed 19 November 2012.

2 E. Mitchell, 'Film Review: The Moor Shoots Hoops', www.nytimes.com/2001/08/31/movies/film-review-the-moor-shoots-hoops.html, last accessed 19 November 2012.

3 Tatara, 'Review'.

4 T. Leitch, *Film Adaptation and Its Discontents: From* Gone with the Wind *to* The Passion of the Christ (Baltimore: The Johns Hopkins University Press, 2007), 100.

5 R. Stam, 'Beyond Fidelity: The Dialogics of Adaptation', in T. Corrigan (ed.), *Film and Literature. An Introduction and Reader*, 2nd edition (Oxford and New York: Routledge, 2012), 83 [first published in J. Naremore (ed.), *Film Adaptation* (New Brunswick: Rutgers University Press, 2000), 54–76].

6 L. Hutcheon, with S. O'Flynn, *A Theory of Adaptation*, 2nd edition (London and New York: Routledge, 2006), 6.

7 D. Vitkus, 'The "O" in *Othello*: Tropes of Damnation and Nothingness', in P. C. Kolin (ed.), *Othello: New Critical Essays* (New York and London: Routledge, 2002), 349.

8 The parallel between the basketball court and the wooden O of the Globe Theatre is also pointed out by Eric C. Brown in 'Cinema in the Round: Self-Reflexivity in Tim Blake Nelson's *"O"*', in J. R. Keller and L. Stratyner (eds.), *Almost Shakespeare: Reinventing his Works for Cinema and Television* (Jefferson and London: McFarland, 2004), 74.

9 The sexual innuendo in the letter 'O' is pointed out by Vitkus, according to whom 'the "O" in *Othello* has a great deal to do with the patriarchal joke about female sexual anatomy as "nothing", as opposed to a man's "thing"' (Vitkus, 'The "O" in *Othello*', 351).

10 M. T. Burnett, *Filming Shakespeare in the Global Marketplace* (Basingstoke: Palgrave Macmillan, 2012 [2007]), 76.

11 B. Hodgdon, 'Race-ing *Othello*, Re-engendering White-Out, II', in R. Burt and L. E. Boose (eds.), *Shakespeare The Movie II: Popularizing the plays on Film, TV, Video, and DVD* (London and New York: Routledge, 2003), 103.

12 S. Greenblatt, *Renaissance Self-Fashioning: From More to Shakespeare* (Chicago: The University of Chicago Press, 1980), 236.

13 M. S. Kimmel, *Manhood in America. A Cultural History*, 2nd edition (Oxford and New York: Oxford University Press, 2006), 5.

14 As M. R. Ridley indicates in a footnote of his Arden edition, it was believed that the raven was 'not only a bird of ill-omen and the harbinger of death, but also a carrier of infection' (136). M. R. Ridley, ed., *William Shakespeare's Othello*, Arden series (London and New York: Routledge, 1992 [1958]).

15 The line may also hint at Othello's epileptic fit in Shakespeare's tragedy.

16 R. Ebert, 'O', www.rogerebert.com/reviews/o-2001, 31 August 2001, last accessed 24 June 2014.

17 Mitchell's review, 'The Moor Shoots Hoops'.

18 Ansen's review, 'Final Score: O, What a Pity'.

19 M. Pope, 'Shakespeare's Falconry', *Shakespeare Survey* 44 (1992), 131.

20 Indeed, Winchester and Gloucester's argument is interrupted by Saunder Simpcox and his wife who burst onto the stage. This episode stresses the commons' lack of economic resources (as Simpcox's wife tells Gloucester: 'Alas, sir, we did it for pure need.' 2.1.157), but it also expresses the social superiority of the aristocracy insofar as the Simpcoxs fail to fool their betters.

21 W. J. Ong, *Fighting for Life: Contest, Sexuality and Consciousness* (Ithaca, London: Cornell University Press, 1981), 96. Shakespeare may also indirectly echo a proverb of his time: 'High flying hawks are fit for princes.' See M. P. Tilley, *A Dictionary of the Proverbs in England in the Sixteenth and Seventeenth Centuries* (Ann Arbor: University of Michigan Press, 1950), H229.

22 Burnett, *Filming Shakespeare*, 78.

23 Vitkus, 'The "O" in *Othello*', 348.

24 C. R. Daileader, *Racism, Misogyny, and the Othello Myth: Inter-racial Couples from Shakespeare to Spike Lee* (Cambridge: Cambridge University Press, 2005), 215–17.

25 Ridley (ed.), *Othello*, 7.

26 Greenblatt, *Renaissance Self-Fashioning*, 235–6.

27 Stam, 'Beyond Fidelity', 76.

28 The allusion is also mentioned by Hodgdon, 'Race-ing *Othello*', 102.

29 Burnett, *Filming Shakespeare*, 84.

30 One may also argue that the soundtrack of the film, which includes both rap and opera music, blurs the line between 'highbrow' and 'lowbrow' cultures. While opera music might be seen as a legitimizing strategy, popular culture also permeates the Shakespearean corpus through the use of rap music.

31 Hutcheon, *A Theory of Adaptation*, 8, 21.

32 Burnett, *Filming Shakespeare*, 82.

33 Similarly, the *Shakespeare Re-Told Macbeth* aired by BBC One in 2005 was a free adaptation from the play which did not keep the original script, although it recycled lines from other Shakespeare plays.

WORKS CITED

Ansen, D., 'Final Score: O, What a Pity', www.newsweek.com/final-score-owhat-pity-152007, 9 September 2001, last accessed 24 June 2014.

Brown, E. C., 'Cinema in the Round: Self-Reflexivity in Tim Blake Nelson's *"O"*', in J. R. Keller and L. Stratyner (eds.), *Almost Shakespeare: Reinventing his Works for Cinema and Television* (Jefferson and London: McFarland, 2004), 73–85.

Burnett, M. T., *Filming Shakespeare in the Global Marketplace* (Basingstoke: Palgrave Macmillan, 2012 [2007]).

Daileader, C. R., *Racism, Misogyny, and the Othello Myth: Inter-racial Couples from Shakespeare to Spike Lee* (Cambridge: Cambridge University Press, 2005).

Ebert, R., 'O', www.rogerebert.com/reviews/o-2001, 31 August 2001, last accessed 24 June 2014.

Greenblatt, S., *Renaissance Self-Fashioning: From More to Shakespeare* (Chicago and London: The University of Chicago Press, 1980).

Hodgdon, B., 'Race-ing *Othello*, Re-Engendering White-Out, II', in Richard Burt and L. E. Boose (eds.), *Shakespeare The Movie II: Popularizing the Plays on Film, TV, Video, and DVD* (London and New York: Routledge, 2003), 89–104.

Hutcheon, L., with S. O'Flynn, *A Theory of Adaptation*, 2nd edition (London and New York: Routledge, 2006).

Kimmel, M. S., *Manhood in America. A Cultural History*, 2nd edition (Oxford and New York: Oxford University Press, 2006).

Leitch, T., *Film Adaptation and Its Discontents: From Gone with the Wind to The Passion of the Christ* (Baltimore: The Johns Hopkins University Press, 2007).

Mitchell, E., 'Film Review: The Moor Shoots Hoops', www.nytimes.com/2001/08/31/movies/film-review-the-moor-shoots-hoops.html, 31 August 2001, accessed 19 November 2012.

Ong, W. J., *Fighting for Life: Contest, Sexuality and Consciousness* (Ithaca and London: Cornell University Press, 1981).

Pope, M., 'Shakespeare's Falconry', *Shakespeare Survey* 44 (1992), 131–43.

Ridley, M. R., ed., *William Shakespeare's Othello*, Arden series (London and New York: Routledge, 1992 [1958]).

Stam, R., 'Beyond Fidelity: the Dialogics of Adaptation', in T. Corrigan (ed.), *Film and Literature. An Introduction and Reader*, 2nd edition (Oxford and New York: Routledge, 2012), 74–88. [First published in J. Naremore (ed.), *Film Adaptation* (New Brunswick: Rutgers University Press, 2000), 54–76].

Tilley M. P., *A Dictionary of the Proverbs in England in the Sixteenth and Seventeenth Centuries* (Ann Arbor: University of Michigan Press, 1950).

Vitkus, D., 'The "O" in *Othello*: Tropes of Damnation and Nothingness', in P. C. Kolin (ed.), *Othello: New Critical Essays* (New York and London: Routledge, 2002), 347–62.

CHAPTER 7

Indianizing Othello
Vishal Bhardwaj's *Omkara*

Florence Cabaret

This chapter partakes of what is now well-known as 'postcolonial Shake-speare' and focuses on the Hindi adaptation of *Othello* by Indian film-maker Vishal Bhardwaj, a film which is itself part of a trend originating in the colonial history of India and its early familiarization with Shakespear-ean plays performed there for both an English and Indian elite. More specifically, we could say that *Omkara* participates in a recent phenom-enon of appropriation and adoption of the British literary canon and its transposition onto the Indian cinematic screen.[1] As an icon of British culture, its adaptation by the Bollywood film industry also reflects what Richard Burt has described as 'the indigenization and subversive appropri-ation of Shakespeare in postcolonial and developing nations' triggered by globalization.[2] But this cinematic adaptation of *Othello* also rests on a well-established tradition of Shakespearean performances on the Indian stage,[3] starting with prominent Bengali playhouses when Bengal came under the rule of the East India Company in 1757, leading to the 1848 first perform-ance of *Othello* with an Indian actor in the lead role up to the post-1947 British drama groups performing British Council-supported plays by Shakespeare, and to Indian drama groups performing home-grown pro-ductions of Shakespeare's plays, some of them such as *Macbeth* and *Othello* being translated into Hindi in the 1950s and 1960s. Still, the transposition of Shakespeare from stage to screen in an Indian context has already been undertaken in the Merchant-Ivory *Shakespeare Wallah* (1965) – a film relating the 1947 experience of the famous Shakespearana drama group and showing part of a performance of *Othello* – and by Indian filmmaker Gulzar when he shot *Angoor* (1982) based on the *Comedy of Errors*. So that we may go as far as to say that Shakespeare has become part and parcel of Indian culture, just like the English language, which Rushdie described in the 1980s as one of the many Indian languages potentially available for Indian artists and speakers.[4]

As to Vishal Bhardwaj, he was familiar with Shakespeare when he directed *Omkara* since he had made an adaptation of *Macbeth* entitled *Maqbool* in 2003, transposing Shakespeare to the contemporary Indian underworld, with a focus on Mumbai and the war of gangs and dons. If *Maqbool* gained him more international than strictly national recognition,[5] *Omkara* did very well at the Indian box office,[6] and it kept on promoting Bhardwaj abroad since the film was shown at the 2006 Cannes Festival. This time, *Omkara* takes place in rural north India, in the state of Uttar Pradesh, where the original Shakespearean plot is broadly followed, with a few displacements, among which I shall mention three, to start with: Omkara/Othello is not a noble general but he heads a gang of outlaws supporting a local politician; he first elopes with Dolly/Desdemona whom he marries only at the end of the film, just before killing her out of misconstrued jealousy; at the end of the film as well, the manipulative Langda/Iago is killed by his wife, who is also Omkara's sister and a friendly companion of Dolly.

Bearing in mind the film's attachment to Hindu caste hierarchies (more than to race hierarchies) and its belonging to the genre of the masala mafia film (i.e., a popular 'spicy' kind of film, that may be heavy-handed in its combination of action, crime, romance, comedy with song-and-dance scenes), I would like to show how *Omkara* is an Indian example of the many possible contextual readings of Shakespeare and how it departs from a strictly postcolonial reading of the text. Indeed, the film appears to be less a direct commentary on postcolonial relations between India and the UK than a reading of contemporary liberal (independent) India negotiating the fast rhythm of domestic changes in terms of politics, economics and social as well as moral values.[7] As Nandi Bhatia points out,

> Bhardwaj's refusal to place race at the heart of his adaptation of *Othello* is to bring attention to other kinds of urgencies that mark the contemporary postcolonial milieu in India: problems and crime related to caste warfare and the violence against women that remains at the center of these crimes, along with lawlessness, clan rivalry and political deceit. To this end, *Omkara*'s achievement lies in establishing, for a global audience, the ability of the Shakespearean play to speak to India's local ethos.[8]

That is why I will first examine how *Omkara* transposes *Othello*'s race issue into a caste issue, where religion and skin colour may also serve as indexes of one's place in the Indian scale of beings in a country which has both erased and maintained the notion of 'caste' in its 1950 constitution.[9] Then, I will envisage the translation of Othello's jealousy crime into an 'honour crime', which is said to involve both religious expectations of female sexual purity and patriarchal domination of women by men, and which questions India's current negotiation of gender equality and rights both in the private and public spheres. Lastly, I will turn to the way the song-and-dance dimension of the film qualifies its belonging to the successful mob movie genre by turning the famous handkerchief into a richly adorned waistband, which addresses more directly the question of men and women's approach of bodily desires and gender roles in this film.

My point here is to show that *Omkara* is representative of a post-independence way of approaching Shakespeare rather than a postcolonial reclaiming of Shakespeare. Indeed, the film transposes the classical colonial and postcolonial trope of black vs white into a more Indian appropriation of colour stigmatization, through a specific choice of actors, but also of costumes and light effects.

From the outset, we cannot but notice that Vishal Bhardwaj made the choice of an all-Indian cast so that he stands beyond a divide that has long been used to comment upon the colonizer/colonized relationship in colonial and postcolonial appropriations of *Othello*. This does not mean that Vishal Bhardwaj ignores the black vs white dichotomy: he introduces a subtle play on the issue of colour by displacing it onto costumes, with a tendency to oppose black and white in the colours of the clothes worn by the protagonists, especially in the middle of the film. Other scenes at the opening and closing of the film show the characters, and especially the male protagonist, wearing white and colourful shirts, and even on one occasion lending his black jacket to his beloved. We may interpret such an alternation between black and white as a way of reminding us of an opposition that does not necessarily have the same symbolism in India and in Europe:[10] the adapted play has to be watched through lenses that cannot be strictly European. This regular play on black and white tells us that the film is aware that Indian and diasporic audiences are familiar with this Western opposition between black/evil and white/good, but also with the dramatic impact of the visual contrast between the two colours, especially in numerous scenes taking place at night, in the shadowy wings of public life, not to mention the striking visual effect produced by white costumes when they are worn by wounded characters. One may, for instance, refer to the moment when Dolly first meets Omkara, who has just been shot in the upper chest. In this scene, Dolly is literally marked by Omkara's blood, underlining that, from the origin of their relationship, and in spite of their different complexions, they share the same colour – that of lethal passion. Yet, by showing a Dolly who is fairer than Omkara, the film recuperates the issue of skin complexion and skin hues within the

Indian context where skin colour is regarded as an index of caste belonging and as a beauty criteria. We may thus say that Omkara addresses first and foremost a coloured/Indian audience, whose perception of skin colour may not so much oppose black and white as light brown and dark brown. Still, by choosing a darker actor for the male lead role, Vishal Bhardwaj also points to the underlying presence of a tawny North African Othello and black actor to perform the role, as was often debated among stage directors and academics dealing with this particular Shakespearian play.

However, the film explicitly enhances a domestic hierarchy pointing to social and religious status based on skin colour in India. Indeed, as Lalita Pandit Hogan has also underlined, Vishal Bhardwaj's film obviously engages with Hindu mythology and deities and their association with specific colours. Thus, Omkara is reminiscent of the central Hindu figure Krishna (which means 'dark-blue' in Sanskrit), while Dolly would stand for his consort, the milkmaid Radha (connecting her to the colour white).[11] Thus, on the first day when Dolly arrives at Omkara's place, she is greeted by all the villagers and by an old woman in particular, who cannot suppress her surprise at seeing such a white girl in her village of Uttar Pradesh where people have much darker skins ('Looking whether she has been white-coated!', as if her whole body had been covered with a thin layer of white). Simultaneously, Omkara is depicted as having a low social origin and partly belonging to a low caste on his mother's side (whereas his father used to be an upper-caste Brahmin). By commenting publicly on Dolly's social superiority to her lover, the old woman openly questions the legitimacy of Omkara's breach of decency as he has an affair beyond caste divisions and beyond religious, legal tradition – and, what is more, it is the woman who is regarded as superior to the man. But the film also shows that arrangements can be made in the underworld: Omkara introduces insecurity and disturbance in the world he rules as he has eventually managed to become the local leader of a Brahmin-led party. By upsetting the traditional laws of religious hierarchy and political power, Omkara is staged as the trespasser imposing new behaviours and attitudes in a strictly regulated spiritual and moral world – which does not refrain from resorting to corruption though.

By transposing the race problem into caste politics, the film touches a prickly topic in an India which had hoped independence could be a way of redressing cast inequalities and boundaries but which had not imagined that bribing and plotting could contribute to such an evolution of mores. The fact that Omkara/Othello has shifted from noble general to mafia ringleader supporting a local politician also provides a form of commentary on the difficulties of democratic India to cope with one of its most troubling current woes, i.e. corruption and organized crime. Moreover, in the underworld, the code of honour is omnipresent and goes along with a great fear of treason and betrayal, rekindling in its own way the dread of 'the enemy within' as illustrated by the parts played by Langda/Iago and Dolly/Desdemona. Indeed, Langda actually plots against his superior by having Dolly accused of cheating on her lover. In the two configurations, treachery and opposition (real and potential) are depicted as thriving in the circles that are closest to the leader of the gang. The question of faithfulness and proximity appears to be all the more relevant in this Indian version as Langda is married to Omkara's sister and therefore belongs to his family. This definitely emphasizes the sense of betrayal, especially in an Indian popular film where extended families and family ties are frequent ingredients.[12] What is more, for an audience who is aware of India's history, this fabricated betrayal meant to hide Langda's true betrayal may echo tragic episodes that marked the life of post-independence India, from the trauma of the 1947 Partition with the numerous riots and slaughters that opposed former brothers (i.e., Muslims and Hindus), to the circumstances of Gandhi's assassination in 1948 and Indira Gandhi's assassination in 1981 (as they were killed by former supporters), not to mention the bomb attacks which started in India in the 1990s and which were initiated by Indian groups of internal opponents. Thus, *Othello* appears to be quite an apt play to stage "the full range of contemporary fears" in India. As Frances Dolan indicates, commenting on Elizabethan fears that are traceable in Shakespeare's plays: 'the racial other; the traitor who schemes against the nation from within; the witch; the plotting subordinate; the abusive authority figure. Granting Othello with [sic] protagonist status, the play yet allies him with each of these spectres of disorder'.[13] In his own approach of *Omkara*, Alfredo Michel Modenessi also underlines the public consequences of an insider's betrayal as the Indian film even appears to lay the emphasis more than Shakespeare on the spreading of the tragedy beyond the private circle of the protagonists:

> The destructive process, then, is set between 'brothers' – violent men used to having one another's back – one of whom will no longer trust the other, because the other has chosen to trust outside his circle. A tragedy of difference is thus triggered, but it runs opposite to Shakespeare's. *Omkara* explores systemic violence more overtly than its source does: it proceeds inside-out instead of outside-in, foregrounding disaffiliation from the original outlawed group over flawed assimilation to the legally hegemonic social body.[14]

Contrary to the false perception many Western people may have of India as a non-violent mystical country, the film obliquely sketches the picture of an independent India as a strongly unequal and violent country where the fear of betrayal within the public sphere goes hand in hand with the fear of betrayal within the private sphere.

Indeed, what is striking in *Omkara* is that it puts to the fore a crucial issue in Shakespeare's play, which has been accounted for by Frances Dolan who describes *Othello* as the embodiment of a shift of representation and budding concern for the figure of the murderous husband. Dolan analyses how Shakespeare's *Othello* originally questioned popular accounts constructing 'a wife's murder of her husband as petty treason' and 'a husband's murder of his wife as petty tyranny'[15] and how those popular accounts did 'not represent this petty tyranny as threatening social order in the same ways that petty treason did'.[16] In a country regularly shaken by sorry tales of violence against baby girls and women (from feticides to faked or forced suicides), the implicit tolerance of certain assaults against females inevitably informs our perception of *Omkara* as it recycles the Shakespearean approach of the greater criminal nature of petty treason over petty tyranny depending on the sex of the perpetrator.

In the film, the loss of a man's honour, which is introduced as early as the third scene, is to be blamed on the daughter's or the wife's lack of responsibility. In this initial scene, Dolly, even though depicted as a supposedly kidnapped daughter, appears to be lost in her father's eyes because her (and therefore his) honour has been soiled by this moral lapse. The lapse is all the more unbearable as Dolly makes it clear that she followed Omkara of her own accord. From that moment, Dolly will bear the burden of the poisonous fatherly accusation of frailty and treason, which will keep gnawing at Omkara's conscience and trust in Dolly. By underlining the shift of shame from father to husband, the film dramatizes the fact that a woman's life and honour necessarily rest in their hands. It therefore addresses the contemporary issue of honour crimes, regarded as the most tyrannical form of domestic violence committed by men and families against so-called fallen women.

Still, the film also adapts the play's script in a way that shows women as trying to redress the course of male-dominated events. There is already a hint to such a possible development in Shakespeare's *Othello*, as Dolan writes:

> As Iago joins the two plots, Emilia disentangles them. Choosing her role as loyal servant over her role as wife, she identifies Iago as a petty traitor, Othello as a domestic tyrant and Desdemona as the victim of them both.[17]

This narrative potentiality is actually carried out by Vishal Bhardwaj when, at the end of the film, the faithful servant Indu/Emilia is not killed by Langda/Iago. It is even quite the reverse which takes places as Indu slashes Langda's throat after she understands his and her role in the murder of Dillo/Desdemona and the suicide of Omkara – and especially how Langda manipulated her to avenge himself. Because it ends with the murder of Langda by his wife, the film suggests a form of female agency and empowerment – even though Indu resorts to the same violence as men, as opposed to the legal condemnation Iago has to face in *Othello*. By resorting to such a final option, the film also shows the power of the contamination of violence in a corrupt world where its least protected actors know they can no longer turn to lawful remedies.

Thus, the film reorients the spectators' perspective onto the motif of the honour crime in various ways. By resorting to colour-blindness (as the cast is an all-Indian cast), it contests the orientalist pattern of the black man's violence against the white woman. By choosing to locate the plot in a Hindu community, the film also challenges another biased perception of honour crime as taking place in Muslim countries and communities. One should not forget that even before 9/11 India suffered from religious tensions, riots and political rivalry involving Muslim and Hindu people, so that the film may contribute to a less dichotomist perception of India both at home and abroad: obviously, Muslim people cannot be accused of being the only perpetrators of intolerance, and patriarchy is depicted as a more general evil afflicting various religions. We could even go as far as to say that the well-known motif of marriage, which keeps recurring in Indian films to the point that it has become a trademark of Indian cinema, is being questioned as the embodiment of absolute tyranny, arbitrary authority and domination. Countering the folkloric approach of wedding ceremonies used for the delight of the spectators' eyes, *Omkara* may be interpreted as a film using the popular genre of the mafia film to raise both a social and cinematic question about the nature of marriage in Indian society, and in the way it is staged in most Indian films. Dolan already indicated that *Othello* could be read as a way of interrogating the meaning of marriage, once we have understood that the final murder may only be there to distract our attention from the true question raised by the play:

> Yet by dwelling on murder – the most extreme abuse of authority – and demonizing it as the work of Tyrants, lunatics and Moors, the representations of wife-killing avoid implying that marriage is arbitrary, tyrannous and exploitative, or that wives' rebellion might be justified.[18]

Indeed, the film does insist on Dolly's fate as trapped between two marriages: one she decides to put an end to from the outset of the plot, and the other one which she chooses for herself and which is responsible for her death. We may simply say that it is a way of underlining the risk she took in opposing her parents' arranged marriage to favour a love marriage, pointing to the changing mores that characterize contemporary India. But Indu's final murder of her husband Langda shows that rebelling is not only a daughter-parents issue. For all these reasons, we may assert that the film leads us to reconsider the repressed violence that hides behind the glamorous images of wedding ceremonies regularly displayed by so-called Bollywood sentimental comedies. Relocating *Othello* in an Indian underworld context would not only be a way of prolonging other contemporary appropriations of Shakespeare's tragedies turned into mob movies,[19] it would also be a means to denounce the connection between violence in public life and violence in private life and to counter the idea that marriage is necessarily the happy ending of a film and of people's lives: it may well be the beginning of a tragic film and of a tragic life.

The hybrid nature of *Omkara* as a mob film regularly interspersed with song-and-dance sequences between lovers and a few item numbers also leads us back to the Indian and filmic adaptation of the play.[20] Indeed, the necessary dance ingredient of the masala film actively contributes to the metamorphosis of Othello's 'ocular proof' (3.3.365) (i.e., the handkerchief he offers to Desdemona), into a richly adorned waistband that physically displaces our visual interpretation of the Shakespearean plot, rekindles various sexual bonds that already exist in the play and illustrates the creativity of Indian filmmakers appropriating the British canon.

The shift from handkerchief to waistband provides a relevant equivalent of the Shakespearean token and its association with sexual consummation. It is reminiscent of the legendary belts of chastity offered by knights and military leaders to their wives when they went to war, even though it is explicitly worn as a belt of seduction by Dolly herself. Further on in the film, it is conceived as a belt of more crude lust by Indu, who appears to have coveted and stolen the beautiful object on her own. Indeed, she is never shown to be urged by Langda to rob the waistband and she appears to act of her own free will and desire. Later though, she is definitely not aware of the use her husband makes of the belt. From these few details, we grasp that it acts as a polysemic prop, both bounding and unbounding female sexuality, but also both empowering and disempowering women. Indeed, it may appear to be an echo of the orientalist motif of the belly dance, which connects Dolly, the faithful woman, to Billo – the equivalent of Bianca in *Othello* – the fallen woman who performs the item number even before she has received this trapped gift from her lover Kesu, instrumented by Langda. Indeed, when Omkara offers the waistband to Dolly, he tells her that it belonged to his mother, who is said to have been a low caste woman who seduced a Brahmin and who is often equated to a prostitute. It clearly points to the sexual ensnaring charm of the piece of jewellery (see Figure 11), reminding us of the day when Dolly got engaged with the fiancé chosen for her by her parents and yet put her ring in a coffee cup that was explicitly meant for Omkara. In its own way the film conjures up 'the magic in the web' mentioned in *Othello* (3.4.67), enthralling in turn both men and women.

Visually speaking, the waistband proves a much more cinematic prop than the handkerchief: it is clearly an expansion of the small piece of cloth, which was itself the reduction of the nuptial sheets with the virginal blood,[21] and its glittering and colourful material is made to catch the eye. Still, though attractive, it fits the codes of propriety and censorship of Indian cinema, especially when it is used in Billo's dance scene, which is an accepted transposition of a seduction and love scene. But it is clearly staged as a teasing object, both for those who watch it inside the film and for the spectators of the film since it keeps appearing and disappearing and regularly changes hands. Such is particularly the case of Billo's bar dance scene, when she wears the waistband Kesu offered her: Omkara attends the show but he fails to notice the jewel because Langda distracts his attention. While the spectator is expecting the moment when Omkara discovers that the waistband is no longer in the possession of Dolly, the script writer chooses to postpone the revelation and make it happen through a conversation between Omkara and Langda: 'It was so sparkling and it was shining so much on her [Billo] waist that one did not need electricity in the room.'

Figure 11:   The waistband in Vishal Bhardwaj's 2006 *Omkara*.

Paradoxically, the ocular nature of the proof lies in the spectators' eyes more than in Omkara's eye, in spite of its visual prominence on the screen. It does underscore Langda's agency in Omkara's manipulation but it also reflexively points to efficient narrative figures such as spying, voyeurism, dissemblance and suggests other possible readings of the play (as we showed previously) and of the prop itself.

For instance, a certain number of shots manage to visually turn the waistband into another object which passes from shot to shot and gradually acquires a different visual meaning in the chronological process. We may think of the love scene between Langda and Indu, when Langda holds up the piece of jewellery and brandishes it like a murderous weapon over his wife's body: the prop definitely looks like a dagger, or even a sabre, as a proleptic vision of the final moment when Indu actually holds such a weapon and rips her husband's throat with it.[22]

The shift from a man's hands to a woman's hands again underlines the film's tendency to promote some form of female agency in the face of men's domination. But the prop may also transform men into ritual lovers: in the very same love scene between Langda and Indu, Langda wears the waistband like a Hindu floral veil traditionally worn by the groom – the *sehra*. Even though he displays it mockingly on his face, Langda thus betrays a repressed desire to be both the future bride seducing Omkara with her charm and Omkara himself, the soon-to-be-groom wearing the *sehra* over his face, and ruling over his gang of outlaws. In such a case, the waistband may be queering the relationship between Omkara and Langda, recycling a frequent interpretation of the homoerotic attraction that exists between Othello and Iago.

Drawing on this approach of an Indian appropriation of certain specific elements of Shakespeare's *Othello*, I would now like to offer three conclusive remarks showing how domestic issues, filmic issues and Shakespearean issues are interwoven in *Omkara*, as I have shown through the treatment of caste and colours, the connection between crime of passion and honour crime and the change from handkerchief to waistband.

By blurring roles, functions and gender identities, the visual circulation and metamorphosis of the waistband raises the question of the centrality of Omkara as the protagonist of the film plot. Indeed, those who manipulate this metamorphic prop appear as the most agentive characters in the film, and it is particularly true of Langda. The choice of gorgeous actor Saif Ali Khan to play the part of Langda also reinforces the impression that he may steal the show from Omkara.

He is the one who opens the film and introduces the plot and characters as if he were drawing the curtain on a stage. From the start he is shot in towering position, limping like Richard III (as the Hindi meaning of 'langda' points to somebody with a limp), up to the ending of the film that nearly closes on his being killed in a scene that is more dramatically shot than that of Omkara's suicide (Omkara's body is visually eclipsed by the gentle swaying of Dolly's bed).

In terms of Indian film history, this contest between close protagonists revives and prolongs the figure of the 'angry young man' of the 1970s. In those days, young male characters became outlaws to challenge the unreliable Indian state and Establishment as depicted in *Deewaar* with Amitabh Bachchan, the arch embodiment of the actor who impersonated this new type of rebellious hero.[23] But, since the 2000s, a new generation of dacoit characters have appeared as they oppose the older leaders of the gangs they belong to in order to oppose what they regard as injustice and unrewarded sacrifices for the gang.[24] Obviously, Langda (more than Omkara) embodies today's angry young man (i.e., a character who rebels against his destiny and resorts to plotting to obtain what the ringleader does not want to share). Intestine hostility and power transmission are definitely at stake in such films which appear to consider colonial dependence and influence as history – or which show that British traditional scenarios can aptly be recycled to both entertain and teach audiences about contemporary India and contemporary political tensions.[25]

Contemporary India at its most modern and technological development is also present in the film through the technical mastery of camera shots and movements, sound editing and lightning, but also through visual clues reminding the spectator that India is not only a countryside land inhabited by folkloric peasants, cows and sari-clad women. Taking up the idea of the dissemination of the belt as an ocular proof in so many shots and varieties of settings (from women to men, from waist to head to buildings, from bedroom to bar to outdoor landscapes), we may wonder whether it does not question the validity of Omkara's quest for an ocular proof to justify his growing anger against Dolly. A number of counter clues are regularly dispersed all along the film, through the presence of cameras, videos on mobile phones, overheard phone calls, discarded mobiles which regularly crop up on the screen, sometimes even eclipsing the actors and occupying centre stage. Paradoxically, in this age of omnipresent 'ocular-ity', the film, after Shakespeare, would also remind us that there is more than meets the eye.

Notes

1 One may think, for instance, of adaptations of Jane Austen's *Sense and Sensibility* and *Emma* with *I Have Found It* by Rajiv Menon (2000) starring Aishwarya Rai and *Aisha* by Rajshree Ojha (2010).

2 R. Burt, 'Shakespeare and Asia in Post-Diasporic Cinemas. Spin-offs and Citations of the Play from Bollywood to Hollywood', in R. Burt and L. E. Boose (eds.), *Shakespeare, The Movie II: Popularizing the Plays on Film, TV, Video and DVD* (New York: Routledge, 2003), 266.

3 One may fruitfully refer to the chapter 'Multiple Mediations of "Shakespeare"', in N. Bhatia, *Acts of Authority/ Acts of Resistance: Theater and Politics in Colonial and Postcolonial India* (Ann Arbor: University of Michigan Press, 2004), 51–75.

4 S. Rushdie, '"Commonwealth Literature" Does Not Exist', in *Imaginary Homelands: Essays and Criticism, 1981–1991* (London: Granta Books, 1991), 61–70.

5 Bhardwaj adapted other literary British works, borrowing from two texts by the contemporary Indian author of British descent, Ruskin Bond: *The Blue Umbrella* (2007) from the novel of the same title, and *7 Khoon Maaf,* from Ruskin Bond's short story 'Susanna's Seven Husbands', which he turned into a novella published along with the film script by Penguin Books India in 2011.

6 Vishal Bhardwaj had hired three major Indian film stars to play the lead parts of Omkara, Dolly and Langda, which obviously played a crucial role in the film's success: 'The film stars some of India's biggest actors. Kareena Kapoor, whose career has rested on a string of romantic leads, plays the role adapted from Desdemona. One of Bollywood's leading men, Saif Ali Khan, also departs from his trademark Romeo roles to take on a limping, scheming Iago. And the veteran Bollywood heartthrob, Ajay Devgan, is the character adapted from Othello'; R. Ramesh, 'A Matter of Caste as Bollywood Embraces the Bard', *Guardian*, 29 July 2006, www.theguardian.com/world/2006/jul/29/books.filmnews, accessed 8 August 2013.

7 The fact that it is a film also contributes to this shift of focus from British Indian relations since Indian filmmakers, like other filmmakers all over the world, are more in touch with North American than British models and references given the momentousness of the US's film industry when compared to that of Great Britain. See the analysis undertaken by Susanne Gruss about the reciprocal influences of Hollywood/Bollywood in her study of *Omkara*: S. Gruss, 'Shakespeare in Bollywood?: Vishal Bhardwaj's *Omkara*', in S. Säckel, W. Göbel, N. Hamdy (eds.), *Semiotic Encounters: Text, Image, and Trans-Nation,* (Amsterdam and New York: Rodopi, 2009), 223–38.

8 N. Bhatia, 'Different *Othello*(s) and Contentious Spectators: Changing Responses in India', *GRAMMA* 15 (2007), 155–74, Special Issue, T. Krontris and J. Singh (eds.), *Shakespeare Worldwide and the Idea of an Audience.*

9 In that way, *Omkara* both recycles and departs from an American tradition of adaptation of *Othello* for the screen, as highlighted by S. Gruss: '*Othello* has thus often been used to shed light on contemporary – and in these cases American – issues of race and violence', (Gruss, 'Shakespeare in Bollywood?', 224).

10 For instance, in India, people usually wear white at funerals.

11 L. P. Hogan, 'The Sacred and the Profane in *Omkara*: Vishal Bhardwaj's Hindi adaptation of *Othello*', *Image & Narrative* 11.2 (2010), 49–61.

12 For a further analysis of the integration of Omkara's family into the plot (contrary to Shakespeare's hero, who is an isolated character), see Gruss, 'Shakespeare in Bollywood?', 230.

13 F. Dolan, 'Revolutions, Petty Tyranny and the Murderous Husband', in K. Chedgzoy (ed.) *Shakespeare, Feminism and Gender* (Basingstoke and New York: Palgrave, 2001), 202.

14 A. M. Modenessi draws a similar conclusion about the Mexican adaptation of the play, *Huapango* (dir. Iván Lipkies, 2003): '"Is This the Noble Moor?" Reviewing *Othello* on Screen through "Indian" (and Indian) Eyes', *Borrowers and Lenders: The Journal of Shakespeare and Appropriation* 7.2 (2012–13): www.borrowers.uga.edu/490/display, accessed 8 November 2013.

15 Dolan, 'Revolutions', 202.

16 *Ibid.*, 203.

17 *Ibid.*, 207.

18 *Ibid.*, 211.

19 From Mervyn LeRoy's 1931 gangster movie *Little Caesar,* to *Looking for Richard* (1996) by Al Pacino, an otherwise emblematic godfather figure, to Geoffrey Wright's 2006 adaptation of *Macbeth*, to the recent Italian docu-drama film by the Taviani brothers, *Caesar Must Die* (2012), for which they hired real inmates to perform *Julius Caesar* in prison. Not to mention *Joe MacBeth* (1955) by Ken Hughes, and *Men of Respect* (1990) by William Reilly starring John Turturro.

20 As to R. M. Garcia Periago, she defends the idea that *Omkara* plays with Bollywood conventions, especially as far as dance-and-song sequences are concerned, as she locates the film in the broader context of what C. Jess-Cooke, 'Screening the McShakespeare in Post-Millennial Shakespeare Cinema', in M. T. Burnett and R. Wray (eds.), *Screening Shakespeare in the Twenty-first Century* (Edinburgh: Edinburgh University Press, 2006), 163–85, has dubbed 'McShakespeare' ('where the global is signified within the local'): 'In spite of the fact that the movies take Bollywood conventions as the point of departure, "bollywoodizing" themselves, they cleverly draw freely upon them, suggesting a movement towards transnational cinema.' R. M. Garcia Periago, *Shakespeare, Bollywood and Beyond*, unpublished PhD thesis, University of Murcia, 2013, 182; 195. http://digitum.um.es/xmlui/handle/10201/36721, accessed 27 May 2014. Conversely, M. T. Burnett prefers to approach Vishal Bhardwaj from a more regional perspective, which avoids 'succumbing to a unitary modality which would favour only the nation-state as an option for analysis' (6). See in particular his chapter 2, 'Vishal Bhardwaj and Jayaraaj Rajasekharan Nair' (55–87) but also his chapter 4, 'Shakespeare, Cinema, Asia' (125–61), in *Shakespeare and World Cinema* (Cambridge: Cambridge University Press, 2013).

21 L. E. Boose, 'Othello's Handkerchief: "The Recognizance and Pledge of Love"', in E. Pechter (ed.), *Othello* (New York: W.W. Norton, 2004), 262–75.

22 See as well the dance-and-song sequence between Omkara and Dolly chasing
    each other, which ends with Dolly playfully challenging Omkara with a gun
    that she holds to his chest.

23 Today, *Deewaar* (dir. Yash Chopra, 1975) is regarded as a classic film which
    contributed to shape the archetype of the underdog hero resorting to criminal
    action so as to fight an inadequate and corrupt ruling system. One may also
    refer to *Zanjeer* (dir. Prakash Mehra, 1973,) and *Sholay* (dir. Ramesh Sippy,
    1975) in which Amitabh Bachchan was given the lead role as well.

24 In Hindi, 'dacoity' means 'banditry'. It has become a colloquial Anglo-Indian
    word referring to people who rob and kill in roving gangs.

25 Internal rebellion may follow diverse patterns. In *Company* (dir. Ram Gopal
    Varma, 2002), which is set in contemporary India, two former friends who
    have become fierce gangsters in Mumbai eventually turn against each other.
    While in *Sarkar* (dir. Ram Gopal Varma, 2005), a man who runs a parallel
    government is being threatened by rivals and sees his son coming to the rescue
    so as to fight his enemies. As to *Once Upon a Time in Mumbai* (dir. Milan
    Luthria, 2010), it goes back to the 1970s to stage internal strife already at work
    between a young gangster and a smuggler who has always considered the
    younger man to be his protégé.

WORKS CITED

Bhatia, N., *Acts of Authority/Acts of Resistance: Theater and Politics in Colonial and
    Postcolonial India* (Ann Arbor: University of Michigan Press, 2004).
    'Different *Othello*(s) and Contentious Spectators: Changing Responses in
    India', *GRAMMA* 15 (2007), 155–74. Special Issue, T. Krontris and
    J. Singh (eds.), *Shakespeare Worldwide and the Idea of an Audience*.
Boose, L. E.. 'Othello's Handkerchief: "The Recognizance and Pledge of Love"',
    in E. Pechter (ed.), *Othello* (New York: W.W. Norton, 2004), 262–75.
Burnett, M. T., *Shakespeare and World Cinema* (Cambridge: Cambridge
    University Press, 2013).
Burt, R., 'Shakespeare and Asia in Post-Diasporic Cinemas. Spin-offs and
    Citations of the Play from Bollywood to Hollywood', in R. Burt and L. E.
    Boose (eds.), *Shakespeare, The Movie II: Popularizing the Plays on Film, TV,
    Video and DVD* (New York: Routledge, 2003), 265–303.
Dolan, F., 'Revolutions, Petty Tyranny and the Murderous Husband', in
    K. Chedgzoy (ed.), *Shakespeare, Feminism and Gender* (Basingstoke and
    New York: Palgrave, 2001), 202–15.
Garcia Periago, R. M., *Shakespeare, Bollywood and Beyond*, unpublished PhD
    thesis, University of Murcia, 2013. http://digitum.um.es/xmlui/handle/
    10201/36721, accessed 27 May 2014.
Gruss, S., 'Shakespeare in Bollywood?: Vishal Bhardwaj's *Omkara*', in S. Säckel,
    W. Göbel, N. Hamdy (eds.), *Semiotic Encounters: Text, Image, and Trans-
    Nation* (Amsterdam and New York: Rodopi, 2009), 223–38.

Hogan, L. P., 'The Sacred and the Profane in *Omkara*: Vishal Bhardwaj's Hindi adaptation of *Othello*', *Image & Narrative* 11.2 (2010), 49–61.

Jess-Cooke, C. 'Screening the McShakespeare in Post-Millennial Shakespeare Cinema', in M. T. Burnett and R. Wray (eds.), *Screening Shakespeare in the Twenty-first Century* (Edinburgh: Edinburgh University Press, 2006), 163–85.

Modenessi, A. M., '"Is This the Noble Moor?" Re-viewing *Othello* on Screen through "Indian" (and Indian) Eyes', *Borrowers and Lenders: The Journal of Shakespeare and Appropriation* 7. 2 (2012–13), www.borrowers.uga.edu/490/display, accessed 8 November 2013.

Ramesh, R., 'A Matter of Caste as Bollywood Embraces the Bard', *Guardian*, 29 July 2006, www.theguardian.com/world/2006/jul/29/books.filmnews, accessed 8 August 2013.

Rushdie, S., '"Commonwealth Literature" Does Not Exist', in *Imaginary Homelands: Essays and Criticism, 1981–1991* (London: Granta Books, 1991), 61–70.

CHAPTER 8

Othello *in Latin America*
Otelo de Oliveira *and* Huapango

Aimara da Cunha Resende

Basing his reflection on Roman Jakobson (1959),[1] Umberto Eco proposes the term *transmutation* instead of *translation* or *adaptation* for the transposition of texts from one language/production to another.[2] This word implies a wide range of possible movements in the process of re-creating the main aspects of such texts in another context, language or medium. Due to its connotation of movement and change, this is the term to be used here.

Any work of translation or adaptation must be based on previous choices of form, content and expression, depending on the contexts of both the source and the target texts. Imbued with various elements, the text thus appropriated becomes the same and another, as it is now, though unconsciously so, charged with new characteristics found in the target culture. According to Patrice Pavis,

> Globally one may say that culture is a system of signification (a molding system, in Lotman's theory) thanks to which a society or a group understands itself in its relationship with the world.

And he goes on to quote Clifford Geertz:

> [culture] is a system of symbols thanks to which man confers meaning to his own experience. The systems of symbols created by man, shared, conventional, ordained and evidently apprehended, provide men with a scheme containing some meaning so that they may guide themselves one in relation to the others, or through the relation with the environment and with themselves.[3]

Transmuting a play by Shakespeare into a different culture thus requires some awareness on the part of the person appropriating it – whether a translator, a theatre director or a film adaptor – of the elements pertaining to either cultural system. The 'transmuter' must know the temporal, historical, social, political and economic elements forming the basis of the source text as well as those pertinent to the culture he/she is re-creating it for:

I am grateful to Mark Thornton Burnett for having called my attention to *Huapango*.

such adaptors always place themselves under the receptors' perspective when they simplify and mold some key elements in the source-culture. Thus they necessarily have an ethnocentric position, but as they are aware of this deforming perspective, they may relativise such discrepancy and search for some conscious understanding of the differences.[4]

According to Pavis, the process of adaptation or appropriation takes place just like sand moving from the upper to the lower bulb in an hourglass. When the sand moves downwards, it is rearranged in the lower bulb according to a system of interrelated connections proper to that bulb. The same is true of any transmutation: there are some relations in the target culture that confer meanings which belong to that culture and are alien to the source culture. As the source text is appropriated, the adaptor/translator must be aware of these relations to make the important elements in the source understood by the receptors:

> cultural transference does not offer an automatic, passive flow from one culture to another. On the contrary, it is an activity much more directed by the 'lower' bulb of the target-culture which consists in actively searching in the source-culture, as if through magnetization, that which is necessary to satisfy its concrete needs.[5]

When he offers the metaphor of the hourglass, Pavis stresses the adaptors' need to be aware of dissimilarities and to place themselves under the receptors' perspective when they simplify and mould some key elements in the source. The appropriation of a dramatic construct may thus be a demanding task if the adaptor wishes both to keep the main elements found in the source and create others that will appeal to his contemporaneous receptors. The transmuter/adaptor/director must first of all define his/her own reading so as to create a consistent product. The message to be conveyed (in accordance with or deviant from that found in the source text), of setting and time, of cultural symbols and beliefs, has to conform to a single view which he/she has decided to adopt. And when it is a product for the screen, whether filmic or televised, he/she must also be aware of the fact that the screen performance has its own codes and that such codes will vary from the cinema to television.

As Shakespeare's *Othello* is transmuted to the screen, in countries and languages other than England and English, it must conform to techniques proper to that medium and to some elements that belong only to the target culture, requiring significations natural to it. The receptors may not realize that their decoding of the appropriated construct is greatly due to their life experience, cultural background, and sociopolitical milieu, or to their knowledge of the culture, time or sociopolitical constraints found in the source text. But they will understand the central ideas the adaptor has chosen to highlight.

Paulo Afonso Grisolli's 1983 Brazilian *Otelo de Oliveira*, adapted by Aguinaldo Silva as a 'recreation of *Othello, the Moor of Venice* by William Shakespeare' (as seen in the credits) and Iván Lipkies's 2003 Mexican *Huapango*, a film which the credits indicate to have been 'inspired by *Othello*, by W. Shakespeare', have been subjected to such choices when transmuted to the screen. There are similarities as well as differences not only between either and Shakespeare's *Othello* but also between the two of them, for although they are products of the same wider regional culture, Latin America, they carry the marks of two different nationalities as well as those of diversified constructs for the screen: a Globo TV production – *Otelo de Oliveira* – and a film – *Huapango*. An aspect to be noticed is the fact that, in both productions, the transmuted Moor is not a Negro, but in either case bears the mark of an outsider: he appears as a white-skinned rancher in *Huapango* and as a dark-skinned – but not black – gypsy in *Otelo de Oliveira*.

In Shakespeare's play, Iago appears from the very beginning as the main conductor of the narrative. He opens Act 1 scene 1 when he talks to Roderigo about their General, whom he swears he hates, claiming that his having been passed over in the General's choice of his second is the reason for his hatred, and reveals his own character to the audience through his rude and ill-mannered speech. Nobody in the audience knows then who his superior is as the Moor's name has not yet been spoken. Iago's use of animal imagery, when he tells Brabanzio that his daughter has eloped to marry Othello, suggests a sort of bestial sexuality:

> Even now, now, very now, an old black ram
> Is tupping your white ewe. Arise, arise!
> Awake the snorting citizens with the bell,
> Or else the devil will make a grandsire of you.
>   (1.1.88–91)

And:

> Because we come to do you service and you think we are ruffians, you'll have your daughter covered with a Barbary horse, you'll have your nephews neigh to you, you'll have coursers for cousins and jennets for germans.
> (1.1.111–15)

This imagery will be recaptured in both *Huapango* and *Otelo de Oliveira*, but now connoting different ideas. As the former is mainly concerned with the issues of national/regional identity and women's condition in a *macho* society, highlighting the importance of folklore as a conveyor of nationality, especially the *huapango* dance, the animal imagery displayed is, in this production, directly related to everyday life in Mexican rural areas where the cattle ranch still maintains its splendour and the wealthy rancher has considerable social and political control. No 'ram' appears here, and the horses and bulls re-enact the function they have in the regional festivities of such communities. In these festivities, as pointed out by Mark Thornton Burnett,[6] horses and bulls offer an opportunity for a display of masculinity by the men who mount and dominate them.

Otelo de Oliveira focuses on social issues and on the worldwide imagery related to Brazilian national identity: the stereotypes of the *tropical paradise* of samba and *mulatas* (women born of the miscegenation of white and black people). Tinted with violence and voodoo, other components of the country's image, the production caters to audiences both at home and abroad, in accordance with Globo TV's commercial scheme. Thus when Tiago/Iago (played by Milton Gonçalves) talks to Rodrigo/Roderigo (Daniel Dantas) about his unfruitful attempts to convince Dé/Desdemona (Júlia Lemmertz) of Rodrigo's love for her, he says: 'A black ram came up, guy. Its belly swollen, fetid. Exu's work'. This transposition of Iago's words in Tiago's mouth reinstalls the source character's imagery and simultaneously links it to a previous scene in which Eloína/Bianca (Regina Dourado) performs a *trabalho* (voodoo ritualistic act). In it, the mystical killing of a black chicken whose blood is to be offered to Exu, the evil god in voodoo, substitutes the erotic ram, as she is performing the *trabalho* to destroy Cássio/Cassio (Oswaldo Loureiro) who has forsaken her. There is no horse in the TV film, but the voodoo scene is strongly interspersed with Tiago's contrivance against Otelo.

In Shakespeare, it is mainly through Iago's narration that one comes to know most of the features in the characters' personalities, including Iago's own, and, most important in the case of this play, the cultural and sociopolitical context wherein the story takes place. As shown by Mark Matheson, social, political and familial relationships find in Venice the ideal place for issues of race, gender and hierarchy to be possibly misunderstood and thus lead to chaos:

> The play [*Othello*] is a powerful illustration of his [Shakespeare's] ability to perceive and represent different forms of political organization, and to situate personal relationships and issues of individual subjectivity in a specific institutional context.[7]

Being aware of Othello's feelings of inferiority for being an alien in Venice, as well as of his inability to understand the liberal education of Venetian women and the discrepancy between family relations and those in the Venetian political system, Iago can make up his stories and succeed in telling them.

To transmute the play to the cinema, Lipkies concentrates on the political issues pertinent to 2004 Mexico, that is, the affirmation of national identity with an ironical reading of the United States' economic domination, when, for instance, Otílio/Othello (played by Alejandro Tommasi) says that he doesn't want pizzas and hamburgers to be served at the dance competition. The issue of hierarchy is highlighted because the country has developed, since its colonial time, a political system of stratification according to race, family ties and close acquaintances. Mexico had gone through a series of insurgences, a twenty-year civil war, had *caudillos* as Presidents and formed its admission into democracy out of a hierarchical organization imbued with ideas of subservience. Such ideas were instilled in its native people throughout years of Spanish despotism, when the *peninsulares* (whites born in Spain) were idealized as superior to the rest of the population, followed by the *criollos* or *creoles* (whites born in the new world), many of whom ended up as wealthy ranchers, then the *mestizos* (illegitimate children of Spanish men and Indian women) and, at the bottom, the Indians. There is also a concern with the position of women in a *macho* society, allied to the religious constraints that saw woman as either a saint – a reflection of the Virgin Mary – or a prostitute. Finally, there is, linked to the ideal of national identity, the validation of folklore through the dance that gives its name to the film. *Huapango* begins with a group of folklore dancers from the Huasteca region, the Tamaulipas, rehearsing for a national festival. The dance, *huapango*, strongly rhythmical and composed of sensual choreography, forms the background for the narrative and becomes the main presence in the film. Its beat, systematically made by heels and toes stamping, reverberates on a large platform, also called *huapango*, with holes on its sides to intensify the sound.[8] The *maestra*, a native woman performed by a nationally known comedian, Maria Elena Velasco, Iván Lipkies's mother and co-producer of the film, embodies the country's ideal of commitment to their own values. Fiercely controlling the dancers, she reinforces the regional/national pride of such commitment when she says: 'We must be disciplined, people, even if we don't get paid! Are we competing out of love for our customs or just because we have to?' Subtly ironical is the fact that the camera has just focused on her feet, showing a torn right shoe indicative of her poor social status. She also insists on Julia/Desdemona (Lisset) not having a honeymoon, as it will coincide with the rehearsals and Julia is the main female dancer in the troupe. The focus on the *maestra* is simultaneously a glorification of national values and a 'tongue-in-cheek' statement, for as the troupe depends financially on Julia's future husband, who wishes both to get married and to have the Tamaulipas win the competition, the *maestra*'s demand ironically brings about Julia's emotional division: the bride to be and dancer is thoroughly committed to *huapango* dancing, which gives her a chance to acquire her own identity and limited freedom within a *macho* society, but she is also in love and wants to get married.

Otilio/Othello, Julia's wealthy rancher fiancé embodies the sociopolitical situation the film indirectly portrays. He is white, in contrast to the others, who are either *mestizos*, in the majority, or descendants from the Indians (I find it hard, however, to see Santiago/Iago [Manuel Landeta] as a *mestizo*. He has white skin, light eyes and features that show more European ascendancy than any mixture of Indian blood). Otilio represents, in that society, the outsider: he neither dances nor shows in his skin and features the marks of hybridism found in most of the others around him. But being a wealthy cattle rancher, he maintains the power acquired by his family as landowners and Spanish descendants. Besides, he is a cousin of the governor's and through this link he is able to reach up to the President and bring the competition to their town. During the celebration of their wedding, when the news comes that the competition has been scheduled for fifteen days from then, exactly when the newlyweds would be on their honeymoon and Julia does not want to give up their honeymoon for the competition, he tells her that he has asked the President to have the competition in 'her town', and thus she must dance. His position in the Tamaulipa community is thus rather paradoxical: of Spanish ascendancy, he nevertheless strives to establish traditional Mexican values, thus reinforcing the country's search for individualization in the global world. As Mark Burnett says,

> Otilio/Othello's defense of traditional cuisine, and the *artesanía* or older skills conjured in the blouse, point to *Mexicanidad* or Mexicaness – a conception of heritage that historians have traced to the 1910–17 revolution.[9]

Another sign of his power – especially financial, this time – appears mixed with an endeavour on the film director's part to show him as a good man, which will tend in the final outcome to darken Santiago's deed: Felipe/Cassio (Alfredo Castillo) asks him what to do in relation to a request from the local priest for some bulls for a *rodeo*, an entertainment typical of rural areas in Latin America, in which untamed horses or bulls are mounted by *vaqueros/vaqueiros* (cowboys) who must dominate them. The priest hopes, with two *rodeos*, to get money for the construction of a church. As the priest cannot pay for the loan of the bulls, the rancher tells his 'second' to send them to him, with no payment.

As the embodiment of the *macho* man, Otilio shows his ability at horsemanship during the wedding party when he nimbly fetches Julia off the ground and puts her up on the horse with him, a feat that, more than a substitute for Shakespeare's animal imagery, as suggested by Burnett,[10] is a demonstration of masculinity in that society, with its rural values of ranch communities. The animals presented in the film are a complement to the scenery, reinforcing regional customs and suggestively re-creating a communal experience characteristic of national/regional traits. Both the horses and the bulls seen during the party are a recurrent *mise-en-scène* of weddings and other festivities among ranchers and their employees. Competitions of wild bulls or horses control are central to such communal festivities.

Otelo de Oliveira, on the other hand, characterizing urban twentieth-century Brazilian life, especially that in Rio de Janeiro, is distanced from the colonial burden and produced at the end of a twenty-year military dictatorship. It has a protagonist who re-creates the myth of the *macho* man, but is closer to the social issues of racism and economic differences in a large Brazilian city. As Skidmore and Smith say,

> Social status in Brazil is not just a function of occupation or wealth. It is also a matter of race. The massive importation of slave labor from Africa brought an additional ethnic dimension into Brazilian society and this in turn has affected customs and attitudes.
>
> There tends to be a strong correlation between race and social standing in Brazil: most on top are white, most blacks are on the bottom, and mixed-bloods are largely in between. Some institutions, such as naval officers and the diplomatic corps, long remained white. But in Brazil race is not defined purely on biological grounds. It is a social concept, open to interpretation. To be 'black' one has to be totally black (in contrast to the U.S., where partly black in ethnic origin means black). Mulattos in Brazil have considerable opportunity for upward mobility, and for this reason miscegenation has been viewed by one scholar as a kind of social 'escape hatch'.[11]

Otelo (played by Roberto Bonfim) is a gypsy and a mulatto, neither black nor white – anyhow, not a man of 'pure' European blood. Black people, in Brazil, compose a large part of the population and as such would never represent an outsider. A gypsy, however, carries the marks of foreignness and mischief with suggestions of witchcraft and deviousness. Thus, in the national imagination, Otelo is the outsider while the black Tiago condenses the untrustworthy, threatening traits still imagined by lots of Brazilian whites to be found in black people.

As in Shakespeare's ensign Iago, in both Mexican and Brazilian TV films, the insidious close subordinate is brought to the front. In *Huapango* he is called Santiago and in *Otelo de Oliveira*, Tiago, both names bearing a clear relation to the source text. The difference in their representation and role is found from the very beginning of the two screen transmutations here discussed: Santiago is a dancer in the Tamaulipa troupe who has fallen in love with Julia. The cause for his hatred of Otilio is quite obviously jealousy. A subtle indication of Santiago's lack of commitment to his community is his being constantly chewing gum, a sign of his approval of stuff imported from the United States.

Tiago is the driver in the house of Dé's wealthy father, Barbosa, and works in the samba school where Otelo is the director of harmony, one of the main positions in such schools. As it happens in the source text, the audience/reader will never be sure of the real motivation for his hatred of Otelo. It seems at first to be the fact that Otelo has chosen Cássio as his second, leaving Tiago aside. He shows his hatred of Cássio also, when he goes to the *terreiro* (voodoo yard) to incite Eloína/Bianca to destroy Cássio with her *trabalho*; he says to her that she must do it very well, for now, as Otelo's second, Cássio will have lots of women after him. But later on, when he goes to the gypsy's house to fetch Dé and bring her to her husband at the samba school, entering their bedroom, by himself, he embraces a pillow and murmurs: 'It's here that she sleeps, like a mermaid, calling ... calling ...'. Thus reasons for Tiago's hatred are, like those of Shakespeare's character, mixed and confusing.

Iago's power lies in his language, his most telling trait, and is transmuted in the Mexican film into Santiago's self-centred exhibition of his strong body, his smile and stance of superiority among the Tamaulipas. Utterly proud of his physical strength, good looks, and unsurpassed dancing ability, he sees himself as a vanquisher. Desperate, during Otilio's and Julia's wedding party, he says to a friend who is frequently with him, and is perhaps intended as a substitute for Roderigo (who is omitted in Lipkies's production): 'I've never lost!' Such a claim is strong enough not to allow him to accept the fact that Julia has never cared for him except as her dancing partner. A *mestizo*, his main problem seems to be his self-regard and inability to accept that he has lost the woman he is infatuated with to a 'white outsider' who does not even dance the *huapango*.

His infiltration into Otilio's mind and soul comes very close to the source in the two scenes where he visits the rancher during Julia's absence and subtly unravels the thread of his venomous story up to the point when he is sure of having convinced the rancher of his wife's adulterous affair with Felipe/Cassio (see Figure 12).

Though insidiously planned to shake Otilio's confidence in Julia, Santiago's words do not follow Shakespeare's Iago's language very closely. He tells the rancher that Felipe is a cheater and Julia, 'very discreet'. And he goes on unravelling the thread of his lies, when Cassio's dream, invented by Iago to intensify the Moor's jealousy, is reproduced, not as a dream, but as a consequence of Felipe's drunkenness that makes him say what lies hidden in his thoughts when he is sober.

Brazilian Tiago also follows his model, as he insidiously suggests to Otelo his suspicion of betrayal at seeing Cássio and Dé so close in the gypsy's house. At the night of Otelo's wedding, an attack on their samba school, with the murder of the watchman, forces the director of harmony to leave his wife behind and stay at the school. Before leaving his house, he tells Cássio to stay there to protect Dé and her maid Emília, Tiago's wife. This is enough for the Negro to set up the scheme to turn his superior's love into

Figure 12:   The 'wooing scene' in Iván Lipkies's 2003 *Huapango*.

jealousy. Due to the demands of a TV production in the format of a *caso especial* that is structured to last around an hour and a half, consisting of four parts, but shown in a single program, and to the techniques of such kind of entertainment on the small screen, Iago's lengthy 'wooing' of the Moor is compressed and placed in Tiago's intense gaze whenever he puts his scheme into motion (one of the main features of TV filmic productions is the constant use of close-ups that highlight facial expression). When Otelo leaves his wife and Emilia in Cassio's care and goes to the samba school, Tiago remains behind and says to Cassio: 'Poor bride, right on her first married night she has to stay alone in the house. That's awful, isn't it, Cassio? Hum?' And his eyes dart an even more disturbing message. The same happens in the scene at the samba school, where Otelo is keeping watch. Tiago seizes the opportunity to begin to insert doubt into the gypsy's mind. Shakespeare is clearly found here as Silva and Grisolli insert Iago's suggestion in 3.3.233–43 into Tiago's speech, when he says, from behind Otelo: 'Cassio is white, middle-class, educated . . .' And once again his eyes seem to probe deeper than what he utters (see Figure 13).

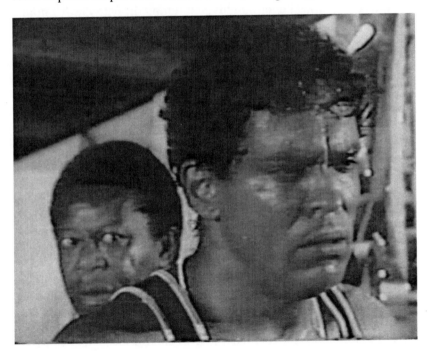

Figure 13:   The 'wooing scene' in Paulo Afonso Grisolli's 1983 *Otelo de Oliveira*.
All rights reserved.

Both appropriations here discussed transform the scenery according to their ideal of national/regional identity. *Huapango* is shot in a typical Mexican environment, with the *Casa de Cultura* (Culture House) as its centre. It is there that the rehearsals take place, since the dance is the main focus in the film. It is also there that Santiago takes the prostitutes whom he engages to trap Felipe, making him drunk to the point of crashing Otilio's truck, after having been robbed by them. Santiago, who has managed to steal the hand-embroidered blouse Otilio had given Julia and place it under the front seat of the wrecked truck, now has the chance to 'prove' to Otilio his wife's adultery. This blouse substitutes the source play's handkerchief, and carries the suggestion both of such transmutation and the value Otilio gives to national craftsmanship, for when a woman dancer praises it and asks if it is hand-embroidered, Julia replies: 'Yes, it is. It is a present from Otilio. His mother made it, you know?' So national craftsmanship and pride in lineage are juxtaposed, linking national and artistic (Shakespearean) identities. The rancher has been in bed since the day of his wedding because, already drunk, thanks to Santiago's pouring liquor into his glass during the party, he fell from a bull he was induced to ride – again by Santiago – during the competition of the *rodeo*. In bed, he has been unable to prove his masculinity, as he said to Santiago in one of the latter's visits to him when Julia was not at home: 'No dancing, no honeymoon, absolutely nothing.' Such an outcome is the utmost catastrophe that may befall a man in a Latin American *macho* culture. The feeling of impotence it creates can easily be turned into an effective weapon, and Santiago knows how to take advantage of the situation.

Like Shakespeare's protagonist, Otilio ends up strangling Julia who has come home from the final competition to tell him they have won. In an attempt to escape his fury and having already difficulty in breathing, Julia beats on Otilio's chest. The beating and the scene of her being murdered are interspersed with the rhythmical dance taking place in the final competition, mixing the central issues of national identity and women's predicament in the *macho* Mexican society. After having rudely tried to make her wear the blouse (now torn as a result of Santiago's attempt at taking it from his sister who had somehow discerned some evil intention in him), the despairing husband murders Julia and lays her dead on their bed with the hand-embroidered blouse carefully placed on her chest. Later on, on being told the truth by Santiago's sister (as Santiago is a bachelor and has no wife, Shakespeare's Emilia is substituted by his sister whose role is rather peripheral), Otilio shoots himself. The film ends with Santiago repeatedly saying he had not killed the couple, a contrastive echo of Iago's final decision to deny speaking.

While the Casa de Cultura is the *locus* of happiness and hopeful endeavour to attain a goal that is filled with the ideal of regional values – the winning of the *huapango* dance competition – Otilio's house, in its refined architecture and its design reminiscent of Spanish heritage, is the *locus* of unhappiness, unfulfilled expectations, treason and death.

Lipkies's use of changing light in the rancher's house between the moment when Julia enters it and that of her death is impressive. Probably due to a power cut, Julia enters her home and goes upstairs to their bedroom in the dark, with candles lit along the stair balustrade, giving the scenery a sombre mood. Later on, as she lies dead, the embroidered blouse on her chest, and flowers on her head, as she had been costumed for the competition, power has been restored and one can see how beautiful she looks when dead. In opposition to the dancer's tragic fate, the Tamaulipas win the competition – partially thanks to her participation – in the splendour of intense light and the bright, diverse colours of the dancers' regional costumes (see Figure 14).

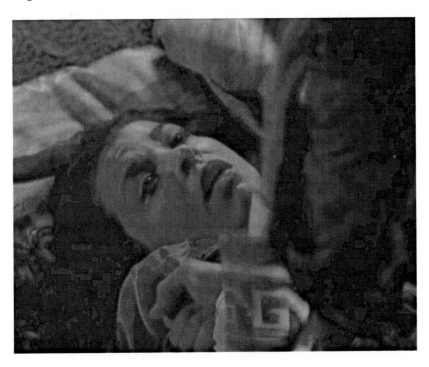

Figure 14: Julia lying dead in Iván Lipkies's 2003 *Huapango*.

Silva's and Grisolli's *Otelo de Oliveira*, whose main concern is related to the unjust social situation in Rio de Janeiro and Brazil in general, has either light or dark colours as the basis for its scenery, even when the shots are taken during the rehearsals for the carnival parade or during the parade itself at the end.

In *Otelo de Oliveira*, the mixture of *loci* conveys the interrelation of carnival, love and treachery, and both Otelo's house and the samba school become places where the different emotional strains compete and are blurred into a single construct. Nevertheless the presentation of two contradictory environments reinforces the idea of a desirable social inclusion not yet achieved in Brazil. Taken separately, the houses representing either side of the socio-economical scale, that of Dé's wealthy father, and that of Otelo's, create the visual transposition of the social, economic and political predicament found in Shakespeare's Venice where Brabanzio is a senator, and Cyprus, the vagrant Moor's place of command. As is noticed in the source text, the two worlds depicted cannot be joined in peaceful agreement either ideally or visually, given the distance between them both geographically and ethically. Barbosa/Brabanzio's house is typical of well-off people, with its antique plates on the walls, decorated furniture, and natural flowers on the small living-room table. Otelo's place, on the contrary, displays the sort of life led in it: on the wall, by the entrance door, a small picture of Christ the Redeemer, a symbol of Rio de Janeiro; on a shelf, an image of the Virgin Mary and another of Saint George; a table with a vase containing artificial flowers; on another wall, a picture and a banner of a football team; in the bedroom, near the simple bed, two small bedside tables, one of them with a little mirror where Tiago's face will be reflected when he is in the bedroom, all alone and embracing the pillow as he smells it and says: 'It's here that she sleeps, like a mermaid, calling, calling ... Until the most stupid falls into the trap: either Cássio or Otelo.' This visual connotation of the revolted subaltern whose cause of anger may also be related to his lust for his superior's wife is a masterpiece of transmutation from Shakespeare's ensign's confused, unclear and psychotic reasons in the written source text to cinematic representation in a production for TV.

In this divided world, where Barbosa respects Otelo as the director of harmony of the samba school he supports, but will not accept him as his son-in-law, and where Otelo, on the other hand, knows his superiority in his job but is also aware of his insurmountable social and racial inferiority, Brazilian socio-economic situation is subliminally hinted at while critical consideration of the issue is subtly provoked.

Despite the transmutation to another place and time, this Brazilian *Othello* follows its source very close: Otelo is a gypsy and consequently prey to the insecurity generated in the fact that he will always be seen as an outsider despite his recognized – and respected – capacity for the function he has in the carnival society. He tries to convince both the community and himself of his importance, as when he says to Tiago, at noticing that the latter does not like the idea of Cássio having been chosen as his second: 'What is the matter? *I* am the director, Tiago'; or when, at the meeting of the Board, as the other members express their disapproval of his choice of Cássio for his second, he threatens to leave the samba school if he cannot decide what is important to their success. At his saying that he wishes to be the only one to control everything, Edmilson/Duke of Venice replies: 'Of course. After all, you are our commander.' And Edmilson says to his companions: 'He sounds like a general, doesn't he? But we need him.' The hint at the source text is obvious here, in the word 'general', which will be reinforced by Edmilson's approving expression later on, at the samba school, after seeing that Otelo has managed to repair their loss: 'You really are our commander.' Nevertheless, like the Moor, Otelo is unable to become a genuine member of that group. Following his source, Tiago will surreptitiously disrupt the feeble thread of Otelo's self-confidence until he manages to convince him of Dé's betrayal. The 'wooing scene' takes place at the samba school, soon after Otelo has asked Tiago to bring Dé to stay with him. Having stolen the ring the gypsy had given his wife as a wedding present, Tiago gives it to Eloína, telling her to use it at the rehearsal of the samba school and say that it was a present from Cássio, which she does. He then tells the director of harmony of his distrust of Dé's and Cássio's close relationship and ends up peremptorily saying that he has seen them exchanging caresses: 'I saw it, Otelo! I saw it!' When Eloína arrives at the samba school showing the ring on her finger, Otelo no longer doubts his wife's infidelity and, maddened by jealousy, destroys the school Carnival props and goes home in search of Dé. On the way, he is met by people already enjoying the approaching carnival and their masques seem to intensify his emotion, as most of them symbolically represent death. In his fury, drunk and desperately disturbed, these apparitions suggest irruptions of his own sentiment. At home, and still like his source, his aggressive attitude and vocabulary confound his young wife as he accuses her of infidelity, asks her if she has prayed and, weeping, finally strangles her (see Figure 15).

This scene comes very close to the source text, when Otelo, already beginning to strangle Dé, reproduces various parts of the Moor's speech.

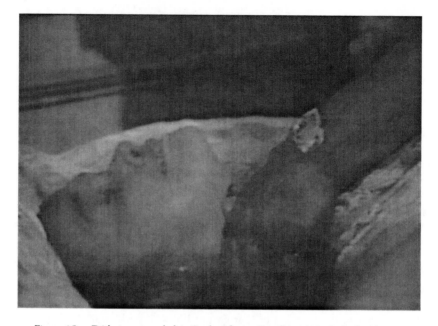

Figure 15:   Dé being strangled in Paulo Afonso Grisolli's 1983 *Otelo de Oliveira*.
All rights reserved.

Here both the Mexican and the Brazilian transmutations are composed of similar representations of Julia and Dé, when, almost dead, in a
last attempt to defend themselves, the camera focuses on their right
hands, in Julia's case slowly passing down Otilio's face, reminiscent of
a gesture she makes twice: the first time when, before getting married,
Otilio takes her to their future house and, once inside, gives her its keys.
Julia passionately says that she loves him, and slowly passes her hand
down his face. At this moment he echoes Shakespeare's hero's famous
words, in Act 3 scene 3, 'when I love thee not,/ Chaos is come again.'
(3.3.92–3), as he replies 'My life without you has no meaning at all'.
Her gesture is seen a second time at the wedding party, when they dance,
then stop, and she repeats the caress before they exchange a long kiss.
In *Otelo de Oliveira*, as Dé is dying, her right hand comes slowly down
her husband's arm, her nails piercing it, leaving their mark on it while he
says: 'Your hand ... so white ... so white ... like the sun ... tearing ...
tearing ...'
    Finally, at being told by Emilia of her husband's scheme to destroy him,
the gypsy does not commit suicide; he kills Tiago instead. Here Tiago's

cold behaviour refracts its source: after being stabbed by Otelo's knife, already vomiting blood, he still has strength to say to Otelo in an ironic last attack: 'Vengeance is sweet, isn't it, Otelo?' The TV *caso especial* ends with interspersed scenes of the samba school parading on the avenue, now directed by Cássio, and of a distracted Otelo crouching behind the bars of the jail while the sound of samba is heard in the background played by the school musicians as the troupe dance by.

Mysticism in the handkerchief, in Shakespeare's play, is also seen in both transmutations. In the Mexican film, Santiago is given to religious syncretism: belonging to a Catholic community, he nevertheless uses magic in his attempt to destroy both Julia and Otilio. As he comes to know that the woman he is infatuated with is engaged to the rancher, he goes home where he tears up a photo of hers, spills salt on a small doll representing her and, putting together the torn photo, the ring he had bought to give her and the doll, envelops them in a scarf. This scarf had served as a pad for a box containing Julia's photo that Santiago had kept in a cupboard with some family souvenirs. He then leaves the house and walks to a river where he throws the scarf containing the salted torn photo, the ring and the doll, thus accomplishing a common practice of incantation. The scarf functions as an extended version of Shakespeare's Moor's handkerchief.

In the Brazilian 1983 version, transmutation of the handkerchief is found in the ring Otelo gives Dé. On the night of their wedding, after Barbosa left the gypsy's house without having killed him, Otelo goes to a cupboard, takes from it a compotier, opens it and takes a scarf that enveloped a box with a ring in it; he then puts the ring on his little finger, telling Tiago and Cássio that his mother had given it to him. He says that she had worn that ring till her death and he wants Dé to wear it in the same way. An indirect suggestion of Othello's handkerchief is constructed through the scarf that enveloped the ring. Like Santiago's scarf, in the Mexican 2003 version, the allusion is obvious to those who know Shakespeare's play. It is that ring that Tiago will use to destroy Otelo. In *Otelo de Oliveira*, mysticism is intensified, exploring the stereotype of Brazilian voodoo when, as already mentioned, Eloína/Bianca performs the ritual to Exu and exhorts the god to help her destroy Cássio.

Women's predicament in Latin America is also represented through the newly constructed *Othellos* here discussed. Both Dé and Julia embody their cultures' concern for the 'pure, loyal wife' who is not expected to have pleasure in sex, and in that they differ from women in Renaissance England. As Catherine Belsey puts it, both Juliet and Desdemona display a sexual frankness which is evidently not inconsistent with early modern propriety. Shakespeare was not a Victorian, and the polarized alternatives of demure virgin or voracious whore are not expected to be sexless, though they were required to be faithful. Domestic conduct books of the period recommend that married sex should be pleasurable for both husband and wife.[12]

Reproducing Mexican *macho* culture and the yoke its women had to bear, Julia's only possibility of being her free self could be through dancing – and that in folklore groups that reinforced the national search for identity. Ironically it was precisely Otilio's decision to make her go back to the competition when she wanted to stay at home, nursing him, that offered the opportunity Santiago was looking for to destroy him. Even in the twentieth century, in various parts of Latin America, men who thought they were betrayed had 'a right' to kill their 'unfaithful wives'. Such crimes were not openly or legally allowed, but passed by unnoticed by the authorities.

In the 1980s, in Brazil, various crimes like these were perpetrated, eventually bringing changes in the legal and sociopolitical systems, when equal rights were given to husband and wife. But domestic violence still persists, though in a much smaller proportion. As *Otelo de Oliveira* was produced at that time, it necessarily brought the issue into focus and has helped to sustain the discussions then beginning. At the time of the production, Dé appears as a very independent girl for her age, and, like Shakespeare's heroine, capable of choosing her husband even without her father's permission, reflecting the Renaissance English playwright's concern with women and their predicament.

In these two transmutations of *Othello, the Moor of Venice*, one can detect the drive towards recognition by the 'central educated world' of their adaptors and directors as artists who know Shakespeare. As already mentioned, the initial credits state that *Huapango* was 'inspired' by Shakespeare's play, and *Otelo de Oliveira* is a 'recreation of *Othello, the Moor of Venice*, by William Shakespeare'. The attempt at placing both Latin American productions at the same level as a canonized text comes simultaneously with the intention to bring to light, through the reinvention of a world masterpiece, issues relevant to their own national cultures. In these hybrid constructs, the guidelines within the 'lower bulb' concentrate enough malleability to reinterpret the 'grains of sand' filtered throughout the tube that links both bulbs, reorganizing them so as to give them a new 'local habitation and a name'. And in so doing, besides suggesting or inviting consideration of their national predicament, they also keep Shakespeare alive.

Notes

1 R. Jakobson, 'Linguistic Aspects on Translation', in R. A. Brower (ed.), *On Translation* (Cambridge, MA: Harvard University Press, 1959), 232–9.
2 U. Eco, *Quase A Mesma Coisa*, trans. E. Aguiar (Rio de Janeiro: Record, 2007).
3 P. Pavis, *O Teatro no Cruzamento de Culturas*, trans. N. Fernandes (São Paulo: Perspectiva, 2008), 8. This and subsequent translations from Pavis are my own.
4 *Ibid.*, 16.
5 *Ibid.*, 3.
6 M. T. Burnett, 'Shakespeare and Contemporary Latin American Cinema', *Shakespeare Quarterly*, 62.3 (2011), 396–419.
7 M. Matheson, 'Venetian Culture and the Politics of *Othello*', *Shakespeare Survey*, 48 (1995), 123.
8 On the 'Huapango' dance, see Burnett, 'Shakespeare and Contemporary Latin American Cinema', 405.
9 M. T. Burnett, 'Shakespeare, Cinema, Latin America', in *Shakespeare and World Cinema* (Cambridge: Cambridge University Press, 2013), 107.
10 *Ibid.*, 100, and Burnett, 'Shakespeare and Contemporary Latin American Cinema', 406.
11 T. E. Skidmore and P. H. Smith, *Modern Latin America* (New York and Oxford: Oxford University Press, 1984), 160.
12 C. Belsey, 'Gender and Family', in C. McEachern (ed.), *The Cambridge Companion to Shakespearean Tragedy* (Cambridge: Cambridge University Press, 2002), 127–8.

WORKS CITED

Belsey, C., 'Gender and Family', in C. McEachern (ed.), *The Cambridge Companion to Shakespearean Tragedy*, (Cambridge: Cambridge University Press, 2002), 123–41.
Burnett, M. T., 'Shakespeare and Contemporary Latin American Cinema', *Shakespeare Quarterly* 62.3 (2011), 396–419.
    'Shakespeare, Cinema, Latin America', in *Shakespeare and World Cinema*, (Cambridge: Cambridge University Press, 2013), 89–124.
Eco, U., *Quase A Mesma Coisa*, Eliana Aguiar, trans. (Rio de Janeiro: Record, 2007).
Jakobson, R., 'Linguistic Aspects on Translation', in R. A. Brower (ed.), *On Translation*, (Cambridge, MA: Harvard University Press, 1959), 232–9.
Matheson, M., 'Venetian Culture and The Politics Of Othello', *Shakespeare Survey* 48, (1995), 123–33.
Pavis, P., *O Teatro No Cruzamento de Culturas*, trans. N. Fernandes (São Paulo: Perspectiva, 2008).
Skidmore, T. E., and P. H. Smith, *Modern Latin America* (New York and Oxford: Oxford University Press, 1984).

CHAPTER 9

Othello *in Québec*

André Forcier's Une histoire inventée

Jennifer Drouin

Une histoire inventée, a cinematic adaptation of Shakespeare released in October 1990, tells the story of a troupe of fledgling actors who perform *Othello* while also acting out aspects of the play in their own lives. Co-written by André Forcier and Jacques Marcotte, and directed by Forcier, the film was selected as Canada's contender for an Oscar nomination in the Best Foreign Language Film category for the March 1991 Academy Awards, although it was not ultimately nominated as one of the films in the running. The script was published the same year the film was released, but the film itself became difficult to obtain, even in Montréal, until it was rereleased on DVD in February 2012. This parallel, metanarrative adaptation differs from Shakespeare's play in terms of its treatment of ethnic difference, female agency and stage violence as blackface, rape and real onstage gun deaths occupy the screen.[1] Set primarily in a small theatre and a jazz club in Montréal, the film reflects Québec's national identity through its collective ethnic, religious, and gender values in contrast to those of the United States. A portrait of Québec's cultural specificity emerges as a nation where progressive, sex-positive feminism has been firmly entrenched for at least a generation, but also where a largely homogenous society is caught between the imposition of two different political philosophies used to manage immigration and ethnic difference. In light of Québec's 'reasonable accommodation' debate about the integration of religious and ethnic difference, the film's rerelease on DVD is timely.[2] *Une histoire inventée*'s embedded staging of *Othello* for a bored captive audience also interrogates Shakespeare's declining cultural value.

The film is driven by the offstage relationship of Jean-Pierre Tibo (Jean-François Pichette),[3] a white man who plays Othello in blackface onstage, and Soledad Desruisseaux (Charlotte Laurier), who plays Desdemona in a translated French production of the play, which appears truncated and occasionally rearranges and cuts lines. Iago is played by a little person named Clément (Paul Cagelet), but no explanation for this casting choice is suggested, and he is a minor character in the film. The film's other main characters are Florence (Louise Marleau), Soledad's mother, who is followed wherever she goes by a throng of broken-hearted ex-lovers, and Gaston Turcotte (Jean Lapointe), the one man who has not been enticed by Florence's charms and with whom, consequently, she is in love. On opening night, between Act 1 scene 3 and the loving reunion of Othello and Desdemona in Act 2 scene 1, Soledad catches Tibo having sex backstage with Arlette (Louise Gagnon), the costume designer, thus putting the actors on a divergent plot path from that of the characters they play. One evening, after several performances, the play-within-the-film culminates with Tibo/Othello shooting Gaston, who has become Soledad/Desdemona's lover in real life and to whom she has been handcuffed before going onstage, forcing her to improvise a line designating him as her '*amant imaginaire*', her imaginary lover.[4] Tibo/Othello then turns the gun on himself. The two real onstage deaths are taken as part of the fiction by the audience of senior citizens who have been bussed in to watch the show each night by the theatre director's ex-mobster uncle, Alfredo (Louis de Santis), who had provided Tibo/Othello with the gun because he could not bear to watch Desdemona suffer a painful, drawn-out death by strangulation. Soledad and Florence reconcile over the dead bodies of Tibo and Gaston, producing a stronger image of female solidarity than the proto-feminism found in Shakespeare's willow scene (4.3). Stealing an ex's taxi, the mother-daughter duo laughingly drive away chased by Florence's inconsolable ex-lovers, leaving behind a horde of men for whom they have no need.

The film thus rewrites the gender norms of Shakespeare's play through its plot, while it engages *Othello*'s race issues through its casting choices. Tibo plays Othello in blackface, but this salient feature of the film is never indicated in the published script. In fact, were a critic to read the script without also viewing the film, she would be led to believe that Tibo is black because Florence twice calls him '*Un beau grand noir*' ['A beautiful, big, black man'] and '*Mon beau grand noir*' ['My beautiful, big, black man'] (44, 56). It is unclear why Florence would call a white actor her 'beautiful, big, black man' when he is not in blackface playing his role, but she may simply be wishfully projecting her desires since, as Lentaignes claims in reference to her ex-lover Théodule (Angelo Cadet), Florence '*l'aime ben son ti-nègre*' ['really likes her little nigger'] (64). There are two black men in the film who could have been cast as Othello instead of Tibo. Florence's ex, Théodule – described in the script as '*un jeune noir de Chicoutimi*' ['a young black man from Chicoutimi'] (23), a northern town whose black population is only 0.2 per cent – drives a taxi. Slim Duson (Warren 'Slim' Williams), 'un grand noir' ['a big black man'] who is a Baptist from the United States (16), plays bass alongside his Québécois fiancée Alys Grenier (France Castel) as part of Gaston's jazz trio. Black actors are thus present in the film itself, both appearing on screen before the audience first sees Tibo/Othello in blackface; yet, like any mention of the use of blackface in the script, they are notably absent from the play-within-the-film. In fact, the cinematic audience does not see Tibo as himself until after the opening night's performance is over, and he is joined soon after by Théodule, producing a clear visual image of their different skin colours.

One explanation for the film's use of an actor in blackface is that it is in keeping with *Othello*'s cinematic production history. The first black actor ever to play Othello on film was Frank H. Wilson, who, as the aspiring actor Lem Anderson, is seen performing the final death scene at the end of Joseph Seiden's 1939 metanarrative adaptation *Paradise in Harlem*;[5] however, the first full-length production to cast a black man was Oliver Parker's 1995 film starring Laurence Fishburne. Forcier's 1990 film thus follows the tradition of blackface in Orson Welles's 1952 film starring himself, Stuart Burge's 1965 film starring Laurence Olivier, and Jonathan Miller's 1981 BBC television movie starring Anthony Hopkins, as well as John Gielgud's 1961 RSC stage production. The play-within-the-film does not, however, align with *Othello*'s longer stage history, which includes the black actors Ira Aldridge (London Covent Garden, 1833), Paul Robeson (London, 1930; New York, 1943), and Willard White (Stratford RSC, 1989).[6]

Contemporary criticism is divided on the use of blackface. Harking back to the first performances starring Richard Burbage, Dympna Callaghan rightly points out that 'Othello was a white man' while poignantly adding 'so was Desdemona'.[7] In analysing Olivier's blackface Othello, which reveals blackness as a layer that 'may be constructed', Barbara Hodgdon claims that 'a made-up Othello ensures that both blackness and whiteness remain separate, unsullied. Putting race matters succinctly, blacking up is whiting out'.[8] Ayanna Thompson discusses the ways in which a blackfaced white actor unsettles and alienates a contemporary audience because he becomes a mere caricature of blackness; on the other hand, a black actor risks legitimizing racial stereotypes.[9] In analysing the photonegative *Othello* directed by Jude Kelly starring Patrick Stewart with a predominantly black cast (Washington DC, 1997–8), Sujata Iyengar argues that 'under certain specific conditions, the use of a white actor in [...] "strategic blackface" can foreground the fact that the category of "race" itself is "the figment of a white man's imagination."[10] Iyengar hits upon Thompson's point about 'the tension between intention, practice, and reception',[11] all of which play a role in the production of meaning no matter what casting choices are made. In putting a blackfaced actor on stage within his film, Forcier seems to be mocking the practice of blackface productions of *Othello* since Soledad/Desdemona also wears gaudy make-up, producing 'racoon eyes' to parody Othello's blackface, and the play-within-the-film frequently falls into farce.[12] The theatrical audience of sleepy senior citizens is indifferent to blackface, but the cinematic audience may be uncomfortable with the disjuncture produced by the presence of black artists in the film in contrast to their absence in the play-within-the-film, and the cinematic audience may arguably be attuned to the onstage performance as a simulacrum of a stereotype.

The film's approach to race is particularly Québécois because Québec's distinct approach to 'ethnicity' is often tied to linguistic rather than racial difference, as demonstrated in the characterization of *'les ethnies'* ['ethnics'] as allophones as well as blacks. Richard Lentaignes (Marc Messier), a cop who is afraid to touch, let alone arrest, *'un ethnie'* ['an ethnic'] (64), reveals to the bartender Gros-Pierre (Marc Gélinas) that *'à police, on a eu des cours sur les ethnies. T'sais c'monde-là, c'est pas comme nous autres'* ['in the police, we had classes on ethnics. Ya know, those people aren't like us'] (118). When two other officers arrive at the theatre after the onstage murder-suicide, Lentaignes's colleague Roger Gingras (Marcel Fournier) warns him to stop beating up Toni Corbo (Tony Nardi), the theatre director: *'C't'un ethnie ça! Arrête ça là!* [...] *Y ont peut-être un vidéo qui filme!'* ['It's an ethnic, that! Stop that! [...] They might have a camera that's filming!'] (137). This is not to say that the police officers are not racist, as Lentaignes clearly is in his description of Théodule as a *'nègre',* but even that word carries a different connotation in Québec since the publication in 1968 of Pierre Vallières's famous *Nègres blancs d'Amérique* [*White Niggers of America*] which attempted to resignify the word in terms of social class in addition to race. Toni and his Italian uncle Alfredo are classified as ethnics not because of their race, or even class, but because of their language. They speak to each other primarily in Italian (21, 27, 74), and Alfredo speaks French with a strong accent in simple sentences (76, 114). Both are allophones, a Québécois term that translates as 'other speaker' and applies to everyone who is neither francophone nor anglophone.[13] They thus slide into the category of *'des ethnies'* even though they are whites of Western origin.[14] Whereas Théodule comes from Chicoutimi, speaks Québécois with a *pure laine* accent,[15] and is desirable to Florence, Toni and Alfredo are objects of ridicule. The film is representative of Québécois attitudes about otherness as primarily a function of an individual's linguistic integration rather than one's race.

Lentaignes is clearly racist,[16] but his comments also point to a wariness about overly politically correct multiculturalism which accords some people special rights, privileges or accommodations that overreach civil norms. In June 1990, as *Une histoire inventée* was being produced, the Meech Lake Accord died. Meech would have recognized Québec as a 'distinct society' and given the provinces more powers with respect to immigration, a condition many Québécois considered a bare minimum in order to endorse the still unsigned 1982 Canadian Constitution. Immigration, diversity, multiculturalism and 'special rights' were thus highly topical at the time. Multiculturalism was, and still is, often perceived in Québec as a political strategy designed to erase the previous discourse of 'two founding nations' (which ignores all the First Nations) by multiplying the number of national identities that compose Canada.[17] Even though the 1963 Royal Commission on Bilingualism and Biculturalism led to Canada becoming a bilingual nation in 1969, Pierre Elliott Trudeau steered the country away from biculturalism to multiculturalism, which was recognized in the 1982 Constitution and further enshrined in the 1988 Canadian Multiculturalism Act. In contrast, Québec espouses an intercultural approach that privileges greater integration of immigrants, thereby eliding multiculturalism's recognition of hyphenated, hybrid identities (which may ultimately reinforce discourses of 'us versus them'). Self-identification as Asian-Québécois, for instance, is much rarer than as Asian-Canadian. The contrast between these two political philosophies is reinforced visually in a shot of a Canadian flag and a Québécois flag hanging side-by-side immediately after one of Lentaignes's comments about '*les ethnies*' (118).

Seeking to integrate immigrants into Québec society, interculturalism exists midway on a spectrum ranging from Canadian multiculturalism (which values differentiation, multilingualism and insertion into society) to French republicanism (which values dedifferentiation, unilingualism and assimilation into a universal vision of society). Québécois interculturalism gives immigrants the liberty to preserve an affiliation with their native ethnic group; however, unlike Canadian multiculturalism which asserts that all cultures within Canada hold equal value and therefore should be promoted and treated equally, Québécois interculturalism insists upon adherence to a common civic culture, that of the francophone majority, with the intent of preventing ghettoization by making immigrants feel fully integrated into their adopted country.[18] In 1990, the Québec government officially adopted interculturalism in its *Énoncé de politique en matière d'immigration et d'intégration* [*Policy Statement on Immigration and Integration*], which states there is a 'moral contract' between Québec as host society and particular cultural groups. Guided by three principles – that French is the common language of public life; that a democratic society requires the participation of everyone; and that a pluralist society is open to the contributions of others within the limits imposed by fundamental democratic values[19] – Québécois interculturalism focuses more strongly on integration and the reciprocal nature of the moral contract than Canadian multiculturalism which supposes a mosaic of juxtaposed ethnocultural groups and which puts more emphasis on individual rights than collective social cohesion.[20]

In addition to its parodic use of blackface and its evocation of the multiculturalism versus interculturalism debate, *Une histoire inventée* interrogates ethnicity through its metatheatrical assessment of the play-within-the-film and its characterization of the play's pompous theatre director. In describing his production, Toni tells Théodule, '*Je ne sais pas si vous pouvez comprendre, hein, puisque nous ne sommes pas tout à fait de la même culture*' ['I don't know if you can understand, eh, since we are not entirely from the same culture'] (73). Toni attempts to create a hierarchy among ethnics based on cultural capital, but his claim to intellectual superiority is undercut by his contradictory statements about the nature of theatre. In response to Théodule pointing out that the glowing review by the critic who left partway through the show due to a '"*bienheureux malaise*"' ['"very happy unease"'] was about Florence rather than the play (24), Toni says, '*Mais c'est sûr. Le spectacle est sur la scène et dans la salle. C'est ça le théâtre*' ['But of course. The show is on the stage and in the auditorium. That's what theatre is'] (72). While Forcier may be alluding to the practice of early modern gallants sitting on the stage in Shakespeare's playhouse in order to be seen as much as to see the play, this remark also reveals Toni's hypocrisy as he struggles to concoct an excuse for the critic getting an erection provoked by Florence (seated next to him by Soledad expressly to garner good reviews). When Théodule pushes the issue further by inquiring about the content of the text – '*Oui... Shakespeare là-dedans? Hein...*' ['Yes... Shakespeare in that? Eh...'] –, Toni replies, '*J'estime que personne dans un théâtre n'a moins d'importance que l'auteur de la pièce*' ['I consider that nobody in a theatre has less importance than the author of the play'] (73). Putting his director's narcissism on display, Toni's espousal of the theory of the death of the author contradicts his assertion just a few lines later: '*Mais mon oncle, je me dois d'être fidèle au texte. Shakespeare aussi est un génie*' ['But my uncle, I must be loyal to the text. Shakespeare, too, is a genius'] (76). Adding that he wants to '*faire des tournées en prison, devant un public captif*' ['tour prisons in front of a captive audience'] (73), much like his current captive audience of bussed-in senior citizens, Toni's ideas about the theatre push the cinematic audience to agree with Soledad's assessment of the play as '*Un* Othello *flyé monté par un metteur en scène capoté*' ['A wild *Othello* staged by a crazy director'] (58). Toni's directorial incompetence influences the entire production, ultimately producing a farce: Soledad and Arlette put itching powder in Clément's costume, but, rather than allowing him to take a shower, Toni orders him to play as he is and tells the women to put itching powder on his costume every night because his contortions agree with Iago's character; Alfredo tells Toni he bought him the theatre in order to see a play that takes place in Venice and he wonders where the gondolas are; the senior citizens fall asleep, knit, play cards, bring feasts of food, and chit-chat during the show; after the break-up with Soledad, Tibo must be forced on stage by Toni who gives him a '*coup de pied au cul*' ['kick in the ass'] which elicits applause from the audience (94), making the ass-kicking a required feature of the subsequent nights' productions just as the handcuffed Gaston becomes a staple after his first onstage appearance. Since this absurd *Othello* would have no audience at all were it not for Alfredo's economic capital, the film confirms that Théodule possesses more cultural capital than Toni who consistently undermines the credibility of his production.

The play-within-the-film's most metatheatrical moment, as Tibo becomes Othello, is closely tied to the film's adaptation of *Othello*'s racial and gender politics. Alfredo's emotional trauma in response to the nightly 'death' of Desdemona incites the cinematic viewer to question whether the distinction between fiction and reality is as clear as one assumes. After having watched the show for several nights, and having been told by Toni, '*Pleure pas, elle n'est pas morte.* [. . .] *C'est comme ça au théâtre*' ['Don't cry; she isn't dead. [. . .] It's like that in the theatre'] (35), Alfredo nevertheless gives 'Othello' a gun: '*Othello! Othello, c'est très bonne la pièce* [. . .] *Mais si Toni demande de touer la femme, touez-la avec mon gun. . . Ne la faites plus souffrir*' ['Othello! Othello, the play is very good [. . .] But if Toni asks to kill the woman, kill her with my gun. . . Don't make her suffer anymore'] (76). Unable to distinguish between actors and characters, Alfredo's reaction to the trauma of witnessing Desdemona die onstage is similar to a story recounted by Stendhal and cited by Michael Bristol:

L'année dernière (août 1822), le soldat qui était en faction dans l'intérieur du théâtre de Baltimore, voyant Othello qui, au cinquième acte de la tragédie de ce nom, allait tuer Desdemona, s'écria: 'Il ne serait jamais dit qu'en ma présence un maudit nègre aura tué une femme blanche.' Au même moment le soldat tire son coup de fusil, et casse un bras à l'acteur qui faisait Othello. Il ne se passe pas d'années sans que les journaux ne rapportent des faits semblables.

The moral that Stendhal wants to draw from the story of the soldier in Baltimore is that only someone who is extremely ignorant or stupid – i.e. an American – fails to distinguish an actual murder from a dramatic representation of one. In the perhaps more definite variant of the anecdote the performance takes place in a barn, and the unlucky actor playing Othello is not merely wounded but killed outright. In this version the soldier's behavior is less a matter of the 'perfect illusion' described by Stendhal than a militant defense of white women notwithstanding the fictional status of Desdemona's 'murder.'[21]

Alfredo's motivations are more altruistic, however, than the racist soldier's since he seeks not to kill Othello but to help him shorten Desdemona's suffering. Lentaignes reminds the retired mob boss, *'pourtant, t'en as tué du monde, hein?'* ['yet you've killed lots of people, eh?'], to which Alfredo replies, *'Oui, mais touer et faire souffrir c'est différent!'* ['Yes, but kill and make suffer are different!'] (115). More crucially, although he provides the gun, the traumatized audience member does not pull the trigger; the actor does:[22]

Soudain Tibo tire sur Gaston avec le gun *de mon oncle Alfredo, puis il se flingue. Desdémone ressuscite en Soledad qui se met à hurler, penchée sur le corps de Tibo. Le rideau tombe sur un Cassio paniqué.* [Suddenly Tibo shoots Gaston with uncle Alfredo's gun, then he shoots himself. Desdemona resuscitates as Soledad who starts screaming, leaning over Tibo's body. The curtain falls on a panicked Cassio.] (134)[23]

Tibo directs his jealousy at Gaston (who actually has slept with Soledad), inciting those familiar with the play to contemplate how Shakespeare's play would have unfolded had Othello confronted and killed Cassio rather than Desdemona. Unlike Othello's, Tibo's suicide is not motivated by guilt over the murder he has just committed but rather his unrequited desire. Although an unintended consequence, Alfredo's inability to distinguish fiction from reality is responsible for the happy ending for the female characters. His confused gift of the gun leads to Soledad/Desdemona's liberation from Tibo/Othello and the ensuing female solidarity that is largely absent among Shakespeare's women until it is too late.

The adaptation of the women characters' fates may also be attributed to Tibo's inability to perform another race adequately. Tibo's onstage suicide in Othello's blackface may be interpreted as an acknowledgement of his failure to perform blackness authentically as he eradicates the inauthentic blackface from the stage in a gesture of irreversible authenticity. In keeping with the casting choices and the comments on ethnics, the blackface Othello's suicide may also be read as Forcier's take on the failure of Canadian multiculturalism, which produces token 'ethnics' rather than the more seamless integration fostered by Québécois interculturalism and represented by Théodule. In fact, the film reveals that Théodule would have made a superior Othello. In his devotion to Florence, Théodule is a more loyal lover than Tibo who is a serial cheater (46). While Tibo becomes a suicidal Othello in life in addition to onstage, Théodule embodies an idealized version of the character, the Othello who could have been, had Shakespeare's play not culminated in tragedy. In having the white man who has usurped the black man's role kill himself off, Forcier may be suggesting that Canadian multiculturalism, which appropriates visible minorities for the political purpose of erasing its history of two founding nations, ought also to be wiped out and replaced by Québec's more holistic approach to immigration, which encourages visible minorities to play out their own cultural identities while simultaneously adopting the cultural practices of the host society, as indeed Othello attempts to do in Venice.

Tibo's suicide may also emanate from his failure to perform masculinity. After Soledad leaves him for cheating, demonstrating her agency compared to the passive character she plays, Tibo proposes marriage, receives no response, and then becomes aggressive:

> *Tibo pousse Soledad contre une voiture, lui arrache son slip et la prend, violemment. Cela ressemble à un acte de possession, c'est fougueux, bref, sans plaisir. Soledad ne résiste presque pas, puis ramasse son vélo et s'en va sans dire mot. Tibo reste planté là à crier 'Soledad'. Il sanglote en s'enfonçant dans le ventre un couteau imaginaire.* [Tibo pushes Soledad against the car, pulls off her panties and takes her, violently. It resembles an act of possession; it's impetuous, brief, without pleasure. Soledad almost doesn't resist, then picks up her bicycle and leaves without saying a word. Tibo stays standing there crying 'Soledad'. He sobs while stabbing his stomach with an imaginary knife.] (84)

In the script, the scene is entitled '*Le demi-viol*', but obviously one cannot have a 'half-rape'. Jonathan Romney's film review states that Tibo 'rapes her' without qualifying it as anything less.[24] The scene title suggests that the act is a rape for Soledad, but Tibo does not perceive it as such because he is trying to reclaim 'possession' of his former partner out of '*la désorbitée maladresse du désespoir*' ['the deorbited awkwardness of despair'] (83, 82).

Regardless of his intentions, Tibo's rape is violent, and even though she 'almost doesn't resist', Soledad does still resist him to some degree, making the act a partner rape that cannot be excused based on their past relationship.[25] The script does not make clear whether or not he later realizes that he has raped his ex and whether guilt for this act plays into his decision to commit suicide, but the self-stabbing gesture he makes as she leaves indicates his emasculation and recognition of his failure to win her back. After his failed attempt to conquer her, Tibo falls into a period of depression and madness as he internalizes Othello more explicitly. Prior to the fatal performance, he madly walks along the balcony railing and then chases the theatre janitor while repeatedly yelling '*Ma femme a un amant!*' ['My wife has a lover!'] (119). His word choice of '*femme*', meaning 'wife', over the more common Québécois term '*blonde*', meaning 'girlfriend', further aligns him with Othello since he and Soledad are not married, yet he feels cuckolded.

In fact, all the men in the film fail to perform masculinity in a way that satisfies the sexually liberated Québécois women who find themselves either insatiable, bored or disappointed by the men in their lives: Florence literally leaves a trail of ex-lovers behind her, none able to satisfy her for long; Alys suffers from a Baptist fiancé whose morals leave her in a constant state of longing; Arlette has given up on relationships entirely; and Soledad dumps Tibo for cheating. Telling him, '*Mange donc d'la marde! J'peux pas aimer un ostie de menteur*' ['Eat shit! I can't love a fucking liar'] (36), Soledad exudes independence in stark contrast to Desdemona whose repeated death scenes in the play-within-the-film highlight her passivity, leaving no possibility of an empowered reading of Shakespeare's text.[26] Each liberated, self-aware woman is too much for the men around her to handle, precisely because she has the sexual agency and emotional self-sufficiency that terrifies Shakespeare's Othello and leads to his murderous rage.

Arlette articulates her sexual liberation when she tells Tibo, '*J'ai pas d'chum pis j'en veux pas. Mais j'ai la cuisse hospitalière et j'en suis fière*' ['I don't have a boyfriend and I don't want one. But I have a welcoming thigh and I'm proud of it'] (47). Putting her own pleasure above the annoyances of a heteronormative relationship, Arlette expresses the sexual independence that Alys suppresses in her relationship with the Baptist American Slim who denies Alys to the point that she touches her breasts and thighs while he is on the other side of a hotel room door because, as she tells Gaston, '*Je l'aime pis y veut pas m'toucher*' ['I love him and he doesn't want to touch me'] (18). Refusing to have sex before marriage, Slim quotes from the Bible,[27] attempting, like Othello, to impose chastity on his future wife's body. Slim's puritan approach to sexuality is antithetical to Québécois feminism. In fact, Slim's religious values construct America as a pre-Quiet Revolution Québec when *la revanche des berceaux* was still the norm,[28] revealing the United States to be thirty years behind the times. Gaston mockingly remarks, '*Slim a pas le droit d'y toucher avant le mariage mais ç'a l'air qu'après y se r'prennent. Hey, sa mère a eu quatorze enfants, cinquante-sept petits-enfants pis vingt-deux arrière-petits-enfants*' ['Slim isn't allowed to touch her before marriage but it looks like they catch up afterwards. Hey, his mother had fourteen children, fifty-seven grandchildren and twenty-two great-grandchildren'] (40). Premarital abstinence, coupled with a lack of marital birth control, harks back to an inconceivably retrograde time Québécois women have gladly left in the past. Lentaignes's conservative girlfriend Nicole (Léo Munger) illustrates how these attitudes are antiquated in Québec, even for those few women who still adhere to elements of Catholicism. Although she wears conservative clothes and a large crucifix hangs prominently outside her blouse, Nicole first proposes sex (98), she uses the promise of sex to make Lentaignes quit his previously excessive drinking (105), and she has no qualms about making out with him during the play (132). The Catholic Québécois woman is thus far more sexually liberated than the Baptist American man. Although the representation of Slim as sexually conservative challenges stereotypes about miscegenation between the lustful black man and the shy white woman, his repressed desires also draw attention to how Québec's progressive gender politics have given women more sexual freedom than enjoyed in the United States, linking Québécois women's agency to their national identity.

In his review of the film, Jonathan Romney claims, 'The invented story which underpins André Forcier's tale is Iago's deception of Othello – a parallel made clear when Soledad drags a bewildered Gaston on stage and speaks Desdemona's line "Behold my imaginary lover"' (52). Romney's reading is valid, but Forcier's title can also be interpreted as a commentary on the nature of adaptation itself and on Shakespeare's cultural value. Evoking adaptation as just one invented story among many variations, the film depicts one instantiation of *Othello* while emphasizing the plurality of possibilities through subtle differences in each night's performance of the death scene as well as the radical ending created by Alfredo's gun. Translated as *An Imaginary Tale*, the film's title also reveals that the framing story is fiction just as much as the play, thereby associating the cinematic audience with the theatrical audience and Alfredo's inability to discern fiction. Should we perhaps all be more like Alfredo, for, if the frame of the story is imaginary, are we any less duped than he when we engage emotionally with a film? And, if Shakespeare's stories are all just imaginary stories he re-invented from others, in this case Cinthio's *Hecatommithi* (1565), what exactly makes Shakespeare more worthy of our esteem than Toni or others who re-invent him?

The film further questions Shakespeare's cultural value by emphasizing his obscurity. In this fictionalized representation of Montréal (which does not accurately depict Shakespeare's draw at Montréal's Théâtre du Nouveau Monde), not only does Shakespeare require busloads of senior citizens to fill a theatre (a phenomenon not unknown in Stratford or at other festivals), but he also does not confer status on actors. When Gaston meets Soledad, he exclaims, '*J'vous connais, j'vous ai vue à la télévision. C'est vous qui annoncez les Tampax*' ['I know you; I saw you on television. You're the one who advertises Tampax'] (44). If starring in a Tampax commercial brings her more fame and admiration than playing Desdemona, why should she want to act in a misogynist play that subjects her to death, erasure and obscurity on a nightly basis? In the increasingly capitalist world of popular culture, Shakespeare's name does not carry the cultural weight it once did, leaving us to wonder whether Shakespeare is losing his 'big-time' status 'in the idiomatic sense of cultural success, high visibility, and notoriety'.[29] If big-time Shakespeare is a product of what Bristol calls 'the supply side of culture' and 'Shakespeare retains his authority, at least in part, because suppliers of cultural goods have been skilful at generating a social desire for products that bear his trademark and in creating merchandise to satisfy that desire',[30] what if there is no more demand for his plays? If Tampax is a bigger brand name than Shakespeare and captive audiences must be bussed in to watch him, what is the current state of the Bardbiz, Shakespeare's cultural authority or as scholars our own? Given Toni's contradictory assertions that Shakespeare is a genius yet the author is the least important person in the theatre, the film suggests that Shakespeare's cultural authority is becoming increasingly ambivalent, retaining some degree of eighteenth-century bardolatry but undermined both by the popular culture and new media represented in the Tampax ad and by critics since post-structuralism who have deliberately challenged that authority.

As a parallel, metanarrative adaptation that is more *about* Shakespeare than an adaptation *of* Shakespeare, *Une histoire inventée* raises a number of important questions about Québec society and the Bardbiz more broadly. First, in light of changing attitudes about race over the last few decades, and especially in light of different approaches to managing ethnocultural and racial diversity, such as multiculturalism versus interculturalism, the film asks how directors should cast an African character originally played by a white Englishman. The absurdity of the film's stage production suggests that blackface is equally absurd and that in an intercultural society black men should be artists, like Slim, rather than confined to jobs driving taxis, like Théodule. Second, the film interrogates how religion circumscribes the sexual freedom of women through both the celibacy imposed on Alys by the Baptist faith and the spectre of unending child-bearing and -rearing under pre-Quiet Revolution Catholicism. Such religious ideologies, the film suggests, are subject, however, to national contexts since moral attitudes prevalent today in many areas of the United States were a source of derision in Québec over twenty years ago. Finally, *Une histoire inventée* asks if Shakespeare's cultural authority is diminishing steadily and, if so, whether it is worth defending. Forcier's film replies that such authority remains relatively intact only if we – actors, directors, and critics – do not go too far in making a mockery of him.[31]

Notes

1 In the chapter 'A Theory of Shakespearean Adaptation' in *Shakespeare in Québec: Nation, Gender, and Adaptation* (Toronto: University of Toronto Press, 2014), I argue the need for greater definitional precision in classifying adaptations through an open-ended adjectival system. *Une histoire inventée* is both a parallel narrative adaptation because Tibo lives out aspects of Othello's life unknowingly and a metanarrative adaptation because it is about characters struggling to act in a Shakespearean play.

2 In 2006, a series of cases of 'reasonable accommodation' hit the media. See Drouin, *Shakespeare in Québec*, 178–9, 247–50n14–21, for a full account. The intersection of race, ethnicity and religion in the public sphere remains a hot topic in Québec today.

3 Tibo's last name may be a transformation of the more common surname Thibault and is likely to be heard as such by a cinematic audience. Thibault is particularly prevalent in *Acadie*, but Tibo does not speak with an Acadian accent and there is no evidence that he hails from the Maritimes. Acadians deported in 1755 did, however, resettle in Québec, particularly in the Montérégie, Lanaudière, Centre-du-Québec, Chaudière-Appalaches, and Bas-Saint-Laurent areas, so the implication may be that the character is not a native Montréalais, thereby aligning him with Othello as an outsider.

4 A. Forcier and J. Marcotte, *Une histoire inventée* (Montréal: Du Roseau, 1990), 110. All references from the film (including stage directions) are from the

published script, which follows the film exactly, and are hereafter provided in parentheses. All translations from French to English are mine.

5 Thanks to Mariangela Tempera for providing information about *Paradise in Harlem* which is viewable on *YouTube.*

6 For a critical reaction to each actor's performance, see S. Iyengar, 'White Faces, Blackface: The Production of "Race" in *Othello*', in P. C. Kolin (ed.), *Othello: New Critical Essays* (London: Routledge, 2002), 103–31. See also B. Hodgdon, 'Race-ing *Othello*: Re-Engendering White Out', in L. Cowen Orlin (ed.), *Othello* (New York: Palgrave Macmillan, 2004), 190–219, for descriptions of Robeson's, Olivier's and White's performances.

7 D. Callaghan, *Shakespeare Without Women: Representing Gender and Race on the Renaissance Stage* (London: Routledge, 2000), 76.

8 Hodgdon, 'Race-ing *Othello*', 194.

9 A. Thompson, *Passing Strange: Shakespeare, Race, and Contemporary America* (Oxford: Oxford University Press, 2011), 99.

10 Iyengar, 'White Faces, Blackface, 105.

11 Thompson, *Passing Strange*, 110.

12 While Soledad's 'racoon-eye' make-up alludes to the racist slur 'coon' in English, the French term for the animal, 'raton laveur', does not carry the same racist connotations in Québec, although 'raton', meaning 'little rat', may be used in France as a racist term for inhabitants of North Africa. A Québécois cinematic audience would be more likely to associate Soledad's gaudy make-up with the farcical nature of the play-within-the-film than with an unspoken English term. Clément/Iago and the other actors also wear black eye make-up since theatre requires heavier make-up than television or film.

13 The film includes two other 'others' who contribute to urban diversity. The actor playing Iago is a '*nain*' ['dwarf'] and we see a blind piano tuner (20, 40).

14 Released five years before Jacques Parizeau's referendum night statement about '*l'argent puis des votes ethniques*' ['money and ethnic votes'], the film testifies to *pure laine* Québécois's growing recognition of '*des communautés culturelles*' ['cultural communities']. For a full discussion of Parizeau's infamous declaration, see Drouin, *Shakespeare in Québec*, 214–17n51.

15 *Pure laine* is generally translated in English as 'dyed in the wool'. The term refers to Québécois who are born and raised in Québec, speak with a Québécois accent, and show no traces of any particular immigrant origin.

16 He drunkenly says, '*J'aimerais ça aller à un mariage de nègres, ça doit être comique*' ['I'd like to go to a marriage of niggers; that must be funny'] (68).

17 For further discussion of 'two founding nations', multiculturalism and interculturalism, see Drouin, *Shakespeare in Québec*, 151, 171–91.

18 For a comprehensive study of the differences between Canadian multiculturalism, Québécois interculturalism and French republicanism, see G. Rousseau, *La Nation à l'épreuve de l'immigration* (Québec: Éditions du Québécois, 2006). The graphic illustration of the values of these three ideologies, 118, is particularly helpful.

19 Gouvernement du Québec, *Au Québec pour bâtir ensemble : Énoncé de politique en matière d'immigration et d'intégration*, Ministère des Communautés culturelles et de l'Immigration du Québec, Direction des communications, Québec, (1990), www.micc.gouv.qc.ca/publications/fr/ministere/Enonce-poli tique-immigration-integration-Quebec1991.pdf, 16.

20 For further scholarship on Québécois interculturalism in contrast to Canadian multiculturalism, see A. G. Gagnon, 'Plaidoyer pour l'interculturalisme', *Possibles*, 24.4 (2000), 11–25; and A. G. Gagnon and R. Iacovino, 'Interculturalism: Expanding the Boundaries of Citizenship', in R. Máiz and F. Requejo (eds.), *Democracy, Nationalism and Multiculturalism* (London: Frank Cass, 2005), 25–42.

21 M. Bristol, *Big-time Shakespeare* (London: Routledge, 1996), 195–6. Italics in source. Bristol provides the following translation: 'Last year (August of 1822), the soldier standing guard at the interior of the theatre in Baltimore, seeing Othello who, in the fifth act of the tragedy of that name, was going to kill Desdemona, cried out "It will never be said that in my presence a damned black would kill a white woman." At that moment the soldier fired his gun, and broke the arm of the actor who played Othello. Not a year goes by without newspapers reporting similar facts.'

22 Alfredo does, however, get up on stage earlier in the film before giving 'Othello' the gun: *'Mon oncle Alfredo, n'en pouvant plus, se lève et monte sur scène. Cela réveille le public apathique. Un comédien reconduit mon oncle Alfredo en coulisses avant qu'il ait eu le temps de raisonner Othello'* ['Uncle Alfredo, no longer able to endure it, rises and gets up on stage. This wakes up the apathetic audience. An actor directs uncle Alfredo backstage before he has the time to reason with Othello'] (74). After 'Othello' shoots himself, Alfredo continues to confound theatre and reality and *'est particulièrement heureux de la résurrection de Desdé- mone'* ['is particularly happy about Desdemona's resurrection'], repeating, *'Elle n'est pas morte'* ['She's not dead'] (135). At Tibo's funeral, he tells the hired criers, *'Pleurez pour l'âme d'Othello, plus de larmes'* ['Cry for Othello's soul, more tears'] (140), still calling the actor by the character's name.

23 In this and other stage directions in the script, Alfredo is always identified as *'mon oncle Alfredo'*, rather than the third person *'son oncle'* in reference to his nephew Toni, because *'mon oncle'*, which is often written *'mononcle'* as a single word, is an idiom in Québécois, as is its female equivalent *'matante'*. The word *'mononcle'* may designate someone's uncle and therefore can produce *'mon mononcle'* in the first person and *'son mononcle'* in the third person. However, *'mononcle'* or *'matante'* can also designate any older person, not necessarily a family member, who is old-fashioned or living in the past. Other characteristics of persons called *'mononcle'* or *'matante'* include having bad taste, being *'cochon'* or leering sexually at younger people, driving slowly or erratically, being a busybody or gossip, or expressing retrograde beliefs. See the *Diction- naire québécois*, www.dictionnaire-quebecois.com.

24 J. Romney, '*Une histoire inventée (An Imaginary Tale)* directed by André Forcier', *Sight and Sound*, 2.1 (May 1992), 52.

25 Soledad's emotional response to the rape is ambiguous. She walks away as if she is broken (or simply doesn't care?). She is next seen dancing to samba music (because she is fine or to raise her dejected spirits?) in her mother's apartment (a safe space of refuge?) having just emerged from taking a shower (to wash Tibo off her body?). She does not tell her mother about the incident (because Florence's lover Rolland is there too?), but she does tell her mother that she is going to sleep with her that night (for comfort and security?). Whatever her emotional state, the character's actions throughout the rest of the film construct her as a survivor rather than a victim and her resolve to move on from Tibo remains undaunted.

26 Although empowered readings of Desdemona are rare, in some productions she fights back during the death scene. In the multiple stagings within the film, however, Soledad's Desdemona does not resist Othello's strangulation and dies passively each time.

27 Slim's passage from 1 Corinthians 7:8, not taken from the King James Version, appears thus: "'But I say to the unmarried and to the widows...' '...it is good for them if they remain as I am. If they cannot exercise self control, let them marry: for it is better to marry than to burn with passion'" (70–1). Slim preaches chastity, yet he ignores the prescript to marry and relieve Alys's passion. The onscreen appearance of French subtitles translating his English monologue exposes the 'word of God' as a social construct subject to human translation and interpretation.

28 *La Revanche des berceaux* translates literally as 'the revenge of the cradles', but 'revenge' is too strong for the phrase's connotation. Before the Quiet Revolution, which began in 1960, the Catholic Church encouraged women to have as many children as possible in order to ensure the survival of the French Canadian nation. A family of twenty children, not counting a few stillborns or early deaths, was common.

29 Bristol, *Big-time Shakespeare*, 2.

30 *Ibid.*, 22.

31 In keeping with its embedded metatheatricality, the film participates in this derision. Although the play-within-the-film is supposed to be a tragedy, it comes off as comedy in keeping with the genre of the film. The film's comedy stretches to the level of an absurd circus in the final scene as Alfredo eggs on the hired criers, knocking one over, causing Slim to come to her rescue, causing a fistfight to break out and eventually a gunfight among the tombstones between Alfredo and Lentaignes, who takes the opportunity to teach Nicole how to shoot. During this time, Slim finally gives in to his desires and makes out passionately with Alys between the tombstones, oblivious to the bullets flying around his head but still holding a Bible from the funeral service. As Soledad and Florence steal Théodule's taxi, it is revealed that Florence's latest ex-lover, Rolland, has become the chauffeur of a chartered bus who drives the exes around after her, and they all run down the snowy road after the taxi shouting her name as upbeat, circus-like music plays. The final scene of the film is thus more absurd than the grotesque final performance of the play-within-the-film.

WORKS CITED

Bristol, M., *Big-time Shakespeare* (London: Routledge, 1996).
Callaghan, D., *Shakespeare Without Women: Representing Gender and Race on the Renaissance Stage* (London: Routledge, 2000).
Dictionnaire québécois, www.dictionnaire-quebecois.com
Drouin, J., *Shakespeare in Québec: Nation, Gender, and Adaptation* (Toronto: University of Toronto Press, 2014).
Forcier, A. (dir.), *Une histoire inventée* (DVD, [1990], 2012).
Forcier, A. and J. Marcotte, *Une histoire inventée* (Montréal: Du Roseau, 1990).
Gagnon, A. G., 'Plaidoyer pour l'interculturalisme', *Possibles*, 24.4 (2000), 11–25.
Gagnon, A. G. and R. Iacovino, 'Interculturalism: Expanding the Boundaries of Citizenship', in R. Máiz and F. Requejo (eds.), *Democracy, Nationalism and Multiculturalism* (London: Frank Cass, 2005), 25–42.
Gouvernement du Québec, *Au Québec pour bâtir ensemble : Énoncé de politique en matière d'immigration et d'intégration*, Ministère des Communautés culturelles et de l'Immigration du Québec, Direction des communications, Québec, (1990), www.micc.gouv.qc.ca/publications/fr/ministere/Enonce-politique-immigration-integration-Quebec1991.pdf
Hodgdon, B., 'Race-ing *Othello*: Re-Engendering White Out', in L. Cowen Orlin (ed.), *Othello* (New York: Palgrave Macmillan, 2004), 190–219.
Iyengar, S., 'White Faces, Blackface: The Production of "Race" in *Othello*', in P. C. Kolin (ed.), *Othello: New Critical Essays* (London: Routledge, 2002), 103–31.
Romney, J., '*Une histoire inventée (An Imaginary Tale)* directed by André Forcier', *Sight and Sound*, 2.1 (May 1992), 52.
Rousseau, G., *La Nation à l'épreuve de l'immigration* (Québec: Éditions du Québécois, 2006).
Thompson, A., *Passing Strange: Shakespeare, Race, and Contemporary America* (Oxford: Oxford University Press, 2011).
Vallières, P., *Nègres blancs d'Amérique* (Montréal: Parti pris, 1969).

CHAPTER 10

Anna's Sin *and the circulation of* Othello *on film*

Douglas M. Lanier

Though *Il Peccato di Anna* (aka *Anna's Sin*, 1952)[1] regularly appears in lists of cinematic *Othello* spinoffs, it has remained largely unknown beyond its provocative title. It is a singular curiosity – made in Italy, it treats Othello's racial dynamics in a fashion more characteristic of Anglo-American films of the play than those produced in Europe, where race has typically not been a central concern. Its director and screenplay co-writer, Camillo Mastrocinque, was never again to direct an 'issues' film, becoming far better known as a director of low-budget horror films, instalments of the Totò comedy series and the Italian TV series *Le avventure di Laura Storm*; Anna Vita, the film's principal actress and creator of its story, disappeared from the screen a year after the film was completed, and her co-star, Ben E. Johnson,[2] made only two other films before ending his brief cinematic career in 1955. Nevertheless, *Anna's Sin* is of interest for several reasons. Not only does it use substantial elements of *Othello* (including performance excerpts) in the service of progressive racial politics, and well before the heyday of the civil rights movement, the film also addresses the relationship between European high culture and American popular culture, offering in effect a meditation on mid-century Italian cultural politics filtered through *Othello*.[3] Noteworthy too is the extent to which the film refocuses the Shakespearean narrative on the Desdemona figure, Anna, rather than on Othello, in the process offering a much different, arguably more provocative, analysis of the patriarchal politics at work in Shakespeare's play. Illuminating too is the film's circulation in the United States in 1954 and especially its rerelease in 1961 as an exploitation film, a re-appropriation which, judging from the ad campaign, reshaped the film's original progressive message into something troublingly lurid and politically retrogressive. The history of *Anna's Sin* is a tale of multiple appropriations of *Othello* across national, gender and racial lines, and so it is a reminder that our accounts of screen Shakespeare, particularly in the context of an international film market, need to address contexts of reception that are multiple and local.

Anna's Sin draws upon a venerable metatheatrical approach to the screen adaptation of *Othello* in which characters involved in a production of the play find their romantic lives mirroring Shakespeare's plot. This film version tells the tale of John Ruthford, an accomplished African American Shakespearean who travels to Rome to head up and star in a lavish production of *Othello*. Seeking a new face to be his Desdemona, Ruthford chooses Anna Curti, a young Italian girl at a local drama school without any professional acting experience. Their evident emotional connection upon first meeting soon blossoms into a secret interracial romance, a liaison strongly opposed by Anna's sinister, patrician guardian, Alberto (played by Paul Muller). Jealous and consumed with racism, Alberto sets to work destroying John and Anna's love. Through a black American expatriate jazz player Sam,[4] Alberto learns that John Ruthford was once John Sutton, convicted for molesting a white girl (wrongfully, we learn from Sam, the true culprit). Despite the fact that Alberto knows the truth about John's wrongful conviction, he uses this information to poison Anna's feelings toward John, and he also fuels the jealousy and bigotry of Alley, John's black female assistant who harbours unrequited feelings for him. When his plot is discovered, Alberto murders Sam to cover his tracks, and John, in a fit of rage, nearly strangles him to death, after which John, filled with remorse over what he thinks is his murder of Alberto, threatens to commit suicide by jumping from the upper terrace of a cathedral. Soon enough, however, Anna and John are reconciled. In the film's signature shot (see Figure 16,[5] also shown in the background of the credit sequence), the shadows of Anna and John move toward each other on the cathedral wall before the camera tilts up to the church steeple. Ruthford's line, 'only our shadows are equal, maybe our souls',[6] glosses the image and tentatively voices the theoretical basis for the film's reconciliation of racial tensions.

This variation on the metatheatrical approach to adapting *Othello* is noteworthy in a couple of ways. First, most metatheatrical variations on *Othello* focus on the mounting homicidal rage of the actor playing Othello; Barbara Hodgdon has argued that the erotic dalliances of the Desdemona figures in these films often offer some genuine reason for the Othello figures' jealousy,[7] so that his attack upon Desdemona is presented as, at least in part, justifiable, even though the narrative officially condemns it. In *Anna's Sin*, the focus falls more squarely on the psychology of Anna, the Desdemona figure, and on her victimization by Alberto, who serves as the Iago figure. Second, most metatheatrical variations on *Othello* end with the

PUIS LEURS OMBRES, CELLE D'ANNE ET CELLE DE JOHN, SE DIRIGÈRENT L'UNE VERS L'AUTRE POUR SE FONDRE ENFIN EN UNE SEULE GRANDE OMBRE, QUI SERAIT LE SYMBOLE DE LEUR AMOUR ÉTERNEL.

fin

Figure 16:   The shadows of Anna and John in Camillo Mastrocinque's 1952 *Anna's Sin*. Image taken from the French photoroman version of the film.

attempted onstage murder of the Desdemona figure, after which the Othello figure, his jealous passion spent, comes to his senses.[8] In this case, the attempted murder victim is the Iago figure, and John's motive for the attack upon Alberto is not jealousy but sheer rage at racial injustice, a rage which the film positions the viewer entirely to share. In an almost tragic irony Alberto's actions coax John into a version of the crime – black on white violence – that he was wrongly accused of, and John falls so deeply back into regret and despair at the injustice of his plight that he nearly loses faith in the potential for cross-racial understanding the film so strongly endorses. In the end, it is Anna who serves as the vehicle for John's restoration of faith both in God (who he accuses of crafting a 'destiny against a Negro and a white') and in the possibility of acceptance and racial equality.

Anna's Sin is unusual for the period in its use of *Othello* in the service of an ostensibly progressive social message. Though Shakespeare's play functions first and foremost as the authoritative template for a taboo interracial romance, it also provides a characterological baseline on which Anna Vita rings telling variations. Ruthford (played by Ben E. Johnson), who like Othello is in Italy far from his native land, claims his authority and nobility not from his military exploits but from his being a Shakespearean, and especially from his ambition to play the Moor in 'the country of Othello', as he announces upon arriving in Rome. In fact, Vita wrote the part for Canada Lee, whom she met in Rome in 1950 while Lee was in Europe for medical treatment. Lee's career included fame as a black Shakespearean, political activism, overseas success, racial and political oppression at home, and public interracial relationships. At the time of his death, Lee was planning a colour film version of *Othello* to be produced in Italy, with Anna Vita as Desdemona, a project which, if it had been realized, would have competed with Welles's black and white *Othello*. Lee died unexpectedly in 1952 before *Anna's Sin* went into production.[9]

Nevertheless, Ruthford's status as a Shakespearean celebrity in Europe seems inevitably to remind the viewer of another African American Shakespearean with an international reputation who had played Othello – Paul Robeson, who had in 1930 played the Moor in London to great acclaim and reprised it on Broadway and an American tour in 1943–4. (There is even perhaps a distant reminiscence of 'Robeson' in the name 'Ruthford'.) Ruthford's *doppelgänger* in the film is the nefarious Sam, who, we learn, actually committed the molestation for which Ruthford (as Sutton) went to prison. Like Cassio, Sam is undone by alcohol – he was drunk, he tells us, when he committed his crime – and he serves as a walking embodiment of compromised reputation, the very stereotype of the shiftless or sexually predatory black male that dogs Ruthford (and black male performers like Robeson) unfairly. Even Sam is capable of reform, for he eventually expresses his intention to confess his guilt to Ruthford and beg his forgiveness. Anna, the Desdemona figure, is presented as an innocent inexperienced in both acting and romance, unlike her more worldly and vivacious roommate Laura (played by Giovanna Mazzotti), the counterpart of Emilia. Anna's natural recognition of racial injustice and her capacity for cross-racial empathy are marked from the first by her echoing of Desdemona's words in her audition. Asked by Ruthford why she would like to play Desdemona, Anna replies, 'I pity the Moor. You see, he's great and noble, yet so unfortunate.'[10] This reply is in pointed contrast to the previous auditionee who, focusing on Desdemona rather than Othello, replies to Ruthford's question by saying, 'there's something about her. This innocent Venetian lady, such a pure heart, and yet she has to die.'

We see rather little of Anna's audition itself (the scene cuts away to the arrival of Alberto), but it is revealing that she ends with the final couplet in 4.3, where Desdemona establishes her intention not to follow Emilia's advice to return marital mistreatment with mistreatment: 'Good night, good night: God me such uses send,/ Not to pick bad from bad, but by bad mend!' In the context of the film, these lines establish Anna as a voice for progressive racial reform (rather than rage at the system) and also clarify that she is, despite the film's title, not engaged in sin.

As is often the case with pop appropriations of Shakespeare, the film's attitude toward the Shakespearean text itself is equivocal. On the one hand, there is the impulse to iconoclasm. Shakespearean dialogue first appears in the film as Laura, Anna's roommate, searches for her rather clueless boyfriend Michael. After rambunctiously barging through a dance rehearsal, she finds him in an acting class, performing the balcony scene (badly) with a Juliet perched atop a stack of chairs. Interrupting, she jealously calls Michael away in a hallway, calling his Juliet an 'idiot'; when Michael protests that 'we're doing Shakespeare', she retorts, 'you're doing him to death!' On the other hand, when later on Anna, having gotten the part of Desdemona, rehearses with John, the Shakespearean text has a different valence. In metatheatrical adaptations of *Othello* it is typical for reading or speaking of Shakespeare's words to awaken uncontrollable jealousy and homicidal impulses in the male protagonist. Here the power of the Shakespearean text is directed toward Anna rather than Ruthford, and what it conjures is idealization of him and her deep devotion. The passage Anna gives is Desdemona's entreaty to the Duke in 1.3 to remain with Othello (1.3.243–6, 247–50, 252–3), and as she speaks, her brightening expression makes clear that her heart is becoming, like Desdemona's, 'subdued/ Even to the very quality of my lord' (1.3.250). Anna's developing attachment to Ruthford is figured at once as star-struck worship of a more experienced stage performer, choice of a substitute for the paternalistic Alberto, and studiously non-sexual attraction to the nobility of Ruthford's character. Setting these sequences against each other works to recalibrate the relative authority of Shakespeare's two Italian tragedies about love; *Romeo and Juliet*, the more famous of the two romances, is deflated as a cliché, whereas the words of *Othello* are shown to have contemporary relevance and sway. The power of Shakespeare's words carries with it the inevitable tragic trajectory of the *Othello* narrative, and this emerges as a central issue in the film.

When John and Anna are next on stage, they are rehearsing the opening of the play's final scene, as if Anna's declaration of love for John led inexorably to their tragedy. Amidst the rehearsal, as the two are on the bed, John pauses to speak to Anna and hints at his love for her, and when they resume, the scene immediately cross-fades to an actual performance of the final scene, with John bearded as Othello in precisely the same position, now delivering his suicide speech and then stabbing himself. The scene continues to the end without a cut, though John as Othello never actually kisses Anna as Desdemona on the line 'I kissed thee ere I killed thee. No way but this:/ Killing myself, to die upon a kiss' (5.2.368–9). The film's avoidance of an interracial kiss here and elsewhere is a disappointing bow to racism and censorship, but what Mastrocinque consistently substitutes is an image taken from *Romeo and Juliet*, two hands, white and black, intertwined ('palm to palm is holy palmers' kiss', 1.5.97, see Figure 17). It is noteworthy that the film so dwells on this final section, even rather surprisingly including all of Lodovico's final speech, as if to stress the horrifying consequences of racism for this interracial couple, particularly Othello's drive to self-destruction that flows from his forbidden love for a white woman. *Othello* functions as a catalyst for Anna and John's relationship and a parallel that gives their passion a measure of gravity, but it also provides a destiny from which the two must struggle to

Figure 17:   The lovers' hands, white and black, intertwined in Camillo
Mastrocinque's 1952 *Anna's Sin*.

escape in the end, particularly John as a black man shadowed by past accusation of the rape of a white woman. The avoidance of a kiss in this scene metatheatrically suggests that John's love for Anna is reassuringly platonic, purged of any troubling eroticism or violence. This point is reinforced when immediately after the performance John and Anna take a moonlit walk in the wood and, after holding hands, agree to act together in America and see 'if we still feel our love was meant to be'.

Among those shown watching John and Anna's performance of *Othello* is Alberto, who, as if taking his cues from Shakespeare's play, orchestrates the destruction of the couple's relationship through racist innuendo. Alberto perversely combines qualities of Iago and Brabanzio. Like Iago, he is exceptionally sensitive to the psychological weaknesses of those about him, ferreting out Sam's guilt by watching his panicked reaction upon seeing John at a nightclub and feigning concern for Alley's unrequited love for John. A master manipulator, he squeezes the tale of John Sutton out of Sam by plying him with liquor and alternately pretending to befriend him and threatening him, then he uses what he learns about the rape charge to poison Anna's feelings about John and blackmail him into abandoning his *Othello* production. As Anna's paternally designated guardian, Alberto occupies the position of surrogate father, and like Brabanzio the objections he raises about Anna's liaison with John are openly miscegynistic. After Anna's moonlight stroll with John, Alberto chastises her for being 'the earnest young liberal, the white girl who loses her head over the muscles of the Negro . . . Every year, there's a certain percentage of girls who run off with them. Jazz musicians as a rule, or else boxers or dancers. Hysterical girls, I think they're called . . . They always end up badly. Nobody pities them.' Alberto's ulterior motives, gradually emerging in the narrative, spring from his patrician bearing. First, he is himself jealous of Anna's feelings for John and fearful of her breaking free of his quasi-paternal control now that she is coming into her majority. Although he is old enough to be her father, he proposes marriage to her as the two stroll in a Roman ruin, in a scene redolent with quasi-incestuous desire. Tellingly, at the end of this sequence, a hole in a ruined wall is cross-faded with the onstage bed of Othello and Desdemona, that fraught image of interracial desire visually filling the gap now opened up in Anna's relationship with Alberto. When later Alberto returns to the subject of marriage and Anna refuses, he grotesquely manhandles her, himself becoming the attempted rapist he later accuses John of having been.

Afterwards, however, Alberto's real motives come into view. Brooding in his apartment lavishly decorated with Old Masters paintings and statuettes, he reveals that his object is not Anna's affection but her inherited money, which he intends to use to finance his art collecting and refined lifestyle. Without her inheritance, he says, 'I'd have to sell everything, sacrifice everything.' Elsewhere the film develops this link between traditional high art and Alberto's impulse to possess and control. When he and Anna discuss her acting prospects in their first scene together, he objects to her pursuing theatre because stage performances, unlike *objets d'art*, are ephemeral and cannot be owned; an actress's 'creation ends right at the stroke of midnight, then she's through', whereas a statuette created centuries ago can be held in his hand, a physical object 'to affirm again that moment' of artistic creation, 'and it is I, the collector, who stands ready to pass it on to others'. This attitude toward theatre serves Alberto's purposes, but within the film it positions *Othello* as somewhat outside the elitist circle of the traditional fine arts where Alberto claims supremacy. As connoisseur and collector, Alberto can claim property rights over *objets d'art*, but theatre, communally experienced and evanescent, eludes his grasp, as increasingly does Anna.

That Alberto thinks of Anna as an art object he owns becomes abundantly clear when he confronts John about his past and tells him to leave Italy. The confrontation takes place in a museum, where John has gone to appreciate the artwork. As the two quarrel, they circle a white marble statue of a partially nude woman reclining, with hair very much like Anna's. The visual congruence between John's white suit and the white marble figure suggests that he, not Alberto, is the proper match for her. Nonetheless, at the end of the scene after John refuses Alberto's demands, he puts his hand on the statue's hand, at which Alberto gruffly pulls it off, underlining the connection between his tyranny over Anna and his sense of proprietorship over artistic tradition. John's angry response highlights the grotesque irony: 'This is great art, and a great civilization. You're a part of that civilization. Aren't you ashamed to talk like a savage to a Negro?' Increasingly the film addresses precisely this contradiction – whereas John's (false) past and his status as a black American threatens to tag him as a savage, it is Alberto, the ostensibly cultured, patrician European, who emerges as the real barbarian. The sculpture in question is Canova's *Paolina Bonaparte of Venus Victrix*, and though the dialogue makes nothing explicit of it, the history of the sculpture may be relevant to the film's message. Paolina Bonaparte, Napoleon's sister, was married to Camillo Borghese, sixth Prince of Sulmona, in an attempt to strengthen ties with French-occupied Italy. When Canova was contracted to sculpt her in neoclassical style in 1805, he originally intended to portray her as

Diana, but Paolina insisted upon being presented as Venus. That portrayal was in line with Paolina's reputation for promiscuity, and the use of nudity for a high-ranking woman, along with the clear allusion to the odalisque tradition, was regarded as provocative in the period, though 'Venus Victrix' has since become one of Italy's most beloved artworks.[11] In light of this history, Alberto's conversation with John about control of Anna's desire and his possessive stance toward an erotically charged art object linked to Italy's ruling class has added resonance.

Alberto's (and Anna's) conception of John's cultural heritage, and thus of John's claim to cultural dignity, surfaces with particular force in a scene in which Alberto, Anna, John, Alley, Laura and Michael visit a nightclub. Listening to the jazz tunes, Alley quickly falls under their spell, swaying with delight in her seat; Alberto, eyeing her clinically, observes contemptuously that 'it's very interesting how, with the champagne and the jazz, Alley can return to the African jungle'. For Alberto, disgusted with the modern music, black culture is the very antithesis of civilization, a retrogression into a primal primitivism that lurks just below the surface of black folk. This Alley would seem to confirm when, as if in a trance, she stands up and starts dancing to the music and John smiles approvingly, 'look at Alley . . . she's back in paradise'. At the same time, John insists 'we [blacks] come from a very ancient civilization, perhaps too much so'. His little qualification is clarified when Anna asks John whether he thinks there is any essential difference between the races. Throughout the film Anna's consistent position is that there is no essential difference if one focuses on the person's fundamental decency and honour – just as there is no difference between Anna and John's shadows in the final scene. However, John does identify a distinction:

JOHN.   There is a difference, I believe. If you notice, it's the way in which a Negro gives expression to his religion, to his art. More passionate, much more intense. He's more apt to show it, rage or jealousy, revenge or violence.
ANNA.   And it's the same for love?
JOHN.   Above all, for love.

Without doubt, this conception of blackness as innately more emotional accords with one line of European thinking in the period, which conceives of blacks and black cultural production like jazz as instinctive, exotic, uncensored, exhilaratingly 'natural', unrefined and popular, an alternative (and antidote) to the overly refined, 'rational' and deeply conservative tradition of the European Old Masters. Whereas John at first stresses the destructive aspects of that intense and passionate black nature, precisely those qualities Othello exhibits under Iago's caustic influence, qualities which Alberto is certain John possesses, Anna's question prompts him to move to a different emphasis: love. One might argue that this scene simply perpetuates the stereotype of the dangerously erotic black male, and certainly at some level that is the case. Indeed, the parallel to *Othello* might be taken as further evidence of the threatening volatility of black male passion. But it is possible to suggest that this passage seeks critically, if incompletely and problematically, to engage the racial stereotype it inherits, in effect ideologically reshaping John as a fit lover for Anna within the confines of romantic melodrama. It is notable, then, that until John explodes in fury (arguably justifiably, even heroically so) at Alberto's murder of Sam, his manner is consistently emotionally restrained, even when Anna rejects him under Alberto's influence. When he and Anna first rehearse the deathbed scene, he pauses to say, 'I don't know why it is, but I don't find it easy, knowing I'm going to have to murder you', in what amounts to his first declaration of love for her. It is Alberto who exudes the qualities of 'rage or jealousy, revenge or violence', though in a sinisterly bottled-up fashion which suggests beneath his, oh so rational, exterior lurks danger.

It is noteworthy too that John is repeatedly identified as an American, for many of the same qualities identified with black culture were also identified with American popular culture in Europe in the period. The parallels between Othello and John tend to mute our perception of Othello as a Moor and instead work to identify Othello as, in some sense, American and identify Shakespeare's play less with European high art and more with American pop culture. The parallels between John's narrative and *Othello* work not only to suggest John's innate nobility, but to recast Shakespeare's story as an interracial pop 'potboiler' *avant la lettre*. This ideological move addresses a live issue in post-war Italian culture, where the effects of American popular culture, newly introduced after a hiatus during the war and, for some, alarmingly popular with the Italian public, were much debated. Mary Wood observes that American culture and Americans in Italian films of the fifties were often represented as 'aspirational and exciting, but also shallow and meretricious in contrast to solid patriarchal values', an ambivalent 'antonym to Italian virtues' touted by the church and the fascists.[12] For many Italian consumers, America and its popular culture promised less rigid social roles, more freedom, prosperity, glamour and social equality. Early neorealist films like *Paisan* (dir. Roberto Rossellini, 1946) and *Vivere in Pace* (dir. Luigi Zampa, 1947) hinted at the possibility for identification between American blacks and working-class

Italians, both victims of social oppression.[13] On the other hand, the Catholic Church saw American popular culture as a moral threat and a challenge to its authority (though not as potent a threat as the political leftism espoused in the neorealist films of the late forties). And many Italian intellectuals and *auteur* filmmakers saw American-style pop culture as a threat to native Italian cultural production, particularly so neorealist filmmakers who, after 1950, struggled to interest an Italian public weaned on vulgar American fare in their films (despite the international prestige of neorealism in the day) and so began to pursue more profitable if less political progressive directions like *neorealismo rosa*. Given this background, one might see *Anna's Sin* as an attempt to contribute to the debate by adopting a politically progressive 'both-and' strategy. For Anna, John certainly represents the possibility of American aspiration. He chooses her, an unknown, for a major theatrical part and, as a result of his love, asks her to join him in the States to continue her acting; John provides the opportunity for Anna to break definitively with all Alberto represents – patriarchal control, stultifying high culture, racism – and pursue her freedom and creative fulfilment. There is even a hint at identification between Anna the oppressed Italian woman and John the oppressed American Negro. At the same time, the film establishes that Anna's alliance with John as lover and symbol is utterly moral, in the end consistent with good Catholic doctrine. It is not accidental that John and Anna's reconciliation occurs on the upper terrace of a cathedral. In that scene, Anna is the faithful Catholic voice countering John's despairing pronouncement that 'I'm a Negro and you're a white. There's a destiny against a Negro and a white. Maybe God wants it that way.' Her reply, 'Don't blaspheme; God's just for everyone', provides a religious foundation for remedying the hopelessness John feels because of racism, although it should be added that this narrative 'solution' is never worked out, only gestured at. Even so, the gesture is insistent. Anna's final line is, 'yes, God is just, because you are here', at which the camera tilts up from the wall where her and John's shadows, their equal 'souls', are projected to focus on the cathedral spire, the film's final image. This ending strongly identifies Catholicism with the socially progressive politics of anti-racism, casting the Church as a redeemer, not an opponent, of John the African American. (How this assertion of Christianity's redemptive potential in fighting racism might play out against Othello's Moorishness in Shakespeare's play is never contemplated or addressed in the film.)

There is also a personal dimension to the film's intervention in the Italian cultural debate in the early 1950s. Anna Vita, the actress playing

Anna Curti/Desdemona in the film, wrote the story on which the screen-play, co-written by Eduardo Anton and director Camillo Mastrocinque, was based, and she also produced the film through Giaguaro Films, in which she was co-owner. Before her brief film career, Vita was known primarily for her appearances in *fotoromanzi fumetti*, photographic comic books featuring tales of love and adventure, which were popular through-out Europe and Latin America. In 1950, she and Sergio Raimondi, her frequent partner in *fotoromanzi*, were elected 'Most Beloved Couple' by the readers of the magazine *Tipo*. The year earlier, she had starred with Raimondi (playing themselves) in *L'amorosa menzogna* (aka *Lies of Love*), a short documentary by Michelangelo Antonioni about the *fotoromanzi* industry.[14] The film garnered some buzz at Cannes in 1949 (it was a selection) and at the 1949 Milan Film Festival, where it won a Silver Ribbon for best documentary. We have no evidence of Vita's response to Antonioni's film, which presented *fumetti* as ultimately empty, pop cultural illusions and their consumption an evasion of post-war existential angst. However, her refusal to participate in Federico Fellini's *The White Sheik* in 1952, a film scripted by Antonioni and set in the same *demi-monde* with very similar concerns, suggests that she was not comfort-able with lampooning the genre from which her fame sprang or its readers. Obituaries note that Vita interviewed with several magazines to defend the *fotoromanzi*, creating something of a minor controversy in the early fifties. There is thus some reason to believe that Vita saw *Anna's Sin* as a bid for respectability for herself as an actress-writer and for the pop genre, roman-tic melodrama, in which she was most identified. Undoubtedly *Anna's Sin* draws upon the parallel to *Othello* to elevate the *romanzi* narrative, but particularly in the scenes involving Sam, the film uses the techniques of neorealism – gritty landscapes shot on location, impoverished characters at the social margins, a growing sense of tragic fatedness – in order to distance it from the escapist qualities of *romanzi* and ally it with social critique. Neorealism no longer held the interest for Italian audiences in 1952 that it did in the late forties, so *Anna's Sin* dovetails the social concerns charac-teristic of neorealist film with a pop cultural genre with greater box office appeal. In this, the film offered a different compromise between neorealism and melodrama than did *neorealismo rosa*, where sentimental tales of working-class families were cloaked in some of neorealism's stylistic traits.[15]

   Anna's Sin premiered in the United States in 1954, released by Italian Films Export, and it enjoyed a brief run in Britain in 1955. Because the major white newspapers largely ignored the film and the ad campaign was nearly non-existent, there is little evidence as to how audiences received it.

However, the multi-page spreads on the film done by *Jet* and *Ebony*, two national black periodicals, suggest that it was framed for the African American community as a screen breakthrough for black actors. *Ebony* hailed it as the first film 'to allow [a] Negro lover to win [the] girl' and the pictorial which follows, featuring Vita prominently, makes it abundantly clear that the girl in question is white. Labelling the film 'a message play', the writer stresses how it seeks 'to expose the evil of racial prejudice and bring people of different colors closer together', but emphasis falls equally on the prestige of the production, touting Vita as 'one of Italy's most promising new movie stars'.[16] Though the writer recognizes that the film follows 'boy-meets-girl, boy-loses-girl, boy-gets-girl Hollywood formula', he or she adds that 'the dramatic introduction of the racial theme . . . keeps the movie from being a trite, run of the mill production'.[17] The profile in *Jet*, titled 'Italian Movie Boom for Negro Actors', praises the film even more extravagantly, noting that Italy has 'far out-distanced' Hollywood 'in the use of high-caliber Negro talent' and in 'smoothly integrat[ing] Negroes into roles based on human passions rather than color'.[18] It presents *Anna's Sin* as a prime example of a foreign film in which 'a Negro's role has been allowed to run the full emotional gamut'.[19] A May 1955 article in *The Chicago Defender*, with two publicity photos from the film, seconds the point, noting that 'French and Italian film companies have been producing pictures which treat the problem of love and marriage between Negro and white in a mature, intelligent way'[20] and citing a positive review of *Anna's Sin* in the *West London Observer*. Taken together, these articles suggest that in its first American release *Anna's Sin* was read by the black community primarily as a breaking of the racialized representational codes of 50s Hollywood, as a breakthrough and entirely positive cinematic depiction of interracial romance. Interestingly, the film's parallels to *Othello* are muted – the *Jet* and *Chicago Defender* articles do not mention it at all, and the *Ebony* article mentions it only once, in a caption (and under a photo which pictures not Othello and Desdemona, but John and Anna at the nightclub). It is possible to see this elision as resistance to the tragic trajectory Othello represents – here the emphasis falls on a successful modern black-white relationship with a uniquely happy ending. Despite the positive publicity, whether the film was actually seen by many African American audiences is unclear, since a caption to one of the publicity photos in the *Chicago Defender* article notes pessimistically that *Anna's Sin* 'will hardly be welcomed in America'. An article from April 1961 seems to confirm that prediction, noting that though the film 'gained momentum abroad due to its exposure of racial bias in the United States', it was given 'the cold shoulder from distributors and theatre managements in this country' upon its original release.[21]

The film was rereleased in 1961, this time by low-budget distributor Atlantis Films of New York, *Anna's Sin* being its last release before it went out of business. Atlantis seems to have specialized in repackaging minor foreign releases as exploitation films. *Anna's Sin* was thereby reshaped in its publicity campaign as a scandalous interracial potboiler, with stress on the 'sin' in the film's title. In an ad in *Ebony* (see Figure 18),[22] typical of how it was marketed, the title 'Anna's Sin' is flanked by sensational labels screaming 'IT SEARS THE SCREEN!' and 'IT SCALDS THE SCREEN!' Anna appears in all of the four illustrations from the film, in three pictured in some state of distress; above her picture in one panel is the copy 'SOME CALLED IT SIN ... SOME CALLED IT SHAME! but None DARED call it by it's [sic] Real Name' and, in another panel, Alberto says to Anna 'a normal *white* woman couldn't get involved!' By contrast, John appears only in one picture, in the centre panel with his hand on Anna's face, the two framed by an ominous shadow into which they are receding.[23]

This focus on racial taboo and sexual shame apparently scared off some theatres – the *Chicago Defender* reported that large loop theatres in Chicago turned it down after it opened in New York[24] – enough so that George Morris, the president of Atlantis Films, gave an interview to the *Defender* which seemed to back off from an appeal to prurience, characterizing the film as a 'frank examination of a problem that arises only from ignorance and prejudice' and claiming that there was 'nothing shocking about the love scenes, which are restrained and lyrical'.[25] Even so, the picture seemed to get relatively wide release in theatres in urban black neighbourhoods, since newspaper ads for the film confirm that it ran for one or two weeks in New York, Chicago, Los Angeles and Washington, DC. In rural America, particularly in the South, the film was marketed as a tale of forbidden interracial passion, run at drive-ins and second-string theatres alongside other prurient fare.[26] The white press paid little attention to the film, either treating it as a curiosity (the *New York Times* suggests, wrongly, that Alberto objects to Anna's relationship with John because of John's 'American upbringing' and goes on to note that the director has lost track of his amateur dentist star)[27] or dismissing it as crude interracial melodrama ruined by its unrealistic 'Iago-like villainy'[28] (the only review in a major white periodical in the United States, *Commonweal*). Interestingly enough, this ad campaign did acknowledge the film's *Othello* connection. One publicity photo was a close-up of Anna as Desdemona and John as Othello, lying dead on the marriage bed after Othello's suicide in the play-within-the-film

Figure 18:   The ad for Camillo Mastrocinque's 1952 *Anna's Sin* in *Ebony* 16.5 (March 1961). All rights reserved.

performance; this photo appeared in *The California Eagle*[29] and *Jet*'s 'Movie of the Week' profile on the rerelease, and in both cases the surrounding copy identifies the lovers as playing in *Othello*. Though the *Jet* article promises 'dramatic protestations of love, hand-holding and kissing' (only the hand-holding actually occurs) and hails the film for having broken the colour barrier with its happy ending,[30] the publicity photo that accompanies it seems to send a rather different message, with the interracial couple in bed together – with all the forbidden eroticism that evokes – but also clearly dead. If the film in its original context stressed the intense but non-sexual nature of Anna and John's passion and their triumph over *Othello*'s tragic trajectory, the marketing of the film upon its rerelease seemed to play up the opposite, using the 'loaded bed' (5.2.373) in *Othello* as a shorthand for cross-racial sexual taboo.

Of course, the marketing of a film does not entirely determine its interpretive fortunes with the public. In her 'My Day' column for 5 April 1961,[31] Eleanor Roosevelt, a strong advocate for civil rights, mentions that she saw a preview for *Anna's Sin* and connects its engagement with 'one phase of the color problem here in our country' with the sacrifices made by servicemen in war, which, she notes, were made without reference to 'color or creed or national origin'.[32] As if responding to the interpretive frame the marketing erected around the film, she says, 'though the theme may be deduced from the title, "Anna's Sin", it makes one wonder exactly whose sin it is'. Even so, judging from the ways in which *Anna's Sin* is routinely characterized as an interracial potboiler, the 1961 publicity campaign for *Anna's Sin* still carries considerable force for those few websites and reference books that even acknowledge the film's existence.

We have become accustomed to thinking of film adaptation of Shakespeare as a process whereby the semantic richness of the Shakespearean text (or a notable stage performance) is down-converted into a cinematic product that is in large measure more interpretively stable than its source, a film-object that produces a single discernible (if potentially complex) reading of the Shakespearean source text. As a result, the default approach to understanding a given Shakespearean film adaptation has been to privilege the originary context of its production and first reception. What the history of *Il Peccato di Anna* suggests is that, despite the value of that approach, it may obscure the potential semantic richness of the adaptation itself, especially as it travels, as films so typically do, across various cultural contexts and time periods. A film inevitably reads differently by different audiences situated at different cultural moments, and so too does the Shakespearean material within that film. Though *Il Peccato di Anna* remains substantially the same artefact as it circulates, it becomes in effect different kinds of *Othello* films (and even perhaps not an *Othello* film at all) as it moves from one cultural context to the next, its use of *Othello* changing appreciably in valence, power and social function. *Othello* becomes a text conferring cultural prestige or an icon of scandal, a progressive racial narrative or the template for titillating interracial desire, depending upon the horizons of reception within which the film might be received. Though those horizons of reception are profoundly shaped by marketing materials,[33] specific film traditions and local cultural contexts, the reception of a given film is never entirely constrained by them. *Il Peccato di Anna* thus illustrates something of the full challenge of adopting a global perspective on Shakespearean film adaptation:[34] how to craft a nuanced account not only of how Shakespeare has been appropriated on film in myriad cultural contexts, but also of how those appropriations – and the particular Shakespeares they bear – have circulated and been received.

Notes

1 For clarity's sake, I will refer to the 1952 Italian release as *Il Peccato di Anna*, and the subsequent English language rereleases as *Anna's Sin*.

2 Two magazine profiles of the period note that Johnson, a Trinidadian dentist living in Rome, was an unknown amateur actor when he was cast as John Ruthford. He was married to Pamela Winter, who played Alley (apparently her only film role). *Jet Magazine* includes the detail that Johnson and Winter hoped to parlay their appearances in *Anna's Sin* into film careers, but in 1952 they were only considering scripts that portrayed black characters in non-stereotypical roles. See 'Italy's Movie Boom for Negro Actors', *Jet Magazine* 6.1 (13 May 1954), 60–2. Johnson was a last-minute replacement for Canada Lee, the famous African American actor and civil rights activist whom Vita met in Rome in 1950 and for whom she wrote the part of Ruthford; Lee died unexpectedly in 1952.

3 It is possible to read *Anna's Sin* as an anticipation of Pasolini's *Che Coso Sono Le Nuvole* (1961), in which the oppressively tragic trajectory of the *Othello* narrative and its reinforcement of racial and misogynistic stereotyping are registered then resisted. I thank S. Hatchuel for drawing my attention to this relationship. While *Anna's Sin* takes a social realist approach to this material, Pasolini's approach is more poetic and, with the rising up of the onscreen audience to overthrow the *Othello* performance within the film, far more revolutionary.

4 The role of Sam was played by William Demby, at the time of filming an African American expatriate in Italy. He was known in the Italian film industry primarily for his work as a translator and subtitler of Italian movies. Demby went on to write several notable experimental novels about black experience, including *Beetlecreek* (1950), *The Catacombs* (1965), and *Love Story Black* (1978). See W. Yardley, 'William Demby, Author of Experimental Novels, Dies at 90', *New York Times*, 1 June 2013, D8.

5 See *Le Péché d'Anne*, *Photoroman* 1.19 (15 August 1956), 60 [1–60].

6 All citations from *Anna's Sin* are taken from my transcript of the dubbed English version.

7 B. Hodgdon, 'Kiss Me Deadly, or the Des/Demonized Spectacle', in V. M. Vaughan and K. Cartwright (eds.), *'Othello': New Perspectives* (Newark: Fairleigh Dickinson University Press, 1991), 215–55.

8 Examples of this tradition include August Blom's *Desdemona* (1911), Harley Knowles's *Carnival* (1921), Herbert Wilcox's *Carnival* (aka *Venetian Nights*, 1931), Walter Reisch's *Men Are Not Gods* (1936), and George Cukor's *A Double Life* (1947). For a discussion of these and other films in this tradition, see D. M. Lanier, 'Murdering *Othello*', in D. Cartmell (ed.), *A Companion to Literature, Film and Adaptation* (Malden, MA: Blackwell, 2012), 198–215.

9 See G. E. Gill's chapter '"Swifter than a Weaver's Shuttle": The Days of Canada Lee', in *No Surrender! No Retreat! African American Pioneer Performers of Twentieth-Century American Theater* (New York: St. Martin's Press, 2000), 107–36; and M. Z. Smith, *Becoming Something: The Story of Canada Lee* (New York: Faber & Faber, 2004).

10 Anna's line picks up Othello's description of Desdemona's feelings in his Senate speech: 'She loved me for the dangers I had passed,/ And I loved her that she did pity them' (1.3.166–7).

11 See F. Licht, *Canova* (New York: Abbeville Press, 1983), 130–43; C. M. S. Johns, *Antonio Canova and the Politics of Patronage in Revolutionary and Napoleonic Europe* (Berkeley, CA: University of California Press, 1998), 116–7; and B. Pollitt, 'Canova's Paolina Borghese', at http://smarthistory.khanacademy.org/canovas-paolina-borghese-as-venus-victorious.html. Accessed 31 May 2014.

12 M. P. Wood, *Italian Cinema* (Oxford: Berg, 2005), 139; 140.

13 T. Cripps, *Making Movies Black: The Hollywood Message Movie from World War II to the Civil Rights Era* (New York: Oxford University Press, 1993), 271.

14 Available at www.youtube.com/watch?v=10Mv4uIVNIs. Accessed 31 May 2014.

15 After *Anna's Sin* premiered and toured the States to some modest success, Paramount invited Anna Vita to train as a contract player. Publicity of the period (see 'Triple-Threat Lady', *Toledo Blade Pictorial*, 10 January 1954, 16) suggests that she was being positioned as a smart version of the Italian bombshell type, on the model of Silvana Mangano, Gina Lollobrigida and Sophia Loren. While in Los Angeles she turned to sculpture and decided to follow in the footsteps of her father Mario, an Italian sculptor of some note. She never returned to acting. See 'Una Vita tra Cinema e Arte: È Morta Anna Vita', www.agenziaaise.it/italiani-nel-mondo/94-generale/57630-una-vita-tra-cinema-e-arte-.html. Accessed 9 June 2014.

16 'Anna's Sin', *Ebony* 9.5 (1954), 33 [33–6].

17 *Ibid.*, 34.

18 *Jet Magazine* 6.1 (13 May 1954), 60.

19 *Ibid.*

20 E. Scobie, 'England's Hollywood Frowns on 'Sins of Anna'', *Chicago Defender (National Edition)*, 7 May 1955, 7.

21 R. Roy, 'Behind the Scenes', *Chicago Defender (National Edition)*, 8 April 1961, 19.

22 'Anna's Sin' [advertisement], *Ebony* 16.5 (March 1961), 11. The *Showman's Campaign* flyer for *Anna's Sin*, published by Atlantis Films, notes that 'this ad has also been seen by Negro audiences throughout the country in such leading Negro publications as "Ebony,", "Jet," "Sepia," and "Tan"' (2). The flyer instructs theatre owners to present the film as racially controversial and sensationalistic, dubbing it an 'Interracial H-Bomb' and stressing the courage of George Morris (president of Atlantic Films) in presenting the film to the public.

23 The motif of John's black hand on Anna's white face in close-up was also used in a publicity photo for the film, printed by *The Chicago Daily Defender* on 2 January 1962 in the article 'Hand on the Face', 16.

24 '"Anna's Sin" Too Real for Local Theatre Run', *Chicago Defender (National Edition)*, 4 February 1961, 18.

25 'Picture "Anna's Sins" New Controversial Run', *Chicago Defender (National Edition)*, 25 March 1961, 19.

26 See, just as an example, the advertisement run in *The Morgantown Post* (for Morgantown, West Virginia) for the Grafton Drive-in Theater, which paired *Anna's Sin* with *Sin and Desire* (dir. Willy Rozier, 1949).

27 'Quo Vadis?', *New York Times*, 19 March 1961, X9.

28 P. T. Hartung, 'The Screen: Angry Young Black Man', *Commonweal* 74, 7 April 1961, 47 [46–8].

29 'Togetherness', *California Eagle*, 23 March 1961, 9.

30 'Anna's Sin', *Jet Magazine* 19.14, 26 January 1961, 65.

31 'My Day' was the First Lady's syndicated column which ran in several newspapers between 1936 and 1962.

32 Eleanor Roosevelt, 'My Day', 5 April 1961, www.gwu.edu/~erpapers/myday, accessed 9 June 2014.

33 For a discussion of the ways in which marketing materials shape horizons of reception of Shakespeare on film, see E. French, *Selling Shakespeare to Hollywood: The Marketing of Filmed Shakespeare Adaptations from 1989 into the New Millennium* (Hatfield: University of Hertfordshire Press, 2006).

34 I am thinking here of the exemplary work of M. T. Burnett and A. Huang. See especially M. T. Burnett, *Shakespeare and World Cinema* (Cambridge: Cambridge University Press, 2013), and A. Huang, 'Global Shakespeares as Methodology', *Shakespeare: The Journal of the British Shakespeare Association* 9.3 (2013), 1–18.

WORKS CITED

Burnett, M. T., *Shakespeare and World Cinema* (Cambridge: Cambridge University Press, 2013).

Cripps, T., *Making Movies Black: The Hollywood Message Movie from World War II to the Civil Rights Era* (Oxford: Oxford University Press, 1993).

French, E., *Selling Shakespeare to Hollywood: The Marketing of Filmed Shakespeare Adaptations from 1989 into the New Millennium* (Hatfield: University of Hertfordshire Press, 2006).

Gill, G. E., '"Swifter than a Weaver's Shuttle": The Days of Canada Lee', in *No Surrender! No Retreat!: African American Pioneer Performers of Twentieth-Century American Theater* (New York: St. Martin's Press, 2000), 107–36.

Hodgdon, B., 'Kiss Me Deadly, or the Des/Demonized Spectacle', in V. M. Vaughan and K. Cartwright (eds.), *'Othello': New Perspectives* (Madison, NJ: Fairleigh Dickinson University Press, 1991), 215–55.

Huang, A., 'Global Shakespeares as Methodology', *Shakespeare: The Journal of the British Shakespeare Association* 9.3 (2013), 1–18.

Johns, C. M. S., *Antonio Canova and the Politics of Patronage in Revolutionary and Napoleonic Europe* (Berkeley, CA: University of California Press, 1998).

Lanier, D. M., 'Murdering *Othello*', in D. Cartmell (ed.), *A Companion to Literature, Film and Adaptation* (Malden, MA: Blackwell, 2012), 198–215.

Le Péché d'Anne, *Photoroman* 1.19 (15 August 1956), 1–60.

Licht, F., *Canova* (New York: Abbeville Press, 1983).

Smith, M. Z., *Becoming Something: The Story of Canada Lee* (New York: Faber & Faber, 2004).

Wood, M. P., *Italian Cinema* (New York: Berg, 2005).

Mirroring Othello *in genre films*
A Double Life *and* Stage Beauty

Kinga Földváry

The range of cinematic works of art based on Shakespeare's *Othello* is no less than breathtaking in scope, provided that we acknowledge the existence of not only straightforward and textually faithful adaptations but also extend our investigation to offshoots, derivatives, appropriations – whichever term we apply to films that include some elements of recognizably Shakespearean origin, but discard the main plotline and/or the early modern text altogether. While it is undeniable that the cultural functions that these diverse types of adaptations fulfil and their positions within the Shakespeare cult may vary to a great extent, I am convinced that they testify to the continuing presence of the Bard in modern (mainly popular) culture in the same way as the textually more conservative pieces, which are recognized and canonized representatives of high culture. Still, even if we acknowledge the obvious differences, the sheer amount of films that have some trace of reference to the Shakespearean play invites us to undertake comparisons, to investigate the variety of ways that filmmakers take when shaping the seventeenth-century text to their own liking. When doing so, however, it appears to me that classifying films on the basis of their loyalty to a supposed original (and a subsequent exclusion of a vast portion of looser adaptations from the investigation) is no longer a tenable attitude, since it is precisely the aspect of textual fidelity that is often the least helpful approach we may use. I believe that a successful interpretive approach must take into account the viewpoint of the audience as well, and when seen from this vantage point, it is inevitable that we need to exercise caution when referring to textual fidelity. One reason for our caution must be the tendency Douglas Lanier refers to by claiming that '[w]hen popular culture cites Shakespeare, the overriding concern is often not what the passage "really" means',[1] and he uses Michel de Certeau's term of 'textual poaching'[2] to describe the way contemporary culture appropriates citations from Shakespeare. Moreover, there is growing evidence to suggest that twenty-first-century moviegoers' knowledge of the

Shakespearean text can hardly be taken for granted, and therefore general cinema audiences show less and less interest in textual fidelity (the only exception being filmed cult fiction, but I am afraid that Shakespeare no longer belongs to that category). At the same time, cinemagoers often display a thorough knowledge of the adapting medium, the cinema itself, and are well acquainted with the range of forms and genres that character-ize the art of motion pictures, therefore this type of altered background knowledge can no longer be ignored.

The recognition that elements of cinematic genre can be found not only in the group of films classified as genre films, a term suggestive of inferiority when used by the *auteur* theory, is certainly not a groundbreak-ing new discovery; it is, however, rather uncommon to see the notion of genres as central to a systematic interpretation of cinema as such, rather than as part of the analysis of isolated examples. However, the significance of genres is easily proved if we consider them not only from a theoretical but also from a practical aspect, as the labels used both by producers during the creative process and audiences when making their viewing choices; in Barry Langford's words, 'genre remains an essential critical tool for understanding the ways that films are produced and consumed'.[3] This is equally true even in the adaptation process, as I believe every screen version of literature is adapted into some cinematic genre, and in this way the significance of genres is relevant not only for media studies but also for Shakespeare adaptation scholarship. What is more, by taking into account the generic features of literary film adaptations, we may be in a better position to understand the films' strategies towards their source texts as well.

In order to demonstrate how the cinematic genre may be used as an essential interpretive tool when we examine film versions of Shakespearean plays, in what follows I am going to compare two adaptations of Shake-speare's *Othello*, whose attitude to the original text appears to be similar at first glance – in fact, both belong to the type of adaptations that Kenneth S. Rothwell terms 'mirror movies'[4] and Cary M. Mazer 'rehearsals-of-a-Shakespeare-production-within-a-film'.[5] Both *A Double Life* (dir. George Cukor, 1947) and *Stage Beauty* (dir. Richard Eyre, 2004) are set in the world of the theatre, where a performance of Shakespeare's *Othello* brings about a range of transformations in the personality and behaviour of the actors themselves, who adopt, and adapt to, their roles to a troubling, even dangerous extent. Since theatrical *Othello*s are in the centre of both films, both of them include a number of Shakespearean lines as well, although embedded in a non-Shakespearean main plot, with language and dialogue updated to fit the new settings. Nonetheless, however similar these plots may seem from a textual point of view, what I intend to show is that, instead of their relationship to the source text, it is the adapting cinematic genres – *film noir*/thriller vs romantic comedy – that define the most relevant features of each film.

This is not to claim that there are no similarities between the two films at all, but I believe that these are mainly superficial elements of the plot, rather than any essential feature of either work. Still, it is useful to look at these connections as well, the most obvious one being the popular setting in both films: the world of the theatre.[6]

The earlier film, George Cukor's multiple award-winning *A Double Life* (1947) takes us to Broadway, where the star actor, Anthony John (Ronald Colman), is offered to play the leading role in *Othello*. He is tempted to move on to a tragic role after being typecast as a comic entertainer, but both himself and his ex-wife, Brita, the company's leading lady, are aware that his tendency to identify with each role is a constant threat to his mental balance every time he leaves the safe territory of the comedy behind. Eventually he accepts the role, and the performance is a resounding success, as a result of his extremely plausible impersonation of Othello, and his ingenious idea to murder Desdemona by 'kissing her to death' rather than simply strangling her with or without a pillow. Still, living the life of the tragic hero soon begins to take its toll, and as the show runs on into its third year, the actor is seen to lose his fight against an almost inexplicable inclination to jealousy and madness, with the result that during a performance he nearly strangles Brita on stage in the murder scene. Although he immediately recovers from the fit and afterwards suffers from deep remorse, it is clear that the abyss of madness is pulling him in, and not long after this, in a near trance, he goes to the apartment of a little waitress he occasionally visits for comfort, and kills her with his famous kiss of death. As Douglas Lanier points out in his account of *A Double Life* and similar *Othello* mirrors, Tony's actions are not only prompted by his envisioning the waitress as a fickle Desdemona, but also by seeing in her his jealously desired ex-wife, Brita.[7] On the subsequent theatre performance, realizing both his guilt and the inevitability of punishment, he kills himself in the final scene as the regretful Othello. The film's general atmosphere and the denouement therefore successfully invoke the tragic spirit of the Shakespearean source text, while the updated language and plot connect the film to its mid-twentieth-century American social context.

Stage Beauty, written first as a theatre play by Jeffrey Hatcher under the title *Compleat Female Stage Beauty* in 1999, which Hatcher later adapted to the screen for Richard Eyre's 2004 feature film, appears consciously to steer clear of tragedy. From its very first shot, the film invites audiences to enter the world of an almost farcical comedy, where the centrality of sexuality and romantic love efficiently marginalizes the tragic overtones otherwise present in the plot. *Stage Beauty* is also set in the theatre, but this time with a historical twist. Using references from Pepys' *Diaries*, the film takes us to the Restoration, witnessing the Desdemona performances of the last male actor, Edward Kynaston, and his fall out of favour and of work when his resentment against actresses indirectly provokes Charles II to pass an act prohibiting men from cross-dressing on public stages. Parallel to Kynaston's downfall, we can see the rise of his former seam-stress, Maria, in the film moulded into one with the historical actress Margaret Hughes, the first woman to perform Desdemona on an English stage. Maria quickly rises to fame; her success soon – if only temporarily – begins to overshadow the light of the star Kynaston once was, although her acting style, imitating Kynaston's, shows more affectation than talent. For a final performance, however, the alienated Kynaston is persuaded to come back to the theatre to coach her and even takes the role of Othello opposite Maria's Desdemona, for an epoch-changing, stylistically innovative *Othello*. During this performance, Kynaston almost strangles Maria on stage – possibly out of an instinctive attempt at revenge on the rival star – but spares her in the end, and the romantic developments between the two seem to culminate in a realization of mutual passion for each other.

Seen from a structural point of view, the similarities between *A Double Life* and *Stage Beauty* are indeed noticeable: both films use a metatheatrical framework, and insert several rehearsal and performance scenes from *Othello* into their plot, although the atmosphere these on-screen stages create is far from identical. In *A Double Life*, the world of the theatre is dominated by dark shadows and labyrinthine spaces suggesting a menacing spectre of crime and passion, together with the alienation of the main hero from human society, represented by the brightly lit private spaces sur-rounding Brita. In *Stage Beauty*, however, the theatre is shown as a warmly lit, inclusive community space, and the only type of isolation that appears here is exclusion from this world of artistic and social opportunity.

However different the representation of theatrical atmospheres, the theatre fulfils a similar function in both films: the offstage lives of the performers are shown to reflect the roles they are playing on stage, a functional similarity which serves as the basis for Kenneth S. Rothwell's categorizing them as 'mirror movies' among the seven types of derivatives he lists in his *History of Shakespeare on Screen*. Rothwell defines mirror movies by arguing that they 'meta-cinematically make the movie's back-stage plot about the troubled lives of actors run parallel to the plot of the Shakespearean play that the actors are appearing in'.[8] Rothwell's taxonomy for derivatives, these looser, textually less faithful adaptations, is particularly useful in the sense that it includes several genre-based groups, such as documentaries or animations, and not only the usual fidelity-based categories that have dominated adaptation studies for such a long time.

Still, when examining these two so-called mirror movies, *A Double Life* and *Stage Beauty* (we could add further examples, such as the 1936 *Men Are Not Gods*, directed by Walter Reisch, or several more recent films, e.g. *In Othello*, directed by Roysten Abel in 2003, and *Huapango*, directed by Ivan Lipkies in 2004),[9] we may easily see the shortcomings of such a system, mainly from the very simple recognition that these mirror-plots reflect the source text in such different ways that even if the texts quoted are identical, audiences' perception of the films will never be the same. For one thing, the most elementary test that tells us what type of film we are watching is a glance at the ending: *A Double Life* culminates in real murder, followed by a suicide, in an accumulation of tragic denouements, while *Stage Beauty* ends with no one injured, the protagonists embracing and kissing passionately, implying a romantic happy ending.

However, if we examine films on the basis of their adapting genres, I believe we can find the elements that establish their place among films that audiences may indeed perceive as belonging to a similar kind. Andrew Tudor in his essay on film genre refers to the usefulness of such a generic label by claiming that 'it provides us with a body of films to which our film can be usefully compared – sometimes the only body of films'.[10] The elements, that is, the 'common set of meanings in our culture'[11] that establish such generic connections include the use of textual and narrative devices, thematic conventions and stock characters, cinematic tools and symbolic elements within the *mise-en-scène*, and in particular, the allusions to other films of the same genre that help us place these works in a particular generic context.

To begin with the textual issue, although the two films quote partly identical scenes of *Othello*, there seems to be a considerable difference between their approaches to this embedded source text. *A Double Life*, similarly to *Stage Beauty*, shows no more but the murder scene in full, but Cukor's film nonetheless presents it only as the final stage, as the culmination of a maddening creative process and the result of an equally maddening jealousy. The film focuses on the journey towards that stage, placing madness into the centre within the frame narrative, and providing us with direct textual references accordingly. Several earlier passages of the play, including the well-known references to the 'green-eyed monster' (3.3.170), are used, to underscore the psychological process through which the protagonist loses his grip on reality. The quotations are often internalized by the frame narrative, either as voice-over, or as accidental asides, not meant for others to hear, suggesting the protagonist's inner voice. On other occasions, they are woven into offstage dialogues, sometimes uttered by characters other than the protagonist. In particular, it is the ignorant little waitress who provides the actor Tony with unintentional cues, e.g. when asking 'What is the matter?' and 'Do you want to put out the light?' The recognition of these textual snatches is often left to the audience, and even if we are given clues, the character of the victim is certainly unaware of the threat she is facing, greatly contributing to the suspense and mystery characterizing the film in general.

Richard Eyre's film, *Stage Beauty*, however, makes it clear at the very beginning that it is neither psychology nor the development of madness but only the performance of the death scene that we are interested in – this is what we see performed on stage and rehearsed backstage several times. The opening scene shows Kynaston dying onstage as Desdemona, then complaining immediately afterwards backstage that he still has not 'got the death scene right'. There are only a few scattered references to other scenes, and there is no attempt made at explaining the position of the scene within the context of the whole play; the Iago character is absent as well, either onstage or in the offstage mirror-context. *Stage Beauty* gets rid of the threat represented by Iago's unmotivated villainy entirely, although we may argue that Sir Charles Sedley is temporarily victorious and causes considerable harm when he has Kynaston beaten by a couple of thugs to take revenge for the mockery he had to suffer earlier. Kynaston's career, indeed, takes a turn for the worse after the event: he is out of a job and out of favour with his patrons; nonetheless, Sir Charles is such a clear embodiment of the character of the fop that he is never taken seriously, let alone seen as a Iago-figure. The villain apparently does not fit into the world of comedy, as Charles II's question points to comedy's refusal to be disturbed by such evils: 'Who were you? Not Iago, I hope, didn't like him.' Another possible source of Iago-like treachery may be seen in Maria's betrayal of Kynaston, but this conflict becomes reinterpreted as a simple and inevitable misunderstanding between the lovers, hardly more than a lovers' tiff, a common tool of romantic comedies to provide obstacles in the course of true love.

Stage Beauty also approaches the Shakespearean text with a different attitude from *A Double Life*: practically every single quotation is almost exclusively heard on stage, establishing them as quotations, setting them apart from the offstage dialogue. In this way, when certain phrases are repeated in an offstage setting, they have already been made familiar to the audience from the onstage context, and therefore they acquire a performative quality, preventing us from complete identification with the actual contents of what is said, and making us see the characters as performing, rather than experiencing the often tragic depths their Shakespearean quotes would suggest.

In George Cukor's *A Double Life*, the textual identification between the frame narrative and the metatheatrical plot is infinitely more complete than in *Stage Beauty*, and the atmosphere of tension and fear, together with the increasing threat of jealousy, may serve as essential elements in preparing us for a tragic denouement. Similarly to Othello's obeying orders in Shakespeare's play, in *A Double Life* the main protagonist is denied the opportunity to follow his own desires; it is not national or social but theatrical authorities, the managers of the theatre, who convince Tony to accept the dangerous role, while his ex-wife is trying to dissuade him from entering this abyss which will certainly lead to his damnation. More importantly, in *A Double Life*, there is a Iago character as well, a secret admirer of Tony's ex-wife, who will at the end notify the police of his suspicion of the great actor and in this way bring about his downfall. Robert F. Willson even suggests that 'the role of Othello ... is Anthony John's Iago',[12] pointing out that in the film, at least in part, the menace is internal and thus impossible to avert. I believe nonetheless that the very palpable external threat of the criminal investigation started off by the jealous romantic rival is equally powerful in turning the film into a thriller, beside the numerous other generic features described later.

Through their different attitudes to the Shakespearean text, the films point beyond issues of textual fidelity; in particular, there are a number of specifically cinematographic differences between them that we can read as tell-tale signs pointing to the two adapting cinematic genres that, above all, govern the adaptations. As Catherine L. Preston quotes Tom Ryall on the necessity of a 'background context' to read a film, she refers to 'a range of discourses: the form of the film, its iconography, situational conventions, stock of characters' among other things which contribute to the construction of the generic system.[13]

A Double Life, as its title suggests, represents the split consciousness of a tragic hero, and in this way provides perfect source material for a *noir* film. The narrative focuses on an isolated protagonist's inner struggles with his psychological weakness, added to a variety of social and psychological crises. We can witness not simply the centrality of jealousy, but also that of madness, crime and investigation (complete with victim, suspect and detective), cleverly designed psychological tricks to betray guilt, and the ultimate punishment the criminal deserves. The frame narrative's effective transfer into a crime story, with a close inspection of the psychological motivation of the criminal and the imminence of the crime, fills most of the narrative space, culminating in the brutal murder of the simple waitress; the last stage rounds up the parallel threads of investigation and self-punishment – all natural elements in *film noir*. All the necessary stock characters of thrillers make an appearance, including snoops and decoys, manipulated forensic pathologists and vulture-like journalists, ready to sell their mother's soul to boost circulation numbers. Apart from these common elements of content, the identification of the film with the genre of *film noir*/thriller is inevitable from the opening shots, accompanied by the darkly passionate music composed by Miklós Rózsa. The cinematography of the film reinforces this impression of threat and darkness in several ways.

Steve Neale, while describing the difficulties associated with *film noir* as a label, lists the most typical features that characterize the admittedly rather heterogeneous group of films usually listed under this heading. These features include 'the importance of crime, violence and death';[14] the presence of the *femme fatale*, embodied in *A Double Life* by Pat, the waitress; 'failed or doomed romances, and absent or distorted families and family relations', dramatizing a 'crisis in male identity',[15] and 'an obsession with male figures who are both internally divided and alienated from the culturally permissible (or ideal) parameters of masculine identity, desire and achievement'.[16] The protagonist of *A Double Life* clearly displays signs of a personal crisis, particularly through his dysfunctional family life: however attractive he may appear to women, including his ex-wife, he is unable to perform successfully the role of responsible family man that is required of a positive hero in the idealized world of classical Hollywood cinema.[17]

The reason for the predominantly dark atmosphere of *noir* films is usually explained by a general 'pessimism and anxiety'[18] in post-war American society. It is certainly true that in *A Double Life* a surprising number of shots add to the tension by presenting human existence as essentially isolated, threatened, imprisoned. The film also creates a downright nocturnal impression, and not simply because it is shot in black-and-white – there are hardly any scenes that would imply a possibility to escape into the world of brightness and safety. Tony often prowls the streets, typically after the performances (i.e., at night, among frightening sound and light effects), and he makes clear references to ghosts haunting him day and night. Douglas Lanier argues that 'Tony's wandering through the bleak cityscape becomes a visual correlative for what he has repressed, the seedy streets from which he had escaped and to which he is drawn'[19] and points out the connections between the character of Othello, American Shakespeare and the crisis within the male identity as displayed by Tony. Apart from these issues of social context and identity, the recurring images of overpowering architectural structures, particularly the elevated train tracks and steep flights of stairs also help us associate the film with *noir* productions. It is also interesting to note that the film seems to have exerted its influence on other *noir* filmmakers as well: half a year after *A Double Life*, another *film noir* was released with the title *Kiss of Death*, most probably feeding on the marketing opportunities offered by the success of *A Double Life*.[20]

When looking at *Stage Beauty*, on the other hand, we can observe considerably different narrative and cinematographic conventions at work; indeed, it seems clear that the situational conventions characterizing romantic comedies, as listed by Catherine L. Preston, are fully relevant here: from the commonplace that the central narrative deals with 'the development of love between the two main characters',[21] to less evident conventions, such as the use of a confidant or friend, who provides a shoulder to cry upon, but also offers advice (here the role is shared between the famed diarist, Pepys, and Nell Gwynn, the King's mistress). In *A Double Life*, no such friendship is available for the protagonist, since both potential confidants are female, and are therefore compromised by the past or present sexual attraction between them and Tony. Pat, the blonde waitress, lacks the intelligence and insight to be able to offer advice, and her function as *femme fatale*, drawing the protagonist into dark alleys and into her unlit bedroom, makes her a representative of danger rather than comfort. Brita, Tony's ex-wife, has also turned away from the actor, and her refusal to consider reuniting with him in marriage is another reason for his lack of trust in her. The film thus refuses to offer any comic potential (or relief) through confidant figures, and eventually, both women end up in the role of victim rather than reliable supporter.

Stage Beauty features a variety of further comic devices, including a slightly more marginal element that Preston notes: 'the idea that one of the characters is engaged to the wrong person'.[22] Throughout the first half of the narrative, Ned Kynaston is involved with the Duke of Buckingham, while for a considerable part of the film, Maria is 'patronised' by the aristocratic fop, Sir Charles Sedley. Both partners, clearly not the right ones for the protagonists, are sufficiently unromantic choices to give us hope that they will have to be discarded by the end. The final scene also confirms the film's return to the safe heterosexuality of romantic comedy, which was threatened by the homoerotic relationship between Kynaston and Buckingham. Interestingly enough, homoeroticism is presented here not as a new danger, disrupting the traditional harmony of love and marriage, but rather the opposite: as the regressive by-product of the old world, the unnatural, all male (or rather boys-only) theatrical environment created by Kynaston's old patron. However nostalgically this old master is recalled, at the beginning of the twenty-first century the image of an elderly man surrounded by effeminate young boys invokes charges of paedophilia rather than admiration, which may explain the film's powerful move towards the heterosexual romance of the end.

According to Stanley Cavell, most romantic comedies also need an intimate setting 'in which the pair have the leisure to be together',[23] possibly in nature, which provides, I believe, confirmation that the romantic union of the couple is the 'natural' solution for all conflicts in the narrative. In *Stage Beauty*, this healing power of nature may be exemplified by the scene in the inn, where Maria takes care of the downtrodden Kynaston and the two seem to develop an understanding of their respective roles in a relationship. Another, somewhat surprising element of romantic comedies is defined by Preston as the 'absence of sex before the recognition of true love',[24] which can also be seen in *Stage Beauty*: there are several moments when the possibility of having sex is acknowledged – even rehearsed – by the protagonists, but it never actually takes place. We may argue that this imitates the broken wedding nights of Othello and Desdemona in the Shakespearean drama, but I believe *Stage Beauty* is simply following the conventional narrative development of romantic comedies: after an initial recognition of attraction, the heroes must undergo isolation, and a number of obstacles have to be removed, until the male and female protagonists can eventually be united – here this union suggests also an artistic understanding forged between the two central heroes, with promises of more to come.

Stage Beauty emphasizes the somewhat lower type of entertainment offered by comedies by the inclusion of a number of comic scenes and stock characters, often in comic disguise, whose presence directs the narrative towards an inevitable happy ending. The film abounds in references to nudity, at times seen, at other times only desired or demanded, as when Maria is required to 'show a tit' when sitting for a portrait, to provide convincing evidence of her real femininity. The bodily markers of gender identity are thus consistently employed partly for their comic potential, but also in a metatheatrical reference to the need of authenticating representation by showing flesh-and-blood reality: the creation of identity, in all its public and private, artistic and social aspects, is shown as a performance one must rehearse and prepare for.

Equally significant and typical is the visual world and overall atmosphere, from the warm and mellow colour schemes to the lively and joyful period music, and the cinematography, e.g. 'lingering close-ups' on the faces of star actors.[25] The presence of stars, while characteristic of both films, following the time-honoured tradition of Hollywood cinema, also helps us distinguish between cinematic genres through the metacinematic associations they bring with themselves. In *Stage Beauty*, it is Claire Danes in particular whose face occupies most of the space in posters, DVD covers and other marketing materials, and she is the performer whose 'supposed personality [becomes] a means of describing or specifying a particular film',[26] as John Ellis clarifies the connection between the function of cinema stars and genres. Here the most important cinematic association must be the best-known Shakespeare film from the end of the millennium, and an almost cultic piece for teenage moviegoers, *William Shakespeare's Romeo + Juliet*, directed by Baz Luhrmann in 1996, which helps us locate Danes at the centre of the narrative, with our foreknowledge of her potential as a romantic heroine, equally capable of passion and sacrifice to save her love. This trait may be traced in Danes's later career as well, retrospectively reinforcing such a characterization in the minds of subsequent audiences, with roles as diverse as fallen star Yvaine in *Stardust* (2007) and CIA agent Carrie Mathison in the *Homeland* series (2011–).[27] In all of these cases, her screen persona is seen as drawn towards a man who may bring destruction to herself and all that she holds sacred; still, she does not flinch from following the course of love. The filmmakers even relied, in their marketing and publicity strategies, on the generic associations offered by another recent award-winning Shakespeare offshoot, aligning the film with *Shakespeare in Love*, similarly a romantic comedy using Shakespearean references.[28] It is interesting to note, however, the character of Thomas Betterton, a leading actor admired and applauded by seventeenth-century English theatrical audiences in the same way as later screen stars:[29] in one of many moves the film takes away from historical accuracy, he is deprived of any trace of star appeal in *Stage Beauty*, and presented here as the shrewd business entrepreneur, with a face that is, as Buckingham points out the reason for the king's disappointment, 'the same old thing' everyone has seen plenty of times, a face that has lost its magnetic power to fill the seats.

It comes as no surprise that *A Double Life*, a product of the classical Hollywood studio system, employed its own star protagonist, and the production marketing relied heavily on the reputation of Ronald Colman as 'gentleman of the cinema',[30] a phrase used later by *The New York Times* obituary,[31] biographies and online fan sites alike to describe the character- istic image that brought him fame and appreciation on the international screen. What is interesting, though, is that while the film is clearly seen (and was also marketed) as 'a Ronald Colman vehicle',[32] it used the gentleman image only as a point of departure (the comedy Tony stars in at the beginning of the film is entitled *A Gentleman's Gentleman*), but the narrative shows his gradual and dramatic move away from this stock character, in a similar way as *A Double Life* proved to take Ronald Colman's career in new directions and to his first Academy Award.

Beside textual and cinematographic devices, in any generic system, objects and imagery may acquire significant roles, enhancing our percep- tion of the genre. To exemplify the different uses the same object may be turned to, I will conclude my analysis with an examination of the ways the two films refer to a simple everyday object that, nonetheless, seems to have symbolic representative power in both films: the mirror. Rothwell's category of the mirror movie is clearly justified when we observe the range of manifestations the mirror takes in both films. In fact, this seems to be the case in several other mirror movies as well, particularly Roysten Abel's *In Othello*, which takes an obvious pleasure in the metaphorical potential of reflexive surfaces. However, we need to note here that the use of mirrors in a metaphorical way is not an exclusive quality of Rothwell's mirror movies, as the mirror-plated interiors in Kenneth Branagh's *Hamlet* (1996) testify, to name just the most blatant example. Still, it is undeniable that the mirror as a metaphor is more than apt in the representation of the metatheatrical narratives of the two *Othello* films: it is not only the actors' lives and passions that mirror those of the characters they perform on stage, but the films also abound in other variations of the mirror image, which are equally informative about the films' distinct generic features.

In *Stage Beauty*, the mirror as a physical object is frequently seen, and it is exclusively an actor's mirror, set in a backstage dressing room, which rarely evokes reflections that point beyond the here and now. At the same time, these mirrors focus our attention on the theatricality of identity, how physical appearance provides a way to perform sexual-racial-professional identity, all of which are changeable, and can be rehearsed, practised, put on, but also

shed when necessary. The mirror may also function as a practical cinematographic device to suggest a hierarchical position in a particular scene: when
Betterton is cornered by Kynaston and has to give in to his demands
for shared power in the theatre, Betterton's face is seen within the small
frame of his mirror in the lower half of the screen, looking up from below
at the overpowering Kynaston (see Figure 19). Moreover, we can find in
Stage Beauty a number of human mirrors as well: a number of parallel scenes
force us to recognize Maria and Kynaston in identical situations, in performances and rehearsals, with Maria imitating Kynaston's ridiculously unnatural
acting style, although she fails to achieve the same effect.

This cinematic device of repeated situations works similarly to the 'alien-
ating double', creating 'a distance between the audience and a character thus
made ridiculous and harder to identify with' described by Sarah Hatchuel in
her reflection of mirrors and mirror effects.[33] Here it is precisely this affected
acting style that Kynaston needs to see reflected in Maria's 'mirror' to find
the right way to perform the death scene, and to perform his own identity in
the changed circumstances, getting rid of effeminate gestures and becoming
a 'man' at last, in this way reinforcing our notion of gender as a performed
construct. Maria also seems to recognize her own artistic struggle in the
distorting mirror of Kynaston's desperate attempt at a performance of
Othello (his first male role ever) and his inevitable humiliation at the court.
Her return to an understanding of the real complexities of personal and
professional identity is shown to be dated from this point.

I also believe that, beside the aforementioned metatheatrical devices,
mirror effects in *Stage Beauty* include an example of metacinematic
mirroring as well: the new acting style, introduced as if by accident or by
instinctive artistic harmony between hero and heroine, is in fact characteristic of the cinematic realism of Hollywood, rather than theatrical acting in
any historical period. It is true that this acting style has its roots in the
Stanislavskian theatrical tradition, but it is equally clear that such a style is

Figure 19:   Betterton cornered by Ned Kynaston in Richard Eyre's 2004 *Stage Beauty*.
All rights reserved.

no more historically accurate on a Restoration stage than the earlier, artificial and affected mode would fit twenty-first century cinema; however, the film transposes this 'unmarked' realistic style from the offstage scenes to the onstage performance, the latter previously marked as different, and in this way the world of the cinema unites what has been separated, in a metaphorical way healing the personal and professional breaches caused by the intrusion of public into private life.

The metaphorical and metatheatrical potentials of mirrors are by no means restricted to the world of comedy; thus *A Double Life* similarly abounds in mirrors in several senses of the word. The main protagonist, the leading actor of the theatre, is first seen looking at his own portraits, as if he were looking into mirrors, in the theatre lobby – as we soon realize he is searching for his own identity which keeps eluding him, especially when he is in between roles. He also faces reflective surfaces, often real mirrors, wherever he goes, and they not only present him with the image of his own anxieties, but also project his fears and his imagination, his all-too-powerful identification with the role. We can see mirrors in the window of a travel agent's (advertising trips to Venice, of all places), where he first sees himself in the costume of Othello. There is a mirror next to his table in the Italian restaurant, coincidentally called Café Venezia; another one at the first-night reception, when he is beginning to hear voices; and he also looks into a mirror in the small apartment of Pat, the blonde Italian waitress, in a way that suggests that the boundary between external reality and his internal world has become dangerously blurred (see Figure 20). When we see mirrors in dressing rooms, particularly in the office of the wigmaker who helps to lay a trap for Tony, they also acquire a menacing quality, and the artificial identity constructed by their help leads to no self-understanding but only to the downfall of the hero. When he looks into

Figure 20:   Mirror effects – blurred boundaries between fiction and reality in George Cukor's 1947 *A Double Life*.

a mirror, he does not see himself, but he sees his other, fictional, unreal self, which preys on his mind – and whenever mirrors are used to create extra reflective surfaces, they shatter the illusion of a safe and protective environment, and add to the oppressive atmosphere of destruction. Unlike in *Stage Beauty*, where mirrors were also part of the theatre, in *A Double Life* they have the power to fragment and destroy the central male identity, and what they reflect will never bring about self-knowledge but only result in disturbing a pathologically troubled mind.

The two *Othello* films showed that the method of adapting (and especially fidelity to) the Shakespearean source text does not define essential features of films, and the same textual quotations may be embedded into diverse cinematic works of art, which are recognized as belonging to various genres, independent of the Shakespearean element. This recognition of genres is, in my opinion, the single most important criterion for popular cinema audiences – it is no longer textual fidelity but generic familiarity that we look forward to. Claire Mortimer summarizes the role of genres: 'genre is about mass entertainment, it is about studios maximising their returns on their huge investment in a film, by replicating formulae which have made money in the past'.[34] And even though she may be right in claiming that genre films, as opposed to *auteur* films, have always been looked down on and seen 'as anathema to creativity and artistry, and hence critical merit',[35] I believe that by acknowledging the presence of genres and their significance in literary adaptations and even *auteur* films, we may be in a better position to understand the ways Shakespeare is marketed today, and accept these films' choice of emphasis and interpretation, without expecting them to fulfil promises they never made. The variety of mirrors the two examples used to reflect on *Othello* shows that *A Double Life* found in it a parable of human existence as inevitably doomed, where no spirit of comedy or happiness in the home sphere can protect man from his fate. *Stage Beauty*, however, presents human identity as an ultimately artificial construct, rehearsed and performed endlessly; but if successfully performed, combining the well-known framework with the element of surprise, it will not fail to bring everlasting fame.

Notes

1 D. M. Lanier, *Shakespeare and Modern Popular Culture* (Oxford and New York: Oxford University Press, 2002), 53.

2 M. de Certeau, *The Practice of Everyday Life*, trans. Steven Rendall (Berkeley: University of California Press, 1984), 165–76.

3 B. Langford, *Film Genre: Hollywood and Beyond* (Edinburgh: Edinburgh University Press, 2005), vii.

4 K. S. Rothwell, *A History of Shakespeare on Screen: A Century of Film and Television* (Cambridge: Cambridge University Press, 1999), 219.

5 C. M. Mazer, 'Sense/Memory/Sense-Memory: Reading Narratives of Shakespearian Rehearsals', *Shakespeare Survey*, 62 (2009), 330.

6 Cf. R. Jackson's *Theatres on Film: How the Cinema Imagines the Stage* (Manchester and New York: Manchester University Press, 2013).

7 D. M. Lanier, 'Murdering *Othello*' in D. Cartmell (ed.), *A Companion to Literature, Film, and Adaptation* (Oxford: Blackwell, 2012), 209.

8 Rothwell, *A History of Shakespeare on Screen*, 219.

9 For a more comprehensive list, see Lanier, 'Murdering *Othello*' or R. Burt, 'Backstage Pass(ing): *Stage Beauty, Othello* and the Make-up of Race' in M. T. Burnett and R. Wray (eds.), *Screening Shakespeare in the Twenty-first Century* (Edinburgh: Edinburgh University Press, 2006), 53–71.

10 A. Tudor, 'Genre' in B. K. Grant (ed.), *Film Genre Reader III* (Austin: University of Texas Press, 2003), 3.

11 *Ibid.*, 6.

12 R. F. Willson, Jr, *Shakespeare in Hollywood: 1929–1956* (Madison, NJ: Fairleigh Dickinson University Press, 2000), 93, quoted in H. R. Coursen, *Shakespeare Translated: Derivatives on Film and TV* (New York: Peter Lang, 2005), 100.

13 C. L. Preston: 'Hanging on a Star: The Resurrection of the Romance Film in the 1990s' in W. W. Dixon (ed.), *Film Genre 2000: New Critical Essays* (Albany, NY: State University of New York Press, 2000), 228.

14 S. Neale, *Genre and Hollywood* (London and New York, Routledge, 2000), 146.

15 *Ibid.*, 151.

16 *Ibid.*, 152.

17 See R. Wood, 'Ideology, Genre, Auteur', in B. K. Grant (ed.), *Film Genre Reader III* (Austin: University of Texas Press, 2003), 60–74.

18 Neale, *Genre and Hollywood*, 145.

19 Lanier, 'Murdering *Othello*', 209.

20 In 'Murdering *Othello*', Lanier even hints at the possibility that the 1947 success of *A Double Life* might have paved the way for Laurence Olivier's Academy Award-winning *noir Hamlet*, see 213.

21 Preston, 'Hanging on a Star', 227.

22 *Ibid.*, 232.

23 S. Cavell, quoted in C. Mortimer, *Romantic Comedy* (Abingdon and New York: Routledge, 2010), 9.

24 Preston, 'Hanging on a Star', 233.

25 *Ibid.*, 232.

26 J. Ellis, *Visible Fictions: Cinema Television Video*, revised edition (London and New York: Routledge, 2001), 92.

27 I am indebted to Sarah Hatchuel for drawing my attention to the *Homeland* series.

28 See Burt, 'Backstage Pass(ing)', 53–71.

29 See S. M. Buhler, *Shakespeare in the Cinema: Ocular Proof* (Albany, NY: State University of New York Press, 2001), 52.

30 R. D. Smith, *Ronald Colman, Gentleman of the Cinema: A Biography and Filmography* (Jefferson, NC: McFarland, 1991).
31 'Ronald Colman, Actor, Is Dead', *The New York Times*, 20 May 1958, 33.
32 Buhler, *Shakespeare in the Cinema*, 180.
33 S. Hatchuel, *Shakespeare, from Stage to Screen* (Cambridge: Cambridge University Press, 2004), 107.
34 Mortimer, 1.
35 *Ibid.*

WORKS CITED

Buhler, S. M., *Shakespeare in the Cinema: Ocular Proof* (Albany, NY: State University of New York Press, 2002).
Burt, R., 'Backstage Pass(ing): *Stage Beauty, Othello* and the Make-up of Race', in M. T. Burnett and R. Wray (eds.), *Screening Shakespeare in the Twenty-first Century* (Edinburgh: Edinburgh University Press, 2006), 53–71.
Certeau, M. de, *The Practice of Everyday Life*, trans. Steven Rendall (Berkeley: University of California Press, 1984).
Coursen, H. R., *Shakespeare Translated: Derivatives on Film and TV* (New York: Peter Lang, 2005).
Ellis, J., *Visible Fictions. Cinema Television Video*, revised edition (London and New York: Routledge, 2001 [1982]).
Grant, B. K., ed., *Film Genre Reader III* (Austin: University of Texas Press, 2003).
Hatchuel, S., *Shakespeare, from Stage to Screen* (Cambridge: Cambridge University Press, 2004).
Jackson, R., *Theatres on Film: How the Cinema Imagines the Stage* (Manchester and New York: Manchester University Press, 2013).
Langford, B., *Film Genre: Hollywood and Beyond* (Edinburgh: Edinburgh University Press, 2005).
Lanier, D. M., *Shakespeare and Modern Popular Culture* (Oxford and New York: Oxford University Press, 2002).
"Murdering *Othello*', in D. Cartmell (ed.), *A Companion to Literature, Film, and Adaptation* (Oxford: Blackwell, 2012), 198–215.
Mazer, C. M., 'Sense/Memory/Sense-Memory: Reading Narratives of Shakespearian Rehearsals', *Shakespeare Survey* 62 (2009), 328–48.
Mortimer, C., *Romantic Comedy* (Abingdon and New York: Routledge, 2010).
Neale, S., *Genre and Hollywood*, (London and New York: Routledge, 2000).
Preston, C. L., 'Hanging on a Star: The Resurrection of the Romance Film in the 1990s', in W. W. Dixon (ed.), *Film Genre 2000: New Critical Essays* (Albany, NY: State University of New York Press, 2000), 227–43.
Rothwell, K. S., *A History of Shakespeare on Screen: A Century of Film and Television* (Cambridge: Cambridge University Press, 1999).
Smith, R. D., *Ronald Colman, Gentleman of the Cinema: A Biography and Filmography* (Jefferson, NC: McFarland, 1991).

Tudor, A., 'Genre', in B. K. Grant (ed.), *Film Genre Reader III* (Austin: University of Texas Press, 2003), 3–11.

Willson, R. F. Jr, *Shakespeare in Hollywood: 1929–1956* (Madison, NJ: Fairleigh Dickinson University Press, 2000).

Wood, R., 'Ideology, Genre, Auteur', in B. K. Grant (ed.), *Film Genre Reader III* (Austin: University of Texas Press, 2003), 60–74.

CHAPTER 12

Othello *in Spanish*
Dubbed and subtitled versions

Jesús Tronch

In a 2002 essay on film adaptations of *Henry V* dubbed into Italian, Sara Soncini, while pointing out screen translation as a 'key stage' in the filmic appropriations of Shakespeare across cultures, complained that it had received 'only marginal attention'.[1] Indeed, while Shakespeare in translation regularly features in Shakespearean conferences and publications, Shakespeare as translated in film or television adaptations is seldom discussed in Shakespearean meetings.[2] In the context of an international volume on *Othello* on screen, the present article aims to contribute to this marginal area of Shakespeare studies by analysing aspects of dubbed and subtitled versions in Spanish of the following *Othello* films: Orson Welles's (1952) and Oliver Parker's (1995), with reference to their translation into Spanish, and also Burge's (1965) with reference to the cultural association of their dubbing actors. I will mainly focus on the translation problems that are specific to dubbing and subtitling (the two most common types of audiovisual translation) and on how they affect perceptions of these *Othellos* in Spain.

My primary material is the following: the subtitles in the 2007 Warner Home DVD release of Parker's *Othello*; the subtitles in the Manga Films DVD release of Welles's *Othello* in 2004; and as examples of non-commercial subtitles, available in video-sharing websites, the subtitles for Welles's film posted on YouTube by a user identified as 'luanurbec' (from Chile) and those for Parker's film posted by a YouTube user identified as 'MrLite100' (from Mexico); and finally the dubbed text in the aforementioned Warner DVD of Parker's *Othello*, produced in 1996 at the Barcelona dubbing studio Sonoblok.[3] According to *eldoblaje.com*, dubbed versions of Welles's and of Stuart Burge's films were made in 1952 and 1966 respectively, but unfortunately I have been unable to locate them.

This study benefitted from the research projects Artelope FFI 2012-34347 (2013–2016), and TC/12 Consolider CSD2009-00033, funded by the the Spanish government.

It is worth pointing out the absence of translations of well-known versions such as Yutkevich's, the 1981 BBC's and Trevor Nunn's. There are only two kinds of films on which investment in dubbing and DVD production was deemed worthwhile: films that were part of the mainstream industrial circuit (Parker's, distributed by Columbia; Sax's, for ITV Global Entertainment) and films based on international stars who were also acclaimed in Spain (Welles's and Burge's).[4] Interestingly, Welles's *Othello* in DVD was distributed in Spain by Manga Films, the biggest Spanish independent distribution company, and it was released in 2004, coinciding with theatre productions of *Othello* in Madrid by Cheek by Jowl and by a Russian company, St Petersburg Youth Theatre,[5] in their turn a response to the growing social concern over violence against women in Spain.[6]

Dubbing and subtitling share problems with other kinds of translation and at the same time are characterized by difficulties inherent in their respective processes.[7] In the case of translating Shakespeare, to technical problems such as those enumerated by Dirk Delabastita (elliptical grammar and general compactness of expression, use of homely images, mixed metaphors and iterative imagery, musicality of verse, etc.),[8] dubbing and subtitling add problems deriving from the interaction between word, image and sound, and the constraints imposed by the time-bound and space-bound medium.

Subtitled Othellos

I will start with subtitling, the type of screen translation of which I have the most *Othello* versions. It is important to point out that the subtitled text needs to 'flow with the current speech', and therefore defines 'the pace of reception'.[9] This reception involves the viewer's ability to read typed letters at a certain rhythm (usually twelve characters per second), which conditions the amount of text to be shown, in its turn, conditioned by the size of the screen. Subtitles should contain no more than two lines, with twenty-eight to forty characters per line depending on the medium (twenty-eight for television and forty for DVD), should be syntactically self-contained and distributed in sense blocks and/or grammatical units, and should stay on the screen for no less than one second and no longer than seven seconds.[10]

These constraints, together with the fact that in general more text can be spoken than an average reading rhythm can follow, force the translation for subtitles to be primarily synthetic. Around 40 per cent of the original text usually disappears in subtitles.[11] It should be borne in mind that the purpose of subtitling is not to offer an exact rendering of the original but rather to allow spectators to follow the intent of the original while at the same time enjoying all the other visual and aural features. Even if the speech rhythm allowed word-for-word subtitles, these would enslave the spectator to reading the subtitled lines and cause him to miss the rest of the audiovisual programme.

Subtitling is therefore characterized by omission and condensation of the source text, with frequent omission of repetitions, tags, emphatic expressions, personal names, certain discourse markers, and recurrent use of transposition and modulation in order to find more concise expressions. For example, in Parker's film, Othello's greeting to Cassio and Iago 'The goodness of the night upon you, friends' (1.2.35) is rendered by Luis Astrana (one of the canonical Spanish translators of Shakespeare)[12] as *¡Los plácemes de la noche caigan sobre vosotros, amigos!*, with the verb *caigan* (literally, 'fall') added because its ellipsis would create an unlikely expression, and with a rarely used noun *pláceme* for 'goodness' that contributes to the general elevated register. Within the limits of forty characters per line, Astrana's translation would be too long as a subtitle. The actual subtitle reads '*Recibid el favor de la noche, amigos*', amounting to a total of thirty-seven characters. This subtitle shows a shorter equivalent for 'goodness' ('*favor*' instead of '*pláceme*')[13] and a shorter verb ('*Recibid* = 'receive', in fact a cause-to-effect modulation) instead of the long verbal phrase '*caigan sobre vosotros*' (literally, 'fall upon you').[14]

I have used Astrana's translation, a conventional literary and literal prose translation for silent reading, for comparison purposes only, not to suggest that the subtitler of Parker's film used it. But it is not uncommon for screen translation, often under heavy commercial pressures, to be based on or to adapt previously published translations.[15] This is the case of the subtitled *Othello*s except for Parker's on DVD: the Manga subtitles show close resemblance to the Instituto Shakespeare's verse translation;[16] the 'luanurbec' subtitles adapt Ángel-Luis Pujante's verse translation;[17] and the 'MrLite100' subtitles use a translation in the public domain, that of Jaime Clark,[18] published in 1873, which often resorts to hyperbaton and to amplifications in order to render Shakespeare's blank verse systematically as unrhymed hendecasyllables. The latter presents a number of problems: on the one hand, present-day viewers may perceive the language in Clark's late nineteenth-century translation as old-fashioned; on the other hand, a few of Clark's errors or inadequate translation choices are preserved, as when the accumulative effect of repeating 'whore' in 4.2 is blunted because MrLite100 uncritically reproduces Clark's prudish neutralizations and modulations: '*Es moza astuta*' ('She is a cunning lass' for Shakespeare's 'This is a subtle whore' at 4.2.22), '*astuta cortesana*' ('She is a cunning

courtesan' for Shakespeare's 'cunning whore', 4.2.93), and '*Decir no puedo
"adúltera"*' ('I cannot say "adulteress"' for Shakespeare's 'I cannot say
"whore"' at 4.2.165).

In general, the subtitles in all four versions keep distinctive stylistic
features in Shakespeare's *Othello*, such as recurrent images of rutting
animals,[19] repetitions of phrases such as 'the pity of it' at 4.1.186–7 (a
feature usually omitted in subtitling), and what Honigmann calls the
'dislocated language'.[20] Similarly, the racial reverberations from the use
of 'black' and black-derived terms are not avoided. What the subtitles
cannot entirely keep is the verbal arrangement of the verse as seen on the
page (or screen) of a conventional edition. Although both the conventional
edition and the subtitles contain a readerly text, the subtitles are in fact
subordinated to the oral (and iconographic) code and must represent an
actual delivery of verse and not its 'musical score'. Generally in the
analysed versions, for speeches delivered at a medium to relatively fast
pace, two-line subtitles usually coincide with the text in a pentameter, with
the last words of the subtitle corresponding to the last words in the original
blank verse (this is more evident in the English subtitles). But, of course,
when the actor or actress runs on the line or stops at a point within the
pentameter, the subtitles follow that rhythm. Let's illustrate this with
reference to Branagh's delivery of 4.1.74–87 in Parker's film:

Whilst you were here, o'erwhelmed with your grief . . .	74
Cassio came hither. I shifted him away,	76
And laid good 'scuse upon your ecstasy,	77
Bade him anon return and here speak with me,	78
The which he promised. Do but encave yourself,	79
And mark the fleers, the gibes and notable scorns	80
That dwell in every region of his face.	81
For I will make him tell the tale anew,	82
Where, how, how oft, how long ago, and when	83
He hath and is again to cope your wife.	84
I say, but mark his gesture. Marry, patience . . .	85

The Warner DVD subtitles provide an equivalent for the first pentameter,
but then Branagh pauses after 'Cassio came hither', which is given a short
subtitle '. . . *ha venido Casio*'. Then, since Branagh ties the second part of
the pentameter, 'I shifted him away', with the next line (77), its Spanish
equivalent, '*Le he hecho marchar*', is shown within the next subtitle that
contains this third pentameter. The next line and a half are also shown in
one subtitle to coincide with Branagh's pause at the caesura in line 79. For
the following 'Do but encave yourself', Branagh emphasizes each word,

and then pauses, so this is given a short subtitle, a neutral *'Escondeos'* ('Hide yourself'). The next two pentameters are given full two-line sub-titles. Then, line 83 'Where, how, how oft, how long ago, and when' is uttered by Branagh with a slight pause before each element but without any pause between 'and when' and the next line, so that *'y cuándo'* ('and when') is shown in the following subtitle disregarding the line ending at 83. Finally, after a slight pause, 'Marry, patience' (85) is again uttered with an emphasis on each word, and this is shown in one short subtitle: *'¡Tened paciencia!'*. This slight disruption of the visual perception of blank verse is one of the problematic consequences of one of the limitations inherent to subtitling: the transposition from an oral to a written medium.

The non-commercial subtitled versions from YouTube do not always meet the formal criteria for quality subtitling. For instance, in the 'lua-nurbec' version, when Iago speaks 'Others there are/ Who, ... throwing but shows of service on their lords' (1.1.49–52), a four-line subtitle can be found,[21] while good practice recommends a maximum of two lines in order to keep as much of the image free as possible. Carelessness on the part of the subtitler can also be seen in the fact that the translation includes the phrase 'trimmed in forms and visages of duty' (1.1.50), which is actually cut in Welles's script. Apart from the fact that four lines occupy too much space on the screen, the line division disrupts grammatical units:

> *Otros, revestidos de*
> *aparente sumisión,*
> *dando muestras de*
> *servicio a sus señores*

In *'revestidos de/ aparente'*, the prepositional phrase is split between the preposition *'de'* ('of') and the head; and similarly with *'muestras de/ servicio'*. This is probably due to a computer programme automatically dividing the lines to be shown neatly centred and typographically well-balanced, with total disregard for the recommended grammatical self-containment of each line.

In line with the typographical disruption of lineation, the non-commercial subtitled versions often distort the visual perception of verse more radically than in the DVD subtitles. For instance, for Othello's speech at 3.3.456–63, Ángel-Luis Pujante's free-verse translation manages to keep the emphasis on the last words in Shakespeare:

> *Jamás, Yago. Como el Ponto Euxino,* [... Pontic sea,]
> *cuya fría corriente e indómito curso* [... compulsive course]
> *no siente la baja marea y sigue adelante* [... keeps due on]

> *hacia la Propóntide y el Helesponto,* [. . . Hellespont,]
> *así mis designios, que corren violentos* [. . . violent pace,]
> *jamás refluirán, y no cederán al tierno cariño* [. . . humble love,]
> *hasta vaciarse en un mar de profunda* [. . . wide revenge]
> *e inmensa venganza.* [Swallow them up.]

The Pujante-based 'luanurbec' subtitles reshuffled the position of the last words, here shown in capitals:

> *Jamás, Yago. Como el Ponto* EUXINO,
> . . . *cuya fría corriente e indómito*
> CURSO *no siente la baja marea y* . . .
> . . . *sigue* ADELANTE *hacia la*
> *Propóntide y el* HELESPONTO.
> *Así mis designios, que corren* VIOLENTOS,
> . . . *jamás refluirán, y no*
> *cederán al tierno* CARIÑO . . .
> . . . *hasta vaciarse en un mar*
> *de* PROFUNDA *e inmensa* VENGANZA.

Sometimes the subtitled text does not match the oral text, as when the 'luanurbec' subtitles for Iago's 'Witness you ever-burning lights above' (3.3.466) are synchronous with Othello's prior climatic phrase 'Swallow them up' (3.3.463). This takes place in the middle of two speeches delivered by both Welles's Othello and MacLiammóir's Iago at a brisk, steady pace that makes synchronization difficult. Another deficiency in the non-commercial subtitled *Othello*s is the fact that, in general, they offer too much text in the subtitles, which results in the spectators having too much to read at the expense of missing the films' visual artistry.

It would not be too risky to regard the subtitled versions on YouTube as examples of 'fansub' or fan-subtitling, a mode of translation by enthusiasts (as opposed to translation by professionals), which is fairly common in popular TV series and Japanese animated productions.[22] What is difficult to ascertain is whether these subtitles resulted from co-creational or partici-patory production or were the work of a single amateur. In common with fansubs, they show technical and formal inadequacies, but unlike fansubs they use published translations (in some cases infringing copyright) and therefore diminish the percentage of translation errors, which is relatively high in fansubs in general. All in all, the popularizing effect of these non-commercial translations cannot be denied: as of 27 April 2012, luanurbec's first fifteen-minute clip of Welles's *Othello* had almost 34,000 views, and later clips had an average of 7,200 views; a number of MrLite100's clips of Parker's film had more than 12,000 views on YouTube.

Dubbed *Othello*

A more complex and expensive process, dubbing is the most common type of audiovisual translation in Spain, as it is in France, Italy and Germany.[23] It should be first pointed out that the final product is not only the result of the translator's efforts. Rather the main responsibility lies in the dubbing studio, and especially in the dubbing director. The studio commissions a translation of the verbal content of the film, and this initial version (a rough translation) is then adapted (sometimes by a different translator, often by the dubbing director himself, who in turn may be a professional dubbing actor) in order to provide a script well synchronized with the image, the length of characters' interventions, their gestures, intonation, attitude and lip movements. The adapted script is handed in to the studio, and then the dubbing director, as in any theatre or filmic production, selects a cast of actors and actresses and organizes dubbing sessions for 'takes' or short fragments of the script. In these sessions, the actor or actress watches the 'take' to be recorded, pays attention to the performance of the character to be dubbed, memorizes or prepares the translated-adapted text, and receives instructions from the director. During this process in the studio's recording room, the adapted script may receive further changes, as both the director and the players need to fine-tune phrases that are not totally synchronized, often by reducing or adding words, and often without resorting to the translator and/or adapter or consulting the original script.[24] This is why, on judging a dubbed version, one cannot be entirely sure of laying responsibility for specific features of the final dubbed text on any specific agent (translator, adapter, dubbing director, actor).

As in the case of subtitles, the dubbing translator-adapter is constrained by the subordination of the verbal text to the audiovisual whole, especially by the interplay between image, sound and word. This interaction is more evident when the film conveys an idea by means of images that have a correspondence in the dialogue. For instance, after Iago finishes his vow of allegiance to Othello with 'What bloody business ever' (3.3.472), Parker has Othello and Iago join their bleeding hands in order to seal that covenant. As an equivalent for 'bloody', a translator could opt for a literal rendering (such as '*sangriento*', '*sanguinario*' or '*de sangre*') or for an associated meaning, as in Pujante's '*por cruel que sea la empresa*' ('however cruel that business be'). Yet the fact that the film shows blood after the word 'bloody' has been pronounced limits the translational choices to blood-related terms.

As subtitles have to be synchronized with the pace of the original speech, so the dubbing script has to observe a temporal synchronization (isochrony) so that the dubbing actor can deliver his text for the same length of time. An example of this limitation can be seen in the aforementioned greeting by Othello, 'The goodness of the night upon you, friends' (1.2.35): the dubbed text '*Recibid los plácemes de la noche*' omits the final word 'friends', since the Spanish trisyllabic '*amigos*' (as in the subtitles) would have to be pronounced when Fishburne has already stopped his mouth (or they would force the dubbing actor to speed up his delivery to an unlikely pace in that specific dramatic situation).

Also, dubbing adapters, as well as subtitlers, have to take into account the characters' gestures and movements since their visually conveyed meaning should agree with the verbal meaning. For instance, Iago's 'Lay thy finger thus' addressed to Roderigo (2.1.217) is performed by Branagh by laying *his* own finger on *his* lips.[25] A literal translation, such as Clark's and Astrana's '*Pon el dedo así*', does not quite match Branagh's gesture of bringing his forefinger to his lips. The translation needs to focus more on the pragmatic or illocutionary force of 'Lay thy finger thus' rather than on its lexical content, as in the Instituto Shakespeare's modulation '*¡Shhh! ¡Dedo en boca y a callar!*', in fact a juxtaposition of three units that urge silence: an interjection '*¡Shhh!*', an idiom '*Dedo en boca*' (literally, 'finger on mouth') and an imperative ('*callar*') urging to shut up. This would be adequate for Branagh's performance, were it not that isochrony demands a shorter phrase. The actual dubbed text, '*Punto en boca*', ('stop talking' – literally, 'point on mouth') respects both gestural synchronization and Branagh's quick delivery.

However, unlike subtitlers, dubbing adapters pay attention to the correlation that may exist between characters' gestures and movements and the 'syllables carrying accentual prominence';[26] and are constrained by phonetic or lip synchronization. Mismatches between the lip movements and the replaced spoken word may impair the verisimilitude of the final product. This is specially the case in close-up shots, with the open vowel 'a', the rounded vowels 'o' and 'u', and the bilabial consonants ('b', 'p', 'm') in which the closing of lips is evident. For example, when Desdemona says 'I cannot say "whore"/ It does abhor me now I speak the word' (4.2.165–6), Parker's medium close-up and Irène Jacob's paused delivery make it clear that the line ends with rounded lips pronouncing 'whore'.[27] The subtitles (and other readerly translations) place a lexical equivalent of 'whore' at the end of the sentence, but neither '*puta*' (Warner DVD) nor '*adúltera*' (MrLite100) with their final 'a' can match the roundedness of 'whore'. By contrast, the choice of 'horror' in the dubbed translation achieves this match; '*hasta me causa horror/ pronunciar la palabra "adúltera"* (literally 'in me it causes horror/ to pronounce the word "adulteress"'). There is a problem, however: by rendering 'whore' as *'adúltera'*—as in Clark's 1873 translation – the Spanish Desdemona not only softens the force of her husband's accusation of prostitution but also appears to be so shocked that she distorts reality – while Emilia and Iago had clearly referred to the term *'puta'* ('whore').[28] Previously, the dubbed text also softens Othello's harshness when 'Are not you a strumpet?' (4.2.83) is rendered '*¿No eres infiel?*' ('Are you not unfaithful?'), perhaps because isochrony was better served than with a more literal rendering or perhaps because the Spanish word *'puta'* here would impair the perception of the text as belonging to a tragedy of classical status.[29]

Both at 4.2.165 ('whore') and 4.2.84 ('strumpet'), the DVD subtitles use straight equivalents of 'prostitute' ('*No puedo decir "puta"*', and '*¿No eres una ramera?*' respectively). Unlike dubbing, where the original text is not accessible to receivers of the translated text, subtitles are in a way more constrained by the audiovisual medium since they suffer from what Törnqvist called 'the gossiping effect', that is, the fact that readers of the subtitles can check the translation against the original.[30]

The following example illustrates how these three types of synchronization can sometimes operate together. Parker has Branagh deliver 'I hate the Moor' (1.3.368) in a close-up shot, looking straight into the camera, almost whispering and with a relatively long pause between 'I', 'hate' and 'the Moor' respectively. Here the challenge lies in matching the length of each of the three elements, the oral gesture and the lip movements, especially with the open front unrounded vowel '/a/' in the personal pronoun 'I' and the bilabial 'm' in 'Moor'. The obvious translation into Spanish of 'I hate the Moor' is '*Odio al Moro*' (as is the case in the translations by Astrana, Instituto Shakespeare and Pujante). However, the dubbed text we hear is '*Y es que ... odio ... al moro*', with an added bisyllabic phrase '*Y es que*' (a kind of discourse marker similar to 'The thing is that ...'). Whether this addition was inserted by the adapter or at the dubbing studio, we do not know, but we can infer that a delivery such as '*Odio ... al ... Moro*', with the preposition and the article '*al*' in the middle, would have been judged too strained, and therefore there was need for something to match the original 'I'. Again the obvious option would have been the personal pronoun so that the phrase would be '*Yo odio al moro*' with the personal pronoun explicit (as Clark translated, probably with '*Yo*' added to complete the hendecasyllabic line), but perhaps a delivery such as '*Yo ...*

odio . . . al moro' would have a rounded vowel 'o' in '*Yo*' mismatching the unrounded vowel in 'I'. Consequently, the discourse marker '*Y es que . . .*' was probably brought in to fill up this specific three-part delivery by Branagh.

Lip synchronization poses great challenges to the translator-adapter, and in this DVD it is not always achieved. For instance, Fishburne delivers 'This is a subtle whore' (4.2.22) in a close-up, although at a speedier pace than Jacob does later, and the dubbed text provides a literal translation, '*Es una puta hábil*', in which again the roundedness of 'whore' is not matched. Since phonetic synchronization is aimed at in order to provide verisimilitude to the final dubbed product, one wonders if the dubbing studio handled this constraint more flexibly because viewers were assumed not to expect that degree of verisimilitude in a film based on a classical play, a film in which characters speak in verse and in an older chronological variety of the language. The Spanish in this dubbed *Othello* is characterized by a choice of vocabulary and syntax that projects a variety slightly archaic to a contemporary audience and almost evenly literary and elaborate in style. Despite a register mismatch in those scenes where Iago speaks ordinary prose in English but in a more formal style in Spanish, the general outcome can be judged favourably for the purposes of creating an illusion that it is, after all, a Shakespearean text.[31] Not surprisingly, this dubbed *Othello* resulted from the combined forces of the translator and adapter Guillermo Ramos, a professional who had already adapted over eighty films since 1978, and the experienced actor and dubbing director Ernesto Aura, who had also worked together on two Shakespearean films, Zeffirelli's *Hamlet* (1990) and Branagh's *Much Ado About Nothing* (1993).

The last aspect I will discuss is not linguistic but rather paralinguistic: the way casting (the choice of specific Spanish-speaking actors and actresses) affects the way the dubbed *Othello*s in Spain can be perceived. Dubbed versions efface not only the singular features of actors' and actresses' voices and interpretive decisions but also the cultural values of their accents. Parker's film has non-native accents in Desdemona (impersonated by French Irène Jacob) and the Duke (by Italian Gabriele Ferzetti), so that these characters are not 'the social norm against which Othello is set, they were themselves outside it'.[32] This is no longer perceived in the dubbed version with the neutral Spanish voices of Alba Solà for Desdemona and Pepe Mediavila for the Duke.

In addition, casting has implications in the added meanings of a film as it incorporates the cultural values and reverberations associated with the chosen players. In Parker's film, Laurence Fishburne not only 'supplies a physical and powerful erotic presence as Othello'[33] but also carries reminiscences of his performance as Ike Turner abusing his wife Tina Turner in the 1994 biographical film *What's Love Got to Do with It*.[34] Similarly, dubbing actors' and actresses' voices are somehow associated with the original players they had dubbed before and their roles. In the case of Othello in Welles's film, the 'very deep' voice ('*muy grave*', as described in *eldoblaje.com*) of Eduardo Fajardo was chosen. The decision seems apt since Fajardo had previously dubbed Orson Welles as Michael O'Hara in *The Lady from Shanghai* in 1948; but inevitably spectators could recall Fajardo's voice for actors such as Charles Boyer, Clark Gable, John Wayne, and Tyrone Power, and especially in 1952, when Welles's film was dubbed, for Raf Vallone as the perfume salesman Martín Jordán in the Spanish-Italian film noir *Los ojos dejan huellas* (*Eyes leave traces*), with a story of jealousy and murder. The connection with *Othello* could not be more obvious.

For Laurence Olivier in Burge's *Othello*, again a deep voice, that of Teófilo Martínez, was given cast. Martínez, a regular voice for John Gielgud, had also dubbed Orson Welles in *Mr Arkadin*, *Moby Dick* and *Touch of Evil*, but he had never dubbed Olivier (nor will he), which suggests that in this case, Martínez was chosen because his voice suited preconceived ideas about the role, and not because of the original actor. Closer to 1966, Martínez's voice would be associated by Spanish spectators with Alec Guinness in Anthony Mann's *The Fall of the Roman Empire* (released and dubbed in 1964), with Humphrey Boggart as Fred Dobbs in John Huston's 1948 film *The Treasure of the Sierra Madre* (dubbed for the second time in 1964), with Yul Brynner as Captain Mueller in B. Wicki's *Morituri* (1965) and with Erich von Stroheim as the faithful servant Max in Billy Wilder's *Sunset Boulevard* (released in 1950 / dubbed in 1965). In the same film, William Holden's Joe Gillis was dubbed by Félix Acaso, a middle voice that was also cast for Finlay's Iago in Burge's *Othello*, so that we find here an interesting pairing: the Shakespearean heroes would recall the two male characters starring in Wilder's Hollywood drama, with Acaso voicing the cynicism in both Iago and Gillis, and Martínez the excessive love in Othello and Max.

In the case of Parker's film, Branagh's Iago was dubbed by another middle voice, that of Jordi Brau, the regular dubbing actor for roles impersonated by Branagh. Around 1996, Brau's prolific career as a dubbing actor would lead his Iago to be inevitably associated in cinemas with a variety of actors (Dan Aykroyd, Brad Pitt, Sean Penn, Daniel Day-Lewis, Nicholas Cage, and Steven Seagal in A. Davis' *Under Siege*, released in

1992 and dubbed in 1993), and among them, those Brau regularly dubbed: Tom Hanks, Tom Cruise and Robin Williams. I find the reverberations of Robin Williams's 'Spanish' voice problematic since Iago in Spanish has the same voice as that of the character Alan Parrish in J. Johnston's *Jumanji* (1995/1996), of the protagonist in Coppola's *Jack* (1996), of the drag club owner Armand in M. Nichols' *The Birdcage* (1996, *Jaula de Grillos*) and of John Jacob Jingleheimer Schmidt in B. Kidron's *To Wong Foo* (1995), all four films dubbed in 1996; or later, when the DVD was released in 2007, the same voice as that of the nutty professor in L. Mayfield's *Flubber* (1997/1998) or of the desperate father in W. Becker's *Old Dogs* (2009, dubbed as *Dos Canguros muy maduros*). In my opinion, these reverberations turn the Spanish-speaking Iago into a more amiable and histrionic character, and a less malign villain than that impersonated by Branagh.

In Parker's *Othello*, the voice for Fishburne's Moor was provided by Ernesto Aura, one of the most highly reputed dubbing actors in Spain, who worked for this film as the dubbing director. His is a very deep voice that has a more imposing resonance than Fishburne's, while his acting expertise allows him to reproduce Fishburne's 'slow, quiet, rather frightening strength'.[35] Aura had not dubbed Fishburne as Ike Turner, but he had 'given' his voice to other roles performed by Fishburne: Charles Piper in K. Hooks' *Fled* (1996, *Fugitivos encadenados*), Furious Styles, the hero's father in J. Singleton's *Boyz N the Hood* (1991, *Los chicos del barrio*), and the professor of political science in J. Singleton's *Higher Learning* (1995, *Semillas de rencor*). Since he is also a prolific dubbing actor (the regular voice for Frank Sinatra in the 1960s, and of Clint Eastwood in the late 1960s), spectators in 1996 would not only recognize Aura's timbre in various Anglophone actors (Christopher Plummer, Abraham Murray, John Gielgud, James Coburn and Jeff Bridges, all of them dubbed in 1996), but would hear his voice matched to that of Jordi Brau as Steven Seagal in A. Davis' *Under Siege* (1992/1993), where Aura dubbed Tommy Lee Jones. Again, we find an interesting auditory coupling: Jordi Brau as both Iago and Chief Petty Office Ryback in *Under Siege* versus Aura as both Othello and the renegade, ex-CIA operative, Strannix.

However, the voice Spanish spectators would associate most with Aura, and therefore with Fishburne's Othello may be – again – problematic: that of Arnold Schwarzenegger in films such as R. Fleischer's *Conan the Destroyer* (1984), W. Hill's *Red Heat* (1988, *Danko*), P. M. Glaser's *The Running Man* (1987/1988, *Perseguido*), P. Verhoeven's *Total Recall* (1990, *Desafío total*), I. Reitman's *Kindergarten Cop* (1990/1991, *Poli de guardería*) and *Junior* (1994), J. Cameron's *True Lies* (1994, *Mentiras arriesgadas*),

B. Levant's *Jingle all the Way* (1996, *Un padre en apuros*), C. Russell's *Eraser* (1996), and more recently in *Borat* (2006) as detective John Kimble.[36] If aural connections with Schwarzenegger may be disturbing, this may be counterbalanced by the fact that Othello's blackness is reinforced by Aura's voice being associated with African American actors too, such as Samuel L. Jackson, Morgan Freeman and Sidney Poitier, as well as Mike Tyson as himself in J. Toback's *Black & White* (1999/2000).

Conclusion

The non-commercial subtitles gain from the use of previously published translations but are weak in the technical aspects of subtitling and thus impair an adequate viewing of the whole subtitled film. As for the commercially dubbed and subtitled DVDs, I would point out that they show quite a remarkable job, in the tradition of Spanish dubbing crafts-manship,[37] with leading male roles dubbed by experienced actors. In my personal interview with Guillermo Ramos (translator and adapter for Parker's *Othello*), he reported that this film took him a month (longer than usual), and like other Shakespeare films it was given a little extra time and care in comparison to other films. However, as I have observed earlier, lip synchronization in this dubbed *Othello* is not always satisfactory, and it may be worth exploring whether this objective is not given priority in films based on classical drama as it is in other (more realistic) genres in which verisimilitude is more important. I shared this observation with translator-adapter Guillermo Ramos and he agreed. If so, it may also be worth investigating whether this may constitute a translation norm in Spanish dubbing practices. But that is a matter for another discussion. I hope my comments have aroused an interest in this area of Shakespeare-on-screen studies, or at least have reinforced the idea that dubbed and subtitled 'Shakespeares' are also part of the filmic existence of Shakespeare and of the way Shakespeare is received around the world, and are therefore a cultural phenomenon we should pay more attention to.

Notes

1 S. Soncini, 'Shakespeare and its Dubble: Cultural Negotiations in Italian Audio-visual Transfers of *Henry V*', *Textus – English Studies in Italy* 15.1 (2002), 163.

2 In 2003, D. Delabastita (in 'Introduction. Shakespeare in Translation: A Bird's Eye View of Problems and Perspectives', *Ilha do Desterro* 45 [2003], 103–15) claimed that 'The translation of Shakespeare for film and TV (dubbing,

subtitling) has become a major new application' (113), but among the few
monographic articles on dubbed or subtitled Shakespeares I have been able to
compile, only G. Rabanaus ('Shakespeare in deutscher Fassung. Zur Synchronisation der Inszenierungen für das Fernsehen', *Jahrbuch Deutsche Shakespeare-
Gesellschaft West* (1982), 63–78) and S. Soncini's 'Shakespeare and its Dubble'
and 'Shakespeare e il suo doppio' (in M. Cavecchi and P. Caponi [eds.],
Shakespeare & Scespir [Milano: CUEM, 2005], 61–82) are published in
Shakespeare-related publications. For other publications, see www.uv.es/
tronch/Tra/BibliographyOnTranslation.html#AV_Sh (with due thanks to Sara
Soncini for providing a number of references).

3 Information about dubbing studios, directors and actors and actresses is taken
from www.eldoblaje.com. This database did not record Geoffrey Sax's TV
adaptation, dubbed and subtitled in Spanish and released as a DVD in 2008.
I thank José Ramón Díaz for alerting me to this version.

4 Frank Finlay won Best Actor in the 1966 San Sebastian Film Festival for his
performance of Iago in Burge's film.

5 See the database SHAKREP *Representaciones de Shakespeare en España*,
Universidad de Murcia, www.um.es/shakespeare/representaciones/.

6 At the end of 2004, a specific law was passed to protect women against
domestic violence (*Ley Orgánica, 1/2004*).

7 See F. Chaume, 'Film Studies and Translation Studies: Two Disciplines at
Stake in Audiovisual Translation', *Meta* 49.1 (2004), 12–24.

8 D. Delabastita, 'Shakespeare Translation', in M. Baker (ed.), *Routledge Encyclopedia of Translation Studies* (London and New York: Taylor & Francis
Group, 2005), 222–6.

9 H. Gottlieb, 'Subtitling: Diagonal Translation', *Perspectives: Studies in Translatology* 2.1 (1994), 101.

10 See M. Carroll and J. Ivarsson, 'Code of Good Subtitling Practice', *ESIST,*
www.esist.org/Index.htm; and J. Díaz Cintas, *Teoría y práctica de la subtitulación Inglés-Español* (Madrid: Ariel, 2003).

11 Díaz Cintas, *Teoría*, 202.

12 L. Astrana Marín, trans., *William Shakespeare: Tragedias,* vol. 1 of *Obras
Completas* (Madrid: Santillana, 2003 [1930]).

13 As in English, Spanish '*favor*' has sexual connotations.

14 Another example, now from a multi-line speech, 4.1.75–88: in the Manga Films
DVD for Welles's *Othello*, the equivalents for the adverbial 'all in all' (4.1.86)
and the exclamation 'Marry' (4.1.85) are omitted; the triplet 'the fleers, the gibes
and notable scorns' becomes two nouns without an adjective ('*sonrisas y burlas*'),
with 'fleers', which is '*sonrisas irónicas*' in the Instituto Shakespeare's translation,
becoming a neutral '*sonrisas*' ('smiles'); the details 'in every region of his face'
(4.1.81) are reduced to '*su rostro*' ('his face'), and the almost repetitive 'He hath
and is again to cope' (4.1.84) is condensed to '*ha de gozar*' ('he is to cope').

15 For instance, the Italian dubbed text of Cukor's 1936 *Romeo and Juliet* was
based on Giulio Carcano's nineteenth-century translation. See S. Soncini, 'Relocating Shakespeare: Cultural Negotiations in Italian Dubbed Versions of

Romeo and Juliet', in M. Pfister, and R. Hertel (eds.), *Performing National Identity: Anglo-Italian Cultural Transactions* (Amsterdam: Rodopi, 2008), 238.

16 Instituto Shakespeare, ed. and trans., *Othello* (Madrid: Cátedra, 1985).

17 Á. Pujante, trans., *Otelo* (Madrid: Espasa Calpe, 1991), rpt. in *William Shakespeare: Tragedias* (Madrid: Espasa Libros, 2010).

18 J. Clark, trans., *Obras de Shakespeare*, 5 vols. (Madrid: Medina y Navarro, 1872–6).

19 See W. Clemen, *The Development of Shakespeare's Imagery* (London: Methuen, 1951), 128–30.

20 E. A. J. Honigmann, ed., *Othello*, The Arden Shakespeare (Walton-on-Thames: Thomas Nelson, 1997), 80–1.

21 See Figure 1 at www.uv.es/shaxpere/oth_AV/OTH_Dub_Subt.html.

22 See among others S. Leonard, 'Progress Against the Law: Anime and Fandom, with the Key to the Globalization of Culture', *International Journal of Cultural Studies* 8.3 (September 2005), 281–305; and J. Díaz Cintas and P. Muñoz Sánchez, 'Fansubs: Audiovisual Translation in an Amateur Environment', *The Journal of Specialised Translation* 6 (July 2006), www.jostrans.org/issue06/art_diaz_munoz.pdf, accessed 10 May 2013.

23 For dubbing, see C. Whitman, *Through the Dubbing Glass* (Frankfurt: Peter Lang, 1992), F. Chaume, *Cine y traducción* (Madrid: Cátedra, 2004) and *Audiovisual Translation: Dubbing* (Manchester: St Jerome, 2012). For dubbed Shakespeare, see R. Paquin, 'In the Foot of the Giants: Translating Shakespeare for Dubbing', *Translation Journal* 5.3 (July 2001), www.bokorlang.com/journal/17dubb.htm; and J. Josek, 'A Czech Shakespeare?', in S. Bassnett and P. Bush (eds.), *The Translator as Writer* (London: Continuum, 2006), 92–4.

24 In an interview, Guillermo Ramos, the translator and adapter for Parker's *Othello*, acknowledged that there is quite a good number of changes between his script and the final dubbed version.

25 At 1:42 in MrLite100's 8/30 clip at www.youtube.com/watch?v=9rlGypoY71U, last accessed 25 April 2013. Clip also available as Figure 2 at www.uv.es/shaxpere/oth_AV/OTH_Dub_Subt.html.

26 T. Herbst, 'Dubbing and the Dubbed Text', in A. Trosborg (ed.), *Text Typology and Translation* (Amsterdam: John Benjamins, 1997), 292. Herbst calls this correlation 'nucleus sync'; other theorists, 'dramatic' or 'kinesic' synchronization.

27 At 5:28 in MrLite100's 19/30 clip at www.youtube.com/watch?v=Uoi1khVbKe4, last accessed 25 April 2013. Clip also available as Figure 3 at www.uv.es/shaxpere/oth_AV/OTH_Dub_Subt.html.

28 In Shakespeare, Desdemona does not dare to use the term 'whore' when she replies to Iago 'Such as she said my lord did say I was' (4.2.123), a line preserved in Parker's film.

29 The combined translation choice of '*adúltera*' and '*infiel*' at 4.2.84 can be traced back to the 1881 translation by the reputed scholar Marcelino Menéndez Pelayo (*Dramas de Guillermo Shakespeare: El Mercader de Venecia, Macbeth, Romeo y Julieta y Otelo* [Barcelona: Biblioteca Arte y Letras, 1881]), whose devout Catholicism and conservatism affect his rendition of Shakespeare. For

instance, he translates Othello's 'This is a subtle whore' (4.2.22) as '*Es moza ladina*' ('She is a cunning lass'), and Othello's 'I took you for that cunning whore of Venice' (4.2.93) as '*os confundí con aquella astuta veneciana*', where the equivalent of 'whore' is omitted.

30 E. Törnqvist, 'Fixed Pictures, Changing Words: Subtitling and Dubbing the Film *Babettes Gæstebud*, *Tijdschrift voor Skandinavistiek* 16.1 (1995), 49.

31 C. Koloszar, 'Übersetzen und Film – Probleme der Filmsynchronisation am Beispiel von *Henry V*, in C. Heiss and R. M. Bosinelli Bollettieri (eds.), *Traduzione multimediale per il cinema, la televisione e la scena* (Bologna: CLUEB, 1996), 167, quoted in Soncini, 'Dubble', 165.

32 L. Potter, *Othello: Shakespeare in Performance* (Manchester: Manchester University Press, 2002), 193.

33 M. Hindle, *Studying Shakespeare on Film* (Houndmills: Palgrave, 2007), 55.

34 See Potter, *Othello*, 193.

35 *Ibid.*

36 In pointing out these associations I am not suggesting that one should imagine Fishburne's Othello with the voice of Tommy Lee Jones or that of Arnold Schwarzenegger; rather one should imagine Fishburne, Jones and Schwarzenegger as having the same very deep voice.

37 See Alejandro Ávila, *La historia del doblaje cinematográfico* (Barcelona: CIMS, 1997).

WORKS CITED

Astrana Marín, L, trans., *William Shakespeare: Tragedias*, vol. 1 of *Obras Completas* (Madrid: Santillana, 2003 [1930]).

Ávila, A., *La historia del doblaje cinematográfico* (Barcelona: CIMS, 1997).

Carroll, M. and J. Ivarsson, 'Code of Good Subtitling Practice', *ESIST*, www. esist.org/Index.htm.

Chaume, F., *Audiovisual Translation: Dubbing* (Manchester: St Jerome, 2012).
Cine y traducción (Madrid: Cátedra, 2004).
'Film Studies and Translation Studies: Two Disciplines at Stake in Audiovisual Translation', *Meta* 49.1 (2004), 12–24.

Clark, J., trans., *Obras de Shakespeare*, 5 vols. (Madrid: Medina y Navarro, 1872–6).

Clemen, W., *The Development of Shakespeare's Imagery* (London: Methuen, 1951).

Delabastita, D., 'Introduction: Shakespeare in Translation: A Bird's Eye View of Problems and Perspectives', *Ilha do Desterro* 45 (2003), 103–15.
'Shakespeare Translation', in M. Baker (ed.), *Routledge Encyclopedia of Translation Studies* (London and New York: Taylor & Francis Group, 2005), 222–6.

Díaz Cintas, J., *Teoría y práctica de la subtitulación Inglés-Español* (Madrid: Ariel, 2003).

Díaz Cintas, J. and P. Muñoz Sánchez. 'Fansubs: Audiovisual Translation in an Amateur Environment', *The Journal of Specialised Translation* 6 (July 2006), www.jostrans.org/issue06/art_diaz_munoz.pdf, accessed 10 May 2013.

Gottlieb, H., 'Subtitling: Diagonal Translation', *Perspectives: Studies in Translatology* 2.1 (1994), 101–21.

Herbst, T., 'Dubbing and the Dubbed Text', in A. Trosborg (ed.), *Text Typology and Translation* (Amsterdam: John Benjamins, 1997), 291–308.

Hindle, M., *Studying Shakespeare on Film* (Houndmills: Palgrave, 2007).

Honigmann, E. A. J., ed., *Othello*, The Arden Shakespeare (Walton-on-Thames: Thomas Nelson, 1997).

Instituto Shakespeare, ed. and trans., *Othello* (Madrid: Cátedra, 1985).

Josek, J., 'A Czech Shakespeare?', in S. Bassnett and P. Bush (eds.), *The Translator as Writer* (London: Continuum, 2006), 84–94.

Koloszar, C., 'Übersetzen und Film – Probleme der Filmsynchronisation am Beispiel von Henry *V*', in C. Heiss and R. M. Bosinelli Bollettieri (eds.), *Traduzione multimediale per il cinema, la televisione e la scena* (Atti del convegno internazionale 'Traduzione multimediale per il cinema, la televisione e la scena', Forlì 26–28 ottobre 1995) (Bologna: CLUEB, 1996), 161–7.

Leonard, S., 'Progress Against the Law: Anime and Fandom, with the Key to the Globalization of Culture', *International Journal of Cultural Studies* 8.3 (September 2005), 281–305.

Menéndez Pelayo, M., trans., *Dramas de Guillermo Shakespeare: El Mercader de Venecia, Macbeth, Romeo y Julieta y Otelo* (Barcelona: Biblioteca Arte y Letras, 1881).

Paquin, R., 'In the Foot of the Giants: Translating Shakespeare for Dubbing', *Translation Journal* 5.3 (July 2001), www.bokorlang.com/journal/17dubb.htm.

Potter, L., *Othello: Shakespeare in Performance* (Manchester: Manchester University Press, 2002).

Pujante, Á., trans., *Otelo* (Madrid: Espasa Calpe, 1991), rpt. in *William Shakespeare: Tragedias* (Madrid: Espasa Libros, 2010).

Rabanaus, G., 'Shakespeare in deutscher Fassung. Zur Synchronisation der Inszenierungen für das Fernsehen', *Jahrbuch Deutsche Shakespeare-Gesellschaft West* (1982), 63–78.

Soncini, S., 'Shakespeare and its Dubble: Cultural Negotiations in Italian Audio-visual Transfers of *Henry V*', *Textus – English Studies in Italy* 15.1 (2002), 63–186.

'Shakespeare e il suo doppio', in M. Cavecchi and P. Caponi (eds.), *Shakespeare & Scespir* (Milano: CUEM, 2005), 61–82.

'Re-locating Shakespeare: Cultural Negotiations in Italian Dubbed Versions of *Romeo and Juliet*', in M. Pfister and R. Hertel (eds.), *Performing National Identity: Anglo-Italian Cultural Transactions* (Amsterdam: Rodopi, 2008), 235–48.

Törnqvist, E., 'Fixed Pictures, Changing Words: Subtitling and Dubbing the Film *Babettes Gæstebud*', *Tijdschrift voor Skandinavistiek* 16.1 (1995), 47–64.

Whitman, C., *Through the Dubbing Glass* (Frankfurt: Peter Lang, 1992).

CHAPTER 13

Othello *on screen*
Select film-bibliography

José Ramón Díaz Fernández

The present chapter seeks to provide a selective reference guide to the screen adaptations of *Othello*. This essay is divided into three sections listing films, television adaptations as well as derivatives and selected citations. In each section, adaptations are classified in chronological order followed by an alphabetical list of relevant critical studies, and a system of cross-references has been designed for those entries making reference to two or more screen adaptations. I have included theatrical productions such as Trevor Nunn's *Othello* (1990) in the television section if there are significant changes between the original stage design and the television programme, and in these cases I have only selected studies making specific reference to the recorded version. As far as the derivatives and citations are concerned, I have only listed those which have been discussed by critics. For additional titles and/or bibliographical entries related to *Othello* on screen, the reader may check the comprehensive online version of the present film-bibliography on the Cambridge University Press website. Most entries here have been written in English, but I have also added a few relevant references in French, German and Italian such as Youssef Ishaghpour's three-volume *Orson Welles cinéaste: Une caméra visible* (2001). Where possible, place names usually appear in their English version (e.g., 'Naples' instead of 'Napoli'). All electronic addresses were correct at the time of going to press.

I. FILM ADAPTATIONS

1.1   *Otello.* Dir. Gerolamo Lo Savio (Italy, 1909).

1 Ball, Robert Hamilton, 'Strange Motions: The Continent (1908–1911)', in his *Shakespeare on Silent Film: A Strange Eventful History.* New York: Theatre Arts Books, 1968, 90–134.

I would like to thank the Andalusian Regional Government for funding the research that allowed me to work at the Folger Shakespeare Library and the British Film Institute and led to the writing of this essay (research project no. P07-HUM-02507).

2 Buchanan, Judith, '"Wresting an Alphabet": Continental European Shakespeare Films, 1907–22', in her *Shakespeare on Film*. Harlow: Pearson Longman, 2005, 49–70.

3 Buchanan, Judith, 'Conflicted Allegiances in Shakespeare Films of the Transitional Era', in her *Shakespeare on Silent Film: An Excellent Dumb Discourse*. Cambridge University Press, 2009, 74–104.

1.2   *Otello*. Dir. Arturo Ambrosio and Arrigo Frusta (Italy, 1914).

4 Ball, Robert Hamilton, 'Increase the Reels: 1912 to World War I', in his *Shakespeare on Silent Film: A Strange Eventful History*. New York: Theatre Arts Books, 1968, 135–215.

5 Potter, Lois, 'Interval: Alternative *Othello*s in the Modern Age', in her *Othello*. Manchester University Press, 2002, 86–103.
See also 2.

1.3   *Othello* / *The Moor*. Dir. Dimitri Buchowetzki (Germany, 1922).

6 Ball, Robert Hamilton, 'Let Me Have Leave to Speak: 1920 to Sound', in his *Shakespeare on Silent Film: A Strange Eventful History*. New York: Theatre Arts Books, 1968, 263–99.

7 Buchanan, Judith, 'Asta Nielsen and Emil Jannings: Stars of German Shakespeare Films of the Early 1920s', in her *Shakespeare on Silent Film: An Excellent Dumb Discourse*. Cambridge University Press, 2009, 217–51.

8 Buhler, Stephen M., 'Ocular Proof: Three Versions of *Othello*', in his *Shakespeare in the Cinema: Ocular Proof*. Albany: State University of New York Press, 2002, 11–31.

9 Davies, Anthony, '"An extravagant and wheeling stranger of here and everywhere": Characterising Othello on Film: Exploring Seven Film Adaptations'. *Shakespeare in Southern Africa* 23 (2011): 11–19.

10 Guneratne, Anthony R., 'The Exfoliating Folio, or Transnational and International Avant-Gardes from Bernhardt's *Hamlets* to Hollywood's Europeans', in his *Shakespeare, Film Studies, and the Visual Cultures of Modernity*. New York and Basingstoke: Palgrave Macmillan, 2008, 115–71.

11 Hodgdon, Barbara, 'Kiss Me Deadly; or, the Des/Demonized Spectacle', in *'Othello': New Perspectives*, ed. Virginia Mason Vaughan and Kent Cartwright. Rutherford: Fairleigh Dickinson University Press, 1991, 214–55.

12 Howlett, Kathy M., 'Interpreting the Tragic Loading of the Bed in Cinematic Adaptations of *Othello*', in *Approaches to Teaching Shakespeare's 'Othello'*, ed. Peter Erickson and Maurice Hunt. New York: Modern Language Association, 2005, 169–79.

13 Jackson, Russell, 'Two Silent Shakespeares: *Richard III* and *Othello*'. *Cineaste* 28.2 (Spring 2003): 48–51.

14 Taylor, Neil, 'National and Racial Stereotypes in Shakespeare Films', in *The Cambridge Companion to Shakespeare on Film*, ed. Russell Jackson. 2nd edn. Cambridge University Press, 2007, 267–79.
See also 2, 5.

1.4   *Othello*. Dir. Orson Welles (Morocco and Italy, 1952).

15 Aebischer, Pascale, 'Murderous Male Moors: Gazing at Race in *Titus Andronicus* and *Othello*', in her *Shakespeare's Violated Bodies: Stage and Screen Performance*. Cambridge University Press, 2004, 102–50.

16 Aebischer, Pascale, 'Vampires, Cannibals, and Victim-Revengers: Watching Shakespearean Tragedy through Horror Film'. *Shakespeare Jahrbuch* 143 (2007): 119–31.

17 Anderegg, Michael, *Orson Welles, Shakespeare, and Popular Culture*. New York: Columbia University Press, 1999.

18 Anile, Alberto, *Orson Welles in Italy*. Trans. Marcus Perryman. Bloomington: Indiana University Press, 2013.

19 Bent, Geoffrey, 'Three Green-Eyed Monsters: Acting as Applied Criticism in Shakespeare's *Othello*'. *Antioch Review* 56 (1998): 358–73.

20 Berthomé, Jean-Pierre, 'Les labyrinthes d'*Othello*: Légendes et réalites d'un tournage'. *Positif* 449–50 (Juillet-Août 1998): 40–8.

21 Berthomé, Jean-Pierre, and François Thomas, '*Othello* 1949–1952', in their *Orson Welles at Work*. Trans. Imogen Forster, Roger Leverdier and Trista Selous. London and New York: Phaidon, 2008, 164–85.

22 Buchman, Lorne M., 'Orson Welles's *Othello*: A Study of Time in Shakespeare's Tragedy'. *Shakespeare Survey* 39 (1987): 53–65.

23 Buhler, Stephen M., 'The Revenge of the Actor-Manager', in his *Shakespeare in the Cinema: Ocular Proof*. Albany: State University of New York Press, 2002, 95–123.

24 Caretti, Laura, 'La recita del potere: Orson Welles e Shakespeare', in *Shakespeare al cinema*, ed. Isabella Imperiali. Rome: Bulzoni, 2000, 65–76.

25 Cartmell, Deborah, 'Shakespeare, Film and Race: Screening *Othello* and *The Tempest*', in her *Interpreting Shakespeare on Screen*. Basingstoke: Macmillan, 2000, 67–93.

26 Cartmell, Deborah, 'Shakespeare and Race: *Othello* I.iii', in *Talking Shakespeare: Shakespeare into the Millennium*, ed. Deborah Cartmell and Michael Scott. Basingstoke and New York: Palgrave, 2001, 138–48.

27 Collick, John, 'Symbolism in Shakespeare Film', in his *Shakespeare, Cinema and Society*. Manchester University Press, 1989, 80–106.

28 Crowl, Samuel, 'One Murderous Image: Welles's *Othello*', in his *Shakespeare Observed: Studies in Performance on Stage and Screen*. Athens: Ohio University Press, 1992, 51–63.

29 Davies, Anthony, 'Orson Welles's *Othello*', in his *Filming Shakespeare's Plays: The Adaptations of Laurence Olivier, Orson Welles, Peter Brook and Akira Kurosawa*. Cambridge University Press, 1988, 100–18.

30 Davies, Anthony, 'Filming *Othello*', in *Shakespeare and the Moving Image: The Plays on Film and Television*, ed. Anthony Davies and Stanley Wells. Cambridge University Press, 1994, 196–210.

31 Del Ministro, Maurizio, '*Othello' di Welles*. Rome: Bulzoni, 2000.

32 Donaldson, Peter S., 'Mirrors and M/Others: The Welles *Othello*', in his *Shakespearean Films/Shakespearean Directors*. Boston and London: Unwin Hyman, 1990, 93–126.

33 Garis, Robert, 'Welles's Shakespeare', in his *The Films of Orson Welles*. Cambridge University Press, 2004, 127–66.

34 Gil, Daniel Juan, 'Avant-Garde Technique and the Visual Grammar of Sexuality in Orson Welles's Shakespeare Films'. *Borrowers and Lenders: The Journal of Shakespeare and Appropriation* 1.2 (Fall/Winter 2005): www. borrowers.uga.edu/781447/display.

35 Guneratne, Anthony R., '"Thou Dost Usurp Authority": Beerbohm Tree, Reinhardt, Olivier, Welles, and the Politics of Adapting Shakespeare', in *A Concise Companion to Shakespeare on Screen*, ed. Diana E. Henderson. Malden and Oxford: Blackwell, 2006, 31–53.

36 Guneratne, Anthony R., 'Genre, Style, and the *Politique des Auteurs*: Orson Welles versus "William Shakespeare"', in his *Shakespeare, Film Studies, and the Visual Cultures of Modernity*. New York and Basingstoke: Palgrave Macmillan, 2008, 173–209.

37 Hall, Joan Lord, 'The Play in Performance: *Othello* on Film', in her *'Othello': A Guide to the Play*. Westport and London: Greenwood, 1999, 158–88.

38 Hatchuel, Sarah, 'Case Studies: Trance on Screen: The "Ocular Proof" and "Fainting" Scenes in *Othello*', in her *Shakespeare, from Stage to Screen*. Cambridge University Press, 2004, 162–5.

39 Heylin, Clinton, 'The Jigsaw Pictures', in his *Despite the System: Orson Welles versus the Hollywood Studios*. Edinburgh: Canongate, 2005, 255–77.

40 Holderness, Graham, 'Shakespeare's Venice on Film', in his *Shakespeare and Venice*. Farnham and Burlington: Ashgate, 2010, 123–34.

41 Howlett, Kathy M., 'The Voyeuristic Pleasures of Perversion: Orson Welles's *Othello*', in her *Framing Shakespeare on Film*. Athens: Ohio University Press, 2000, 52–91.

42 Hurwitz, Gregg Andrew, 'Transforming Text: Iago's Infection in Welles' *Othello*'. *Word and Image* 13 (1997): 333–9.

43 Impastato, David, 'Orson Welles's *Othello* and the Welles-Smith Restoration: Definitive Version?' *Shakespeare Bulletin* 10.4 (Fall 1992): 38–41.

44 Ishaghpour, Youssef, 'La transcendance de la forme: *La Tragédie d'Othello*', in his *Orson Welles cinéaste: Une caméra visible*, vol. 3: *Les films de la période nomade*. Paris: Éditions de la Différence, 2001, 79–305.

45 Jacobs, Alfred, 'Orson Welles's *Othello*: Shakespeare Meets Film Noir', in *Shakespeare and the Twentieth Century: The Selected Proceedings of the International Shakespeare Association World Congress, Los Angeles, 1996*, ed. Jonathan Bate, Jill L. Levenson and Dieter Mehl. Newark: University of Delaware Press, 1998, 113–24.

46 Jess-Cooke, Carolyn, 'Film Style', in her *Shakespeare on Film: Such Stuff as Dreams Are Made of*. London: Wallflower, 2007, 55–81.

47 Jones, Nicholas, 'A Bogus Hero: Welles's *Othello* and the Construction of Race'. *Shakespeare Bulletin* 23.1 (Spring 2005): 9–28.

48 Jorgens, Jack J., 'Orson Welles's *Othello*', in his *Shakespeare on Film*. 1977, rpt, Lanham and London: University Press of America, 1991, 175–90.

49 Lake, James H., 'The Effects of Primacy and Recency upon Audience Response to Two Film Versions of *Othello*'. *Shakespeare Newsletter* 56 (2006–07): 45–6.

50 Leutrat, Jean-Louis, 'Décentrements: *Othello* (1952)', in his *Kaléidoscope: Analyses de films*. Presses Universitaires de Lyon, 1988, 39–53.

51 MacLiammóir, Micheál, *Put Money in Thy Purse: The Diary of the Film of 'Othello'*. 1952, rpt as *Put Money in Thy Purse: The Filming of Orson Welles's 'Othello'*. London: Virgin, 1994.

52 Mancini, Carmela Bruna, 'Visioni neobarocche: Shakespeare e il cinema', in *Tragiche risonanze shakespeariane*, ed. Laura Di Michele. Naples: Liguori, 2001, 285–327.

53 Manvell, Roger, 'Shakespeare by Orson Welles', in his *Shakespeare and the Film*. Revised, updated edn. South Brunswick and New York: A. S. Barnes, 1979, 55–71.

54 Marienstras, Richard, 'Orson Welles, interprète et continuateur de Shakespeare'. *Positif* 167 (Mars 1975): 36–44.

55 Mason, Pamela, 'Orson Welles and Filmed Shakespeare', in *The Cambridge Companion to Shakespeare on Film*, ed. Russell Jackson. 2nd edn. Cambridge University Press, 2007, 187–202.

56 McBride, Joseph, 'Welles and Shakespeare: *Macbeth* and *Othello*', in his *Orson Welles*. New York: Da Capo, 1996, 111–28.

57 Mellet, Laurent, and Shannon Wells-Lassagne, 'Adaptation et réadaptation', in their *Étudier l'adaptation filmique: Cinéma anglais – Cinéma américain*. Presses Universitaires de Rennes, 2010, 97–120.

58 Mereghetti, Paolo, 'Shakespeare: *Macbeth*, *Othello*', in his *Orson Welles*. Revised English edn. Paris: Cahiers du cinéma, 2011, 55–65.

59 Morelli, Annamaria, '*Othello* di Orson Welles: La passione dello sguardo nella tragedia *noir*', in her *La scena della visione: L'eccesso barocco e la teatralità shakespeariana*. Rome: Bulzoni, 1997, 145–55.

60 Mullini, Roberta, 'Il paradiso perduto, ovvero *Othello* di Orson Welles'. *Studi Urbinati*, Serie B: *Scienze umane e sociali* 70 (2000): 397–414.

61 Naremore, James, 'The Gypsy: I. *Othello*', in his *The Magic World of Orson Welles*. Revised edn. Dallas: Southern Methodist University Press, 1989, 176–82.

62 Petit, J.-P., 'Note sur deux *Othello*', in *Shakespeare à la télévision*, ed. Michèle Willems. Publications de l'Université de Rouen, 1987, 143–9.

63 Potter, Lois, 'Emilia in *Othello*: The Problem of the Unfilmic Character', in *Shakespeare et le cinéma: Actes du Congrès de 1998*, ed. Patricia Dorval. Paris: Société Française Shakespeare, 1998, 149–57.

64 Potter, Lois, 'The Robeson Legacy I: White Othellos on Film, Stage and Television', in her *Othello*. Manchester University Press, 2002, 135–56.

65 Prümm, Hans-Joachim, 'Orson Welles' *Othello*', in his *Film-Script: William Shakespeare. Eine Untersuchung der Film-Bearbeitung von Shakespeares Dramen*

am Beispiel ausgewählter Tragödien-Verfilmungen von 1945–1985. Amsterdam: Grüner, 1987, 248–71.

66 Quarenghi, Paola, 'Otello, Iago e gli inganni del cinema', in her *Shakespeare e gli inganni del cinema*. Rome: Bulzoni, 2002, 95–137.

67 Rasmus, Agnieszka, '"Life's but a walking shadow": *Mise-en-scène* in Orson Welles's *Macbeth* and *Othello*', in her *Filming Shakespeare, from Metatheatre to Metacinema*. Frankfurt: Peter Lang, 2008, 167–71.

68 Roger, Philippe, 'La seconde mort d'*Othello*: Entretien avec Jean-Pierre Berthomé'. *CinémAction* 97 (2000): 196–8.

69 Rosenbaum, Jonathan, 'Improving Mr Welles'. *Sight and Sound* ns 2.6 (Oct. 1992): 28–30.

70 Rosenbaum, Jonathan, '*Othello* Goes Hollywood', in his *Discovering Orson Welles*. Berkeley: University of California Press, 2007, 163–74.

71 Rothwell, Kenneth S., 'Orson Welles: Shakespeare for the Art Houses', in his *A History of Shakespeare on Screen: A Century of Film and Television*. 2nd edn. Cambridge University Press, 2004, 69–90.

72 Rutter, Carol Chillington, 'Looking at Shakespeare's Women on Film', in *The Cambridge Companion to Shakespeare on Film*, ed. Russell Jackson. 2nd edn. Cambridge University Press, 2007, 245–66.

73 Stone, James W., 'Black and White as Technique in Orson Welles's *Othello*'. *Literature/Film Quarterly* 30 (2002): 189–93.

74 Tarasco, Matteo, 'Marlowe, Welles e il mistero del terzo feretro'. *Cineforum* 36.356 (Iuglio-Agosto 1996): 32–7.

75 Tatspaugh, Patricia, 'The Tragedies of Love on Film', in *The Cambridge Companion to Shakespeare on Film*, ed. Russell Jackson. 2nd edn. Cambridge University Press, 2007, 141–64.

76 Thomas, François, 'La tragédie d'*Othello*'. *Positif* 424 (Juin 1996): 70–6.

77 Thomas, François, 'Orson Welles et le remodelage du texte shakespearien', in *Shakespeare et le cinéma: Actes du Congrès de 1998*, ed. Patricia Dorval. Montpellier: Société Française Shakespeare, 1998, 171–82.

78 Vaughan, Virginia Mason, 'Orson Welles and the Patriarchal Eye', in her *'Othello': A Contextual History*. Cambridge University Press, 1994, 199–216.

79 Willson, Robert F., Jr, 'Strange New Worlds: Constructions of Venice and Cyprus in the Orson Welles and Oliver Parker Films of *Othello*'. *Shakespeare Bulletin* 20.3 (Summer 2002): 37–9.

80 Zambenedetti, Alberto, 'Introducing Shakespeare: The Incipit in Orson Welles's Adaptations'. *Journal of Adaptation in Film & Performance* 4 (2011): 39–52.
See also 9, 11, 12, 14.

1.5 *Othello*. Dir. Sergei Yutkevich (USSR, 1955).

81 Dorval, Patricia, '*Othello*: "A pageant to keep us in false gaze" ou la part de l'invisible aperçu occultement', in *Shakespeare et le cinéma: Actes du Congrès de 1998*, ed. Patricia Dorval. Montpellier: Société Française Shakespeare, 1998, 105–14.

82 Manvell, Roger, 'The Russian Adaptations: Yutkevitch and Kozintsev', in his *Shakespeare and the Film*. Revised, updated edn. South Brunswick and New York: A. S. Barnes, 1979, 72–85.

83 Osborne, Laurie E., 'Filming Shakespeare in a Cultural Thaw: Soviet Appropriations of Shakespearean Treacheries in 1955–6'. *Textual Practice* 9 (1995): 325–47.

84 Prümm, Hans-Joachim, 'Sergej Jutkewitschs *Othello*', in his *Film-Script: William Shakespeare. Eine Untersuchung der Film-Bearbeitung von Shakespeares Dramen am Beispiel ausgewählter Tragödien-Verfilmungen von 1945–1985*. Amsterdam: Grüner, 1987, 197–218.

85 Rothwell, Kenneth S., 'Other Shakespeares: Translation and Expropriation', in his *A History of Shakespeare on Screen: A Century of Film and Television*. 2nd edn. Cambridge University Press, 2004, 160–91.

86 Soncini, Sara, 'Fra teatro, cinema e televisione: La "scena della seduzione" in alcune regie contemporanee di *Othello*', in *'Othello': Voci, echi, risonanze: Seminario interdisciplinare dell'Istituto di Anglistica 1996/97*, ed. Anna Anzi and Paolo Caponi. Milan: CUEM, 1998, 176–98.

87 Yutkevitch, Sergei, 'My Way with Shakespeare'. *Films and Filming* 4.1 (Oct. 1957): 8, 32.

88 Yutkevitch, Sergei, '*Othello*, wie ich ihn sehe', in his *Kontrapunkt der Regie*. Berlin: Henschel, 1965, 229–87.

See also 5, 8, 9, 14, 15, 30, 63, 75.

1.6   *Othello* / *Othello: The Moor of Venice*. Dir. Stuart Burge (Great Britain, 1965).

89 Buhler, Stephen M., 'Documentary Shakespeare', in his *Shakespeare in the Cinema: Ocular Proof*. Albany: State University of New York Press, 2002, 33–49.

90 Fisher, James E., 'Olivier and the Realistic *Othello*'. *Literature/Film Quarterly* 1 (1973): 321–31.

91 Green, Douglas E., 'Estranging Bedfellows: Early Modern Cinema Today', in *Presentism, Gender, and Sexuality in Shakespeare*, ed. Evelyn Gajowski. Basingstoke and New York: Palgrave Macmillan, 2009, 179–91.

92 Jorgens, Jack J., 'Stuart Burge and John Dexter's *Othello*', in his *Shakespeare on Film*. 1977, rpt, Lanham and London: University Press of America, 1991, 191–206.

93 Manvell, Roger, 'Theatre into Film', in his *Shakespeare and the Film*. Revised, updated edn. South Brunswick and New York: A. S. Barnes, 1979, 114–32.

94 McGuire, Philip C., 'Whose Work Is This? Loading the Bed in *Othello*', in *Shakespearean Illuminations: Essays in Honor of Marvin Rosenberg*, ed. Jay L. Halio and Hugh Richmond. Newark: University of Delaware Press, 1998, 70–92.

95 Murray, Timothy, 'Dirty Stills: Arcadian Retrospection, Cinematic Hieroglyphs, and Blackness Run Riot in Olivier's *Othello*', in his *Like a Film: Ideological Fantasy on Screen, Camera and Canvas*. London and New York: Routledge, 1993, 101–23.

96 Pilkington, Ace G., 'Othello's Stature: Three Filmed Versions of the Moor'. *Encyclia: The Journal of the Utah Academy of Sciences, Arts, and Letters* 68 (1991): 301–14.

97 Rothwell, Kenneth S., 'Laurence Olivier Directs Shakespeare', in his *A History of Shakespeare on Screen: A Century of Film and Television.* 2nd edn. Cambridge University Press, 2004, 47–68.
   See also 9, 12, 14, 15, 19, 25, 30, 37, 62, 63, 64, 66, 75, 86.

1.7   *Othello.* Dir. Liz White (USA, 1966).

98 Buhler, Stephen M., 'Shakespeare the Filmmaker', in his *Shakespeare in the Cinema: Ocular Proof.* Albany: State University of New York Press, 2002, 73–94.

99 Donaldson, Peter S., '"Haply for I Am Black": Liz White's *Othello*', in his *Shakespearean Films/Shakespearean Directors.* Boston and London: Unwin Hyman, 1990, 127–43.
   See also 14.

1.8   *Othello.* Dir. Oliver Parker (USA, 1995).

100 Aldama, Frederick Luis, 'Race, Cognition, and Emotion: Shakespeare on Film'. *College Literature* 33.1 (Winter 2006): 197–213.

101 Anderegg, Michael, 'Branagh and the Sons of Ken', in his *Cinematic Shakespeare.* Lanham: Rowman and Littlefield, 2004, 118–47.

102 Berthomieu, Pierre, *Kenneth Branagh: Traînes de feu, rosées de sang.* Paris: Jean-Michel Place, 1998.

103 Buchanan, Judith, 'Virgin and Ape, Venetian and Infidel: Labellings of Otherness in Oliver Parker's *Othello*', in *Shakespeare, Film, Fin de Siècle,* ed. Mark Thornton Burnett and Ramona Wray. Basingstoke: Macmillan, 2000, 179–202.

104 Burnett, Mark Thornton, 'Contemporary Film Versions of the Tragedies', in *A Companion to Shakespeare's Works,* ed. Richard Dutton and Jean E. Howard, vol. 1: *The Tragedies.* Malden and Oxford: Blackwell, 2003, 262–83.

105 Burnett, Mark Thornton, 'Racial Identities, Global Economies', in his *Filming Shakespeare in the Global Marketplace.* Basingstoke and New York: Palgrave Macmillan, 2007, 66–86.

106 Coursen, H. R., 'Two Tragedies of Wrong Conclusions: Parker's *Othello* and Luhrmann's *Romeo + Juliet*', in his *Shakespeare: The Two Traditions.* Madison and Teaneck: Fairleigh Dickinson University Press, 1999, 174–97.

107 Crowl, Samuel, 'Checkmate: Parker's *Othello*', in his *Shakespeare at the Cineplex: The Kenneth Branagh Era.* Athens: Ohio University Press, 2003, 91–104.

108 Crowl, Samuel, '"Ocular Proof": Teaching *Othello* in Performance', in *Approaches to Teaching Shakespeare's 'Othello',* ed. Peter Erickson and Maurice Hunt. New York: Modern Language Association, 2005, 162–8.

109 Daileader, Celia R., 'Nude Shakespeare in Film and Nineties Popular Feminism', in *Shakespeare and Sexuality*, ed. Catherine M. S. Alexander and Stanley Wells. Cambridge University Press, 2001, 183–200.

110 Daileader, Celia R., 'Conclusion: "White women are snaky": *Jungle Fever* and Its Discontents', in her *Racism, Misogyny, and the 'Othello' Myth: Inter-racial Couples from Shakespeare to Spike Lee*. Cambridge University Press, 2005, 208–22.

111 Dorval, Patricia, 'Shakespeare on Screen: Threshold Aesthetics in Oliver Parker's *Othello*'. *Early Modern Literary Studies* 6.1 (May 2000): 1.1–15. extra. shu.ac.uk/emls/06–1/dorvothe.htm.

112 Green, Douglas E., 'Shakespeare, Branagh, and the "Queer Traitor": Close Encounters in the Shakespearean Classroom', in *The Reel Shakespeare: Alternative Cinema and Theory*, ed. Lisa S. Starks and Courtney Lehmann. Madison and Teaneck: Fairleigh Dickinson University Press, 2002, 191–211.

113 Hodgdon, Barbara, 'Race-ing *Othello*, Re-EnGendering White-out', in her *The Shakespeare Trade: Performances and Appropriations*. Philadelphia: University of Pennsylvania Press, 1998, 39–73.

114 Hodgdon, Barbara, 'Race-ing *Othello*, Re-engendering White-out, II', in *Shakespeare, the Movie, II: Popularizing the Plays on Film, TV, Video, and DVD*, ed. Richard Burt and Lynda E. Boose. London and New York: Routledge, 2003, 89–104.

115 Lake, James H., 'Auteurial Control of Audience Response in Some Film Adaptations of Shakespearean Tragedy'. *Shakespeare Bulletin* 16.3 (Summer 1998): 33–5.

116 Mieszkowski, Sylvia, 'Impossible Passions – Shakespeare and Parker: *Othello*'. *Wissenschaftliches Seminar Online* 1 (2003): 15–23. shakespeare-gesellschaft.de/en/publications/seminar/issue2003/mieszkowski.html.

117 Patricia, Anthony Guy, '"Through the Eyes of the Present": Screening the Male Homoerotics of Shakespearean Drama', in *Presentism, Gender, and Sexuality in Shakespeare*, ed. Evelyn Gajowski. Basingstoke and New York: Palgrave Macmillan, 2009, 157–78.

118 Potter, Lois, '*Othello* at the End of the Century: Sex and Soldiers', in her *Othello*. Manchester University Press, 2002, 185–217.

119 Rasmus, Agnieszka, 'When the Villain Meets the Camera's Gaze: Whose Tragedy?', in her *Filming Shakespeare, from Metatheatre to Metacinema*. Frankfurt: Peter Lang, 2008, 68–79.

120 Rasmus, Agnieszka, 'Shakespeare Villains as Cinematographers', in her *Filming Shakespeare, from Metatheatre to Metacinema*. Frankfurt: Peter Lang, 2008, 79–90.

121 Rothwell, Kenneth S., 'The Renaissance of Shakespeare in Moving Images', in his *A History of Shakespeare on Screen: A Century of Film and Television*. 2nd edn. Cambridge University Press, 2004, 219–47.

122 'Shakespeare in the Cinema: A Film Directors' Symposium with Peter Brook, Sir Peter Hall, Richard Loncraine, Baz Luhrmann, [Trevor Nunn,] Oliver Parker, Roman Polanski and Franco Zeffirelli'. *Cineaste* 24.1 (1998): 48–55.

123 Starks, Lisa S., 'The Veiled (Hot) Bed of Race and Desire: Parker's *Othello* and the Stereotype as Screen Fetish'. *Post Script: Essays in Film and the Humanities* 17.1 (Fall 1997): 64–78.

124 Starks, Lisa S., 'An Interview with Michael Maloney'. *Post Script: Essays in Film and the Humanities* 17.1 (Fall 1997): 79–87.

125 White, Mark, 'Sweet Prince', in his *Kenneth Branagh*. London: Faber and Faber, 2005, 190–212.

See also 8, 9, 12, 14, 15, 19, 25, 26, 37, 38, 49, 57, 63, 72, 75, 79, 81, 91, 94.

2. TELEVISION ADAPTATIONS

2.1 *Othello*. Dir. Delbert Mann (NBC, 1950).

126 Anderegg, Michael, 'Electronic Shakespeares: Televisual Histories', in his *Cinematic Shakespeare*. Lanham: Rowman and Littlefield, 2004, 148–76.

127 Coe, Fred, 'Televising Shakespeare'. *Theatre Arts* 35.4 (Apr. 1951): 56, 96.

2.2 *Othello*. Dir. David Greene (CBC, 1953).

128 Griffin, Alice Venezky, 'Shakespeare through the Camera's Eye–*Julius Caesar* in Motion Pictures; *Hamlet* and *Othello* on Television'. *Shakespeare Quarterly* 4 (1953): 331–6.

129 Rosenberg, Marvin, 'Shakespeare on TV: An Optimistic Survey'. *Quarterly of Film, Radio, and Television* 9 (1954): 166–74.

2.3 *Othello*. Dir. Claude Barma (RTF, 1962).

130 Hatchuel, Sarah, and Nathalie Vienne-Guerrin, '"O monstrous": Claude Barma's French 1962 TV *Othello*', in *Shakespeare on Screen in Francophonia*, ed. Patricia Dorval and Nathalie Vienne-Guerrin: www.shakscreen.org/analysis/barma_othello/.

2.4 *Othello*. Dir. Jonathan Miller (BBC, 1981).

131 Boose, Lynda E., 'Grossly Gaping Viewers and Jonathan Miller's *Othello*', in *Shakespeare, the Movie: Popularizing the Plays on Film, TV, and Video*, ed. Lynda E. Boose and Richard Burt. London and New York: Routledge, 1997, 186–97.

132 Fenwick, Henry, 'The Production', in *'Othello': The BBC TV Shakespeare*, ed. Peter Alexander et al. London: British Broadcasting Corporation, 1981, 18–28.

133 Hall, Joan Lord, 'The Play in Performance: *Othello* on Television', in her *'Othello': A Guide to the Play*. Westport and London: Greenwood, 1999, 188–200.

134 Willems, Raymond, 'L'*Othello* de Jonathan Miller', in *Shakespeare à la télévision*, ed. Michèle Willems. Publications de l'Université de Rouen, 1987, 151–5.

135 Willis, Susan, 'Jonathan Miller: Producer and Director', in her *The BBC Shakespeare Plays: Making the Televised Canon*. Chapel Hill and London: University of North Carolina Press, 1991, 107–34.
See also 15, 63, 64, 94, 96.

2.5   *Othello*. Dir. Andrzej Chrzanowski (Telewizja Polska, 1981/84).

136 Fabiszak, Jacek, 'Shakespeare in the Space of the Studio: The 1981/1984 *Othello*, or Iago as Setting', in his *Polish Televised Shakespeares: A Study of Shakespeare Productions within the Television Theatre Format*. Poznań: Motivex, 2005, 142–50.
137 Fabiszak, Jacek, 'Shakespeare's Histories and Polish History: Television Productions of *Henry IV* (1975), *Richard III* (1989) and *Othello* (1981/84)'. *Multicultural Shakespeare: Translation, Appropriation, Performance* 4 (2007): 59–65, multicultural.online.uni.lodz.pl/index.php/content,article,19.

2.6   *Othello / Othello: The Moor of Venice*. Dir. Franklin Melton (Bard Productions, 1985).

138 Cook, Ann Jennalie, 'Bard Productions: *Othello*'. *Shakespeare on Film Newsletter* 12.1 (Dec. 1987): 1, 4.
139 Coursen, H. R., 'A Space for Shakespeare', in his *Shakespearean Performance as Interpretation*. Newark: University of Delaware Press, 1992, 205–16.
140 Potter, Lois, 'The Robeson Legacy II: Casting *Othello*, 1960–97', in her *Othello*. Manchester University Press, 2002, 157–84.
See also 96.

2.7   *Othello*. Dir. Janet Suzman (Channel Four, 1988).

141 Coursen, H. R., 'The Case for a Black Othello', in his *Watching Shakespeare on Television*. Rutherford: Fairleigh Dickinson University Press, 1993, 126–62.
142 Seeff, Adele, '*Othello* at the Market Theatre'. *Shakespeare Bulletin* 27 (2009): 377–98.
See also 9, 15, 25, 63, 86, 94, 113, 140.

2.8   *Othello*. Dir. Trevor Nunn (Channel Four, 1990).

143 Conrad, Peter, 'When Less Means Moor'. *Observer Magazine* 29 Apr. 1990: 24–6.
144 Coursen, H. R., 'Editing the Script', in his *Watching Shakespeare on Television*. Rutherford: Fairleigh Dickinson University Press, 1993, 93–104.
145 Fischer, Susan L., 'Race-ing with the Times: Theatrical Exigency and Performative Politics in Trevor Nunn's *Othello* (1989)'. *Revista Alicantina de Estudios Ingleses* 25 (2012): 167–77.

146 Rutter, Carol Chillington, 'Remembering Emilia: Gossiping Hussies, Revolting Housewives', in her *Enter the Body: Women and Representation on Shakespeare's Stage*. London and New York: Routledge, 2001, 142–77.

147 Vaughan, Virginia Mason, '*Othello* for the 1990s: Trevor Nunn's 1989 Royal Shakespeare Company Production', in her '*Othello*': *A Contextual History*. Cambridge University Press, 1994, 217–32.
See also 9, 15, 63, 72, 86, 94, 108, 113, 118, 133, 141.

3.   DERIVATIVES AND SELECTED CITATIONS

3.1   *Desdemona / For Åbent Tæppe*. Dir. August Blom (Denmark, 1911).

148 Lanier, Douglas M., 'Murdering *Othello*', in *A Companion to Literature, Film, and Adaptation*, ed. Deborah Cartmell. Malden and Oxford: Wiley-Blackwell, 2012, 198–215.
See also 1, 11.

3.2   *Carnival*. Dir. Harley Knowles (Great Britain, 1921).

149 Gledhill, Christine, 'Performing British Cinema', in her *Reframing British Cinema 1918–1928: Between Restraint and Passion*. London: British Film Institute, 2003, 62–89.
See also 148.

3.3   *Carnival / Venetian Nights*. Dir. Herbert Wilcox (Great Britain, 1931).

See 148.

3.4   *Men Are Not Gods*. Dir. Walter Reisch (Great Britain, 1936).

150 Tempera, Mariangela, 'The Play without the Play', in *Shakespeare Graffiti: Il Cigno di Avon nella cultura di massa*, ed. Mariacristina Cavecchi and Sara Soncini. Milan: CUEM, 2002, 44–55.
See also 148.

3.5   *Children of Paradise / Les enfants du paradis*. Dir. Marcel Carné (France, 1945).

151 Ganim, Russell, 'Prévert Reads Shakespeare: Lacenaire as Iago in *Les Enfants du Paradis*'. *Comparative Literature Studies* 38 (2001): 46–67.

152 Jackson, Russell, 'Three *Auteurs* and the Theatre: Carné, Renoir and Rivette', in his *Theatres on Film: How the Cinema Imagines the Stage*. Manchester University Press, 2013, 221–68.

153 Lanier, Douglas M., '*L'homme blanc et l'homme noir: Othello* in *Les Enfants du paradis*', in *Shakespeare on Screen in Francophonia*, ed.

Patricia Dorval and Nathalie Vienne-Guerrin: shakscreen.org/analysis/
analysis_homme_blanc.
154 Tibbetts, John C., 'Backstage with the Bard: Or, Building a Better
Mousetrap', in *The Encyclopedia of Stage Plays into Film*, ed. John C.
Tibbetts and James M. Welsh. New York: Facts on File, 2001, 541–70.
155 Turk, Edward Baron, 'Politics and Theater in *Children of Paradise*',
in his *Child of Paradise: Marcel Carné and the Golden Age of French Cinema*.
Cambridge, MA and London: Harvard University Press, 1989, 245–67.
See also 64, 150.

3.6   *A Double Life*. Dir. George Cukor (USA, 1947).

156 Ardolino, Frank, 'Metadramatic Murder in *A Double Life*'. *Marlowe Society of
America Newsletter* 14.2 (Fall 1994): 3–4.
157 Jackson, Russell, 'The Uncanny Theatre', in his *Theatres on Film: How the
Cinema Imagines the Stage*. Manchester University Press, 2013, 134–79.
158 Phillips, Gene D., 'The Play's the Thing: Drama on Film', in his *George
Cukor*. Boston: Twayne, 1982, 35–58.
159 Potter, Lois, 'Unhaply, for I Am White: Questions of Identity and
Identification when *Othello* Goes to the Movies'. *Times Literary Supplement*
5 March 1999: 18–19.
160 Rippy, Marguerite Hailey, 'All Our *Othellos*: Black Monsters and
White Masks on the American Screen', in *Spectacular Shakespeare:
Critical Theory and Popular Cinema*, ed. Courtney Lehmann and Lisa S.
Starks. Madison and Teaneck: Fairleigh Dickinson University Press, 2002,
25–46.
161 Willson, Robert F., Jr, '*A Double Life*: *Othello* as *Film Noir* Thriller'.
Shakespeare on Film Newsletter 11.1 (Dec. 1986): 3, 10.
162 Willson, Robert F., Jr, 'Selected Offshoots: Shakespeare at War, on
Broadway, in the Mob, in Space, and on the Range', in his *Shakespeare in
Hollywood, 1929–1956*. Madison and Teaneck: Fairleigh Dickinson University
Press, 2000, 74–129.
See also 11, 64, 148, 150, 154.

3.7   *Jubal*. Dir. Delmer Daves (USA, 1956).

163 Coursen, H. R., '*Othello*', in his *Shakespeare Translated: Derivatives on Film
and TV*. New York: Peter Lang, 2005, 95–114.
See also 162.

3.8   *The Lone Ranger*: 'Outlaws in Greasepaint'. Dir. Oscar Rudolph
(ABC, 1957).

164 Burt, Richard, 'Civic ShakesPR: Middlebrow Multiculturalism, White
Television, and the Color Bind', in *Colorblind Shakespeare: New Perspectives*

on Race and Performance, ed. Ayanna Thompson. New York and London: Routledge, 2006, 157–85.

3.9 *Have Gun – Will Travel*: 'The Moor's Revenge'. Dir. Andrew V. McLaglen (CBS, 1958).

See 164.

3.10 *Saptapadi*. Dir. Ajoy Kar (India, 1961).

165 Burt, Richard, 'All That Remains of Shakespeare in Indian Film', in *Shakespeare in Asia: Contemporary Performance*, ed. Dennis Kennedy and Yong Li Lan. Cambridge University Press, 2010, 73–108.

166 Chakravarti, Paromita, 'Modernity, Postcoloniality and *Othello*: The Case of *Saptapadi*', in *Remaking Shakespeare: Performance across Media, Genres and Cultures*, ed. Pascale Aebischer, Edward J. Esche and Nigel Wheale. Basingstoke and New York: Palgrave Macmillan, 2003, 39–55.

3.11 *All Night Long*. Dir. Basil Dearden (Great Britain, 1962).

167 Skrebels, Paul, '*All Night Long*: Jazzing around with *Othello*'. *Literature/Film Quarterly* 36 (2008): 147–56.
See also 11.

3.12 *Shakespeare Wallah*. Dir. James Ivory (India, 1965).

168 Bhatia, Nandi, 'Imperialistic Representations and Spectatorial Reception in *Shakespeare Wallah*'. *Modern Drama* 45 (2002): 61–75.

169 Bhatia, Nandi, 'Multiple Mediations of "Shakespeare"', in her *Acts of Authority/Acts of Resistance: Theater and Politics in Colonial and Postcolonial India*. Ann Arbor: University of Michigan Press, 2004, 51–75.

170 Bhatia, Nandi, 'Different *Othello*(s) and the Contentious Spectators: Changing Responses in India'. *Gramma: Journal of Theory and Criticism* 15 (2007): 155–74.

171 Chaudhry, Lubna, and Saba Khattak, 'Images of White Women and Indian Nationalism: Ambivalent Representations in *Shakespeare Wallah* and *Junoon*', in *Gender and Culture in Literature and Film East and West: Issues of Perception and Interpretation: Selected Conference Papers*, ed. Nitaya Masavisut, George Simson and Larry E. Smith. Honolulu: University of Hawaii Press, 1994, 19–25.

172 Ciocca, Rossella, 'Indian *Othello*s: From Post-Imperial Melancholy to Bollywood Rural Western'. *Stratagemmi* 24–25 (2012–13): 323–38.

173 Contenti, Alessandra, '*Shakespearewallah* (sic): Shakespeare in India. Un episodio', in *Postcolonial Shakespeare: Studi in onore di Viola Papetti*, ed. Masolino d'Amico and Simona Corso. Rome: Edizioni di Storia e Letteratura, 2009, 57–70.

174 Hopkins, Lisa, 'Across the Ocean: *Shakespeare Wallah* and Shakespearean Performance; and *Bride and Prejudice* (2004)', in her *Relocating Shakespeare and Austen on Screen*. Basingstoke and New York: Palgrave Macmillan, 2009, 105–29.

175 Jhaveri, Shanay, 'Being Ferried around Trees in Merchant-Ivory's *Shakespeare Wallah*', in his *Outsider: Films on India 1950–1990*. Mumbai: Shoestring Publisher, 2009, 100–23.

176 Kapadia, Parmita, 'Shakespeare Transposed: The British Stage on the Post-Colonial Screen', in *Almost Shakespeare: Reinventing His Works for Cinema and Television*, ed. James R. Keller and Leslie Stratyner. Jefferson and London: McFarland, 2004, 42–56.

177 Kapadia, Parmita, 'Bollywood Battles the Bard: The Evolving Relationship between Film and Theater in *Shakespeare Wallah*', in *Bollywood Shakespeares*, ed. Craig Dionne and Parmita Kapadia. New York and Basingstoke: Palgrave Macmillan, 2014, 45–60.

178 Long, Robert Emmet, 'The Late Fifties—Mid-Sixties—Beginnings', in his *The Films of Merchant Ivory*. Updated edn. New York: Harry N. Abrams, 1997, 33–52.

179 Long, Robert Emmet, 'Feature Films: India', in his *James Ivory in Conversation: How Merchant Ivory Makes Its Movies*. Berkeley: University of California Press, 2005, 67–116.

180 Mukherjee, Ankhi, 'hamarashakespeare.com: Shakespeare in India', in her *What Is a Classic? Postcolonial Rewriting and Invention of the Canon*. Stanford University Press, 2014, 182–213.

181 Pym, John, 'An Experience of India', in his *The Wandering Company: Twenty-One Years of Merchant-Ivory Films*. London: British Film Institute, 1983, 30–49.

182 Venning, Dan, 'Cultural Imperialism and Intercultural Encounter in Merchant Ivory's *Shakespeare Wallah*'. *Asian Theatre Journal* 28 (2011): 149–67.

183 Wayne, Valerie, '*Shakespeare Wallah* and Colonial Specularity', in *Shakespeare, the Movie: Popularizing the Plays on Film, TV, and Video*, ed. Lynda E. Boose and Richard Burt. London and New York: Routledge, 1997, 95–102.

See also 154, 165.

3.13   *Che cosa sono le nuvole?* Dir. Pier Paolo Pasolini (Italy, 1968).

184 Belleggia, Lino, '*Che cosa sono le nuvole?* di Pier Paolo Pasolini', in *Shakespeare e il Novecento*, ed. Agostino Lombardo. Rome: Bulzoni, 2002, 241–53.

185 Di Meo, Philippe, 'Ce que nous disent les nuages'. *Positif* 467 (Janvier 2000): 81–5.

186 Guneratne, Anthony R., 'Six Authors in Search of a Text: The Shakespeares of Van Sant, Branagh, Godard, Pasolini, Greenaway, and Luhrmann', in his *Shakespeare, Film Studies, and the Visual Cultures of Modernity*. New York and Basingstoke: Palgrave Macmillan, 2008, 211–49.

187 Massai, Sonia, 'Subjection and Redemption in Pasolini's *Othello*', in her *World-Wide Shakespeares: Local Appropriations in Film and Performance*. London and New York: Routledge, 2005, 95–103.

188 Tempera, Mariangela, '"'Twas Me Who Combed Her Hair": Audience Participation in Two Italian Rewritings of *Othello*'. *Gramma: Journal of Theory and Criticism* 15 (2007): 193–210.
See also 66.

3.14   *The Flesh and Blood Show*. Dir. Pete Walker (Great Britain, 1972).

189 Chibnall, Steve, 'Double Exposures: Observations on *The Flesh and Blood Show*', in *Trash Aesthetics: Popular Culture and Its Audience*, ed. Deborah Cartmell, I. Q. Hunter, Heidi Kaye and Imelda Whelehan. London and Chicago: Pluto Press, 1997, 84–102.

190 Hutchings, Peter, 'Theatres of Blood: Shakespeare and the Horror Film', in *Gothic Shakespeares*, ed. John Drakakis and Dale Townshend. London and New York: Routledge, 2008, 153–66.

191 Loiselle, André, '*Cinéma du Grand Guignol*: Theatricality in the Horror Film', in *Stages of Reality: Theatricality in Cinema*, ed. André Loiselle and Jeremy Maron. University of Toronto Press, 2012, 55–80.

3.15   *Theatre of Blood*. Dir. Douglas Hickox (Great Britain, 1973).

192 Ardolino, Frank, 'Metadramatic Grand Guignol in *Theater of Blood*'. *Shakespeare on Film Newsletter* 15.2 (Apr. 1991): 9.

193 Cartmell, Deborah, 'Shakespeare, Film and Violence: Doing Violence to Shakespeare', in her *Interpreting Shakespeare on Screen*. Basingstoke: Macmillan, 2000, 1–20.

194 Gearhart, Stephannie S., '"Only he would have the temerity to rewrite Shakespeare": Douglas Hickox's *Theatre of Blood* as Adaptation'. *Literature/Film Quarterly* 39 (2011): 116–27.

195 Holdefer, Charles, 'Bad Shakespeare: Adapting a Tradition', in *Screening Text: Critical Perspectives on Film Adaptation*, ed. Shannon Wells-Lassagne and Ariane Hudelet. Jefferson and London: McFarland, 2013, 197–206.

196 Lowe, Victoria, '"Stages of Performance": Adaptation and Intermediality in *Theatre of Blood* (1973)'. *Adaptation* 3 (2010): 99–111.

197 Pendleton, Thomas A., 'What [?] Price [?] Shakespeare [?]' *Literature/Film Quarterly* 29 (2001): 135–46.
See also 154, 190, 191.

3.16   *Filming Othello*. Dir. Orson Welles (West Germany, 1978).

198 Berthomé, Jean-Pierre, and François Thomas, '*F for Fake & Filming Othello*', in their *Orson Welles at Work*. Trans. Imogen Forster, Roger Leverdier and Trista Selous. London and New York: Phaidon, 2008, 296–303.

199 Graver, Gary with Andrew J. Rausch, 'You Have to Have Chutzpah!', in their *Making Movies with Orson Welles: A Memoir*. Lanham: Scarecrow Press, 2008, 84–92.
200 Ishaghpour, Youssef, 'Marges, fragments, ruines II', in his *Orson Welles cinéaste: Une caméra visible*, vol. 3: *Les films de la période nomade*. Paris: Éditions de la Différence, 2001, 799–855.
201 Kliman, Bernice W., 'The Making of Welles's *Othello*'. *Shakespeare on Film Newsletter* 11.2 (Apr. 1987): 1, 6.
202 McBride, Joseph, 'All's Welles'. *Film Comment* 14.6 (Nov.-Dec. 1978): 24–7.
203 Petric, Vlada, 'Welles Looks at Himself: An Educational Film: *Filming Othello*'. *Film Library Quarterly* 13.4 (1980): 21–3.
204 Rosenbaum, Jonathan, 'Orson Welles's Essay Films and Documentary Fictions: A Two-Part Speculation', in his *Discovering Orson Welles*. Berkeley: University of California Press, 2007, 129–45.
    See also 17, 36.

3.17   *So Fine*. Dir. Andrew Bergman (USA, 1981).

205 Burt, Richard, 'The Love That Dare Not Speak Shakespeare's Name: New Shakesqueer Cinema', in his *Unspeakable ShaXXXspeares: Queer Theory and American Kiddie Culture*. New York: St Martin's Press, 1998, 29–75.
206 Burt, Richard, 'Slammin' Shakespeare in Acc(id)ents Yet Unknown: Liveness, Cinem(edi)a, and Racial Dis-integration'. *Shakespeare Quarterly* 53 (2002): 201–26.

3.18   *Cheers*: 'Homicidal Ham'. Dir. James Burrows (NBC, 1983).

See 160, 163.

3.19   *Otelo de Oliveira*. Dir. Paulo Afonso Grisolli (Globo TV, 1984).

207 Rothwell, Kenneth S., 'Shakespeare on Film All over the World: *Otelo de Oliveira*'. *Shakespeare on Film Newsletter* 10.2 (Apr. 1986): 5–6.
208 Smith, Cristiane Busato, 'The Brazilian Accent of *Othello*', in *Renaissance Shakespeare: Shakespeare Renaissances: Proceedings of the Ninth World Shakespeare Congress*, ed. Martin Procházka, Michael Dobson, Andreas Höfele and Hanna Scolnicov. Lanham: Rowman & Littlefield, 2014, 296–305.

3.20   *Otello*. Dir. Franco Zeffirelli (Italy, USA and Holland, 1986).

209 Bachmann, Gideon, 'On Set with *Othello*'. *Cinema Papers* 60 (Nov. 1986): 19–22.
210 Bini, Daniela, 'Reticence, a Rhetorical Strategy in *Othello/Otello*: Shakespeare, Verdi-Boito, Zeffirelli'. *Italica* 83 (2006): 238–55.

211 Brèque, Jean-Michel, 'Entretien avec Franco Zeffirelli'. *L'Avant-Scène Opéra* 90/91 (septembre/octobre 1986): 200–11.

212 Brèque, Jean-Michel, 'L'*Otello* de Zeffirelli, ou Quand l'opéra devient un véritable film'. *L'Avant-Scène Opéra* 90/91 (Sept./Oct. 1986): 212–18.

213 Citron, Marcia J., 'A Matter of Belief: *Otello* on Film and Television', in her *Opera on Screen*. New Haven and London: Yale University Press, 2000, 69–111.

214 Citron, Marcia J., 'The Erotics of Masculinity in Zeffirelli's Film *Otello*', in *Masculinity in Opera: Gender, History, and New Musicology*, ed. Philip Purvis. New York and London: Routledge, 2013, 84–101.

215 Grover-Friedlander, Michal, '*Otello*'s One Voice', in her *Vocal Apparitions: The Attraction of Cinema to Opera*. Princeton and Oxford: Princeton University Press, 2005, 53–80.

216 Lorant, André, 'From *Othello* to *Otello*: Zeffirelli's Opera-Film (1990)'. *Shakespeare Yearbook* 4 (1994): 113–42.

217 Napoleone, Caterina, '*Otello*', in her *Franco Zeffirelli: Complete Works – Theatre | Opera | Film*. London: Thames & Hudson, 2010, 458–63.

218 Schroeder, David, 'Finale: Directors' Operas', in his *Cinema's Illusions, Opera's Allure: The Operatic Impulse in Film*. New York and London: Continuum, 2002, 321–40.

219 Tempera, Mariangela, '"What You Have to Do Is All Visual": Zeffirelli's Opera Film of Verdi's *Otello*', in *Enjoying the Spectacle: Word, Image, Gesture: Essays in Honour of Professor Marta Wiszniowska*, ed. Jerzy Sobieraj and Dariusz Pestka. Toruń: Wydawnictwo Uniwersytetu Mikołaja Kopernika, 2006, 75–84.

220 Zeffirelli, Franco, '*Otello*', in his *Zeffirelli: The Autobiography of Franco Zeffirelli*. New York: Weidenfeld & Nicolson, 1986, 327–39.

3.21   *True Identity*. Dir. Charles Lane (USA, 1991).

See 206.

3.22   *Suture*. Dir. Scott McGehee and David Siegel (USA, 1993).

221 Thompson, Ayanna, 'Universalism: Two Films That Brush with the Bard, *Suture* and *Bringing down the House*', in her *Passing Strange: Shakespeare, Race, and Contemporary America*. Oxford University Press, 2011, 21–43.

3.23   *Othello – Shakespeare: The Animated Tales*. Dir. Nikolai Serebryakov (Great Britain and Russia, 1994).

222 Andreas, James R., 'The Canning of a Classic: *Shakespeare, the Animated Tales*'. *Shakespeare Yearbook* 11 (2000): 96–117.

223 Coursen, H. R., 'Animated Shakespeare: Second Season', in his *Shakespeare in Space: Recent Shakespeare Productions on Screen*. New York: Peter Lang, 2002, 113–28.

224 Osborne, Laurie, 'Mixing Media and Animating Shakespeare Tales', in *Shakespeare, the Movie, II: Popularizing the Plays on Film, TV, Video, and DVD*, ed. Richard Burt and Lynda E. Boose. London and New York: Routledge, 2003, 140–53.

225 Rokison, Abigail, '*Shakespeare: The Animated Tales*', in her *Shakespeare for Young People: Productions, Versions and Adaptations*. London and New York: Bloomsbury, 2013, 128–44.
    See also 163.

3.24   *Kaliyattam*. Dir. Jayaraaj Rajasekharan Nair (India, 1997).

226 Burnett, Mark Thornton, 'Vishal Bhardwaj and Jayaraaj Rajasekharan Nair', in his *Shakespeare and World Cinema*. Cambridge University Press, 2013, 55–86.

227 Muraleedharan, T., 'Shakespearing the Orient: Western Gaze and the Technology of Otherness in Jayaraj Films'. *Deep Focus* (March 2002): 31–8.

228 Sandten, Cecile, '*Kaliyattam* (The Play of God) by Jayaraj: Polymorphous and Postcolonial Poetics in an Indian *Othello* Adaptation', in *Postcolonial Studies across the Disciplines*, ed. Jana Gohrisch and Ellen Grünkemeier. Amsterdam and New York: Rodopi, 2013, 305–22.

229 Trivedi, Poonam, '"Filmi" Shakespeare'. *Literature/Film Quarterly* 35 (2007): 148–58.

3.25   *Buffy the Vampire Slayer*: 'Earshot'. Dir. Regis B. Kimble (WB Network, 1999).

230 Grant, Julia L., 'Slaying Shakespeare in High School: Buffy Battles *The Merchant of Venice* and *Othello*', in *Buffy in the Classroom: Essays on Teaching with the Vampire Slayer*, ed. Jodie A. Kreider and Meghan K. Winchell. Jefferson and London: McFarland, 2010, 202–12.

3.26   *O*. Dir. Tim Blake Nelson (USA, 2001).

231 Ardolino, Frank, 'The Story of *O*: Shakespeare's *Othello* and the Tragedy of Columbine'. *Journal of Evolutionary Psychology* 28.1&2 (Apr. 2006): 5–11.

232 Balizet, Ariane M., 'Teen Scenes: Recognizing Shakespeare in Teen Film', in *Almost Shakespeare: Reinventing His Works for Cinema and Television*, ed. James R. Keller and Leslie Stratyner. Jefferson and London: McFarland, 2004, 122–36.

233 Brown, Eric C., 'Cinema in the Round: Self-Reflexivity in Tim Blake Nelson's *O*', in *Almost Shakespeare: Reinventing His Works for Cinema and Television*, ed. James R. Keller and Leslie Stratyner. Jefferson and London: McFarland, 2004, 73–85.

234 Buchanan, Judith, 'Roguish Interventions: American Shakespearean Offshoots', in her *Shakespeare on Film*. Harlow: Pearson-Longman, 2005, 90–118.

235 Criniti, Steve, 'Othello: A Hawk among Birds'. *Literature/Film Quarterly* 32 (2004): 115–21.

236 Deitchman, Elizabeth A., 'Shakespeare Stiles Style: Shakespeare, Julia Stiles, and American Girl Culture', in *A Companion to Shakespeare and Performance*, ed. Barbara Hodgdon and W. B. Worthen. Oxford and Malden: Blackwell, 2005, 478–93.

237 French, Emma, 'Hollywood Teen Shakespeare Movies', in her *Selling Shakespeare to Hollywood: The Marketing of Filmed Shakespeare Adaptations from 1989 into the New Millennium*. Hatfield: University of Hertfordshire Press, 2006, 101–32.

238 Jess-Cooke, Carolyn, 'Screening the McShakespeare in Post-Millennial Shakespeare Cinema', in *Screening Shakespeare in the Twenty-First Century*, ed. Mark Thornton Burnett and Ramona Wray. Edinburgh University Press, 2006, 163–84.

239 Jess-Cooke, Carolyn, 'Popularisation', in her *Shakespeare on Film: Such Stuff as Dreams Are Made of*. London: Wallflower, 2007, 83–102.

240 Leggatt, Alexander, 'Teen Shakespeare: *10 Things I Hate about You* and *O*', in *Acts of Criticism: Performance Matters in Shakespeare and His Contemporaries: Essays in Honor of James P. Lusardi*, ed. Paul Nelsen and June Schlueter. Madison and Teaneck: Fairleigh Dickinson University Press, 2006, 245–58.

241 Maguire, Laurie, 'Language and Genre', in her *'Othello': Language and Writing*. London and New York: Bloomsbury, 2014, 77–128.

242 Phares, Dee Anna, 'Desi "was a ho": Ocular (Re)proof and the Story of *O*'. *Upstart Crow* 31 (2012): 34–53.

243 Rasmus, Agniezska, 'Two 2001 Takes on *Othello*: From a Basketball Court to a Master Bedroom', in *Reading English Drama and Poetry*, ed. Joanna Kazik. Łódź: Wydawnictwo Uniwersytetu Łódzkiego, 2007, 155–63.

244 Sanders, Julie, '"You know the movie song": Contemporary and Hybrid Film Scores', in her *Shakespeare and Music: Afterlives and Borrowings*. Cambridge and Malden: Polity, 2007, 159–81.

245 Semenza, Gregory M. Colón, 'Shakespeare after Columbine: Teen Violence in Tim Blake Nelson's *O*'. *College Literature* 32.4 (Fall 2005): 99–124.

246 Welsh, James M., 'Classic Demolition: Why Shakespeare Is Not Exactly "Our Contemporary", or, "Dude, Where's My Hankie?"' *Literature/Film Quarterly* 30 (2002): 223–7.

247 Whaley, Deborah Elizabeth, 'The Tragedy of Whiteness and Neoliberalism in Brad Kaaya's *O/Othello*', in *The Persistence of Whiteness: Race and Contemporary Hollywood Cinema*, ed. Daniel Bernardi. London and New York: Routledge, 2008, 233–52.

248 York, Robert L., '"Smells like Teen Shakespirit" or, the Shakespearean Films of Julia Stiles', in *Shakespeare and Youth Culture*, ed. Jennifer Hulbert, Kevin J. Wetmore, Jr and Robert L. York. New York and Basingstoke: Palgrave Macmillan, 2006, 57–115.

See also 12, 14, 57, 100, 105, 110, 114, 163.

3.27　*Othello*. Dir. Geoffrey Sax. Script by Andrew Davies (ITV, 2001).

249 Cardwell, Sarah, 'Distinguishing the Televisual', in her *Andrew Davies*. Manchester University Press, 2005, 147–76.

250 Cartelli, Thomas, and Katherine Rowe, 'Channeling *Othello*', in their *New Wave Shakespeare on Screen*. Cambridge and Malden: Polity, 2007, 120–41.

251 Hopkins, Lisa, '*Othello*: Adapted for Television by Andrew Davies'. *Early Modern Literary Studies* 8.1 (May 2002): 11.1–4 extra.shu.ac.uk/emls/08–1/othelrev.htm.

252 Osborne, Laurie E., 'A Local Habitation and a Name: Television and Shakespeare'. *Shakespeare Survey* 61 (2008): 213–26.

253 Walker, Eamonn, 'Othello in Love', in *Living with Shakespeare: Essays by Writers, Actors, and Directors*, ed. Susannah Carson. New York: Vintage Books, 2013, 141–61.

　　See also 114, 163, 241, 243, 246.

3.28　*Brihnnlala Ki Khelkali* / *Dancing Othello*. Dir. Ashish Avikunthak (India, 2002).

254 Calbi, Maurizio, 'Postcolonial Entanglements: Performing Shakespeare and Kathakali in Ashish Avikunthak's *Dancing Othello*'. *Anglistica* 15.2 (2011): 27–32.

255 Calbi, Maurizio, '*Dancing Othello* (*Brihnnlala Ki Khelkali*): An Interview with Ashish Avikunthak'. *Anglistica* 15.2 (2011): 33–46.

3.29　*In Othello*. Dir. Roysten Abel (India, 2003).

256 Burnett, Mark Thornton, 'Post-Millennial Parody', in his *Filming Shakespeare in the Global Marketplace*. Basingstoke and New York: Palgrave, 2007, 129–57.

3.30　*Huapango*. Dir. Iván Lipkies (Mexico, 2003).

257 Burnett, Mark Thornton, 'Shakespeare, Cinema, Latin America', in his *Shakespeare and World Cinema*. Cambridge University Press, 2013, 89–124.

258 Michel Modenessi, Alfredo, '"Is this the Noble Moor?": Re-viewing *Othello* on Screen through "Indian" (and Indian) Eyes'. *Borrowers and Lenders: The Journal of Shakespeare and Appropriation* 7.2 (Fall 2012 / Winter 2013): www.borrowers.uga.edu/490/display.

3.31　*Souli*. Dir. Alexander Abela (France and United Kingdom, 2004).

259 Burnett, Mark Thornton, 'Alexander Abela', in his *Shakespeare and World Cinema*. Cambridge University Press, 2013, 23–54.

260 Calbi, Maurizio, 'Reiterating *Othello*: Spectral Media and the Rhetoric of Silence in Alexander Abela's *Souli*', in his *Spectral Shakespeares: Media Adaptations in the Twenty-First Century*. New York and Basingstoke: Palgrave Macmillan, 2013, 63–79.

3.32   *Stage Beauty*. Dir. Richard Eyre (United Kingdom, USA and Germany, 2004).

261 Burt, Richard, 'Backstage Pass(ing): *Stage Beauty, Othello* and the Make-up of Race', in *Screening Shakespeare in the Twenty-First Century*, ed. Mark Thornton Burnett and Ramona Wray. Edinburgh University Press, 2006, 53–71.

262 Cardullo, Bert, 'Drama into Film, or Films by Dramatists: *Stage Beauty, House of Games*, and *People I Know* as Exempla', in his *Screening the Stage: Studies in Cinedramatic Art*. Bern: Peter Lang, 2006, 251–61.

263 Coursen, H. R., 'Shakespeare on Film: The Web of Allusion', in his *Contemporary Shakespeare Production*. New York: Peter Lang, 2010, 135–59.

264 Gruber, Elizabeth, '"No Woman Would Die like That": *Stage Beauty* as Corrective-Counterpoint to *Othello*', in *Situating the Feminist Gaze and Spectatorship in Postwar Cinema*, ed. Marcelline Block. Newcastle upon Tyne: Cambridge Scholars Publishing, 2008, 226–39.

265 Kamaralli, Anna, 'Rehearsal in Films of the Early Modern Theatre: The Erotic Art of Making Shakespeare'. *Shakespeare Bulletin* 29 (2011): 27–41.

266 Kidnie, Margaret Jane, 'Staging Shakespeare for "Live" Performance in *The Eyre Affair* and *Stage Beauty*', in *Shakespeare/Adaptation/Modern Drama: Essays in Honour of Jill L. Levenson*, ed. Randall Martin and Katherine Scheil. University of Toronto Press, 2011, 76–92.

267 Mora, María José, 'Eyre, Richard (dir.) 2004: *Stage Beauty*'. *SEDERI: Yearbook of the Spanish and Portuguese Society for English Renaissance Studies* 15 (2005): 151–6.

268 Rodgers, Amy, 'Looking up to the Groundlings: Representing the Renaissance Audience in Contemporary Fiction and Film', in *The English Renaissance in Popular Culture: An Age for All Time*, ed. Greg Colón Semenza. New York and Basingstoke: Palgrave Macmillan, 2010, 75–88.
See also 91, 241.

3.33   *Omkara*. Dir. Vishal Bhardwaj (India, 2006).

269 Alter, Stephen, *Fantasies of a Bollywood Love Thief: Inside the World of Indian Moviemaking*. Orlando: Harcourt, 2007.

270 Charry, Brinda, and Gitanjali Shahani, 'The Global as Local / Othello as Omkara', in *Bollywood Shakespeares*, ed. Craig Dionne and Parmita Kapadia. New York and Basingstoke: Palgrave Macmillan, 2014, 107–23.

271 Ciocca, Rossella, 'Omkara e Maqbool: Riconfigurazioni indiane del tragico shakespeariano', in William Shakespeare e il senso del tragico, ed. Simonetta de Filippis. Naples: Loffredo Editore, 2013, 201–9.

272 Gruss, Susanne, 'Shakespeare in Bollywood? Vishal Bhardwaj's Omkara', in Semiotic Encounters: Text, Image and Trans-Nation, ed. Sarah Säckel, Walter Göbel and Noha Hamdy. Amsterdam and New York: Rodopi, 2009, 223–38.

273 Heidenberg, Mike, 'No Country for Young Women: Empowering Emilia in Vishal Bhardwaj's Omkara', in Bollywood Shakespeares, ed. Craig Dionne and Parmita Kapadia. New York and Basingstoke: Palgrave Macmillan, 2014, 87–105.

274 Hogan, Lalita Pandit, 'The Sacred and the Profane in Omkara: Vishal Bhardwaj's Hindi Adaptation of Othello'. Image [&] Narrative 11.2 (2010): 49–62. www.imageandnarrative.be/index.php/imagenarrative/article/view/75/51.

275 Hudelet, Ariane, 'Renversement d'empire: Le cinéma indien et la culture britannique au tournant du XXIᵉ siècle'. CinémAction 138 (2011): 156–62.

276 Milton, John, 'Theorising Omkara', in Translation and Adaptation in Theatre and Film, ed. Katja Krebs. New York and London: Routledge, 2014, 83–98.

277 Pennacchia, Maddalena, 'Othello fiorisce a Bollywood: Omkara di Vishal Bhardwaj', in Postcolonial Shakespeare: Studi in onore di Viola Papetti, ed. Masolino d'Amico and Simona Corso. Rome: Edizioni di Storia e Letteratura, 2009, 231–50.

278 Pulugurtha, Nishi, 'The Moor Recontextualized: Othello to Omkara'. Silhouette 7 (2009): 105–12.

279 Trivedi, Poonam, 'Singing to Shakespeare in Omkara', in Renaissance Shakespeare: Shakespeare Renaissances: Proceedings of the Ninth World Shakespeare Congress, ed. Martin Procházka, Michael Dobson, Andreas Höfele and Hanna Scolnicov. Lanham: Rowman & Littlefield, 2014, 345–53.

280 Verma, Rajiva, 'Shakespeare in Indian Cinema: Appropriation, Assimilation, and Engagement'. Shakespearean International Yearbook 12 (2012): 83–96.

281 White, R. S., Shakespeare's Cinema of Crime: 'Macbeth', 'Hamlet' and Film Genres Including 'Maqbool', 'Omkara' and 'Eklavya'. Kurukshetra: Shakespeare Association, 2012.

See also 170, 172, 180, 226, 258.

Index

235

Brennan, Anthony, 61
Bridges, Jeff, 206
Bristol, 83
Bristol, Michael, 146–7, 151
Britain, 83, 107, 117, 168
British Council, 107
Broadway, 2, 160, 179
Brooks, Duwayne, 88
Brynner, Yul, 205
Buchanan, Judith, 5, 7, 8, 9
Buchowetzki, Dimitri, 5, 9
Buhler, Stephen, 1, 6, 9
Burbage Richard, 2, 142
Burge, Stuart, 5, 16, 43–56, 70, 142, 195, 196, 205
Burnett, Mark Thornton, 7, 8, 9, 15, 24, 94, 99, 103, 125, 127, 128
Burt, Richard, 8, 14, 107

Cabaret, Florence, 12
Cadet, Angelo, 141
Cage, Nicholas, 205
Cagelet, Paul, 140
Callaghan, Dympna, 35, 142
Cameron, David, 83
Cameron, James, 206
Campbell, Sol, 77
Canada, 12, 140, 144–5, 148
Cannes Festival, 108, 168
Canova, Antonio, 164
Cappuccilli, Piero, 50
Carné, Marcel, 16
Carnival (Knowles), 14
Cartelli, Thomas, 88
Castel, France, 142
Castillo, Alfredo, 127
Cat Ballou (Silverstein), 45
Cavell, Stanley, 186
Channel Four, 6
Charles II (King), 180, 182
Che Cosa Sono Le Nuvole? (Pasolini), 3
Cheek by Jowl, 196
Chekhov, Anton, 46
Chicago, 170
Chicoutimi, 141, 143
Cinthio, Giovanni Battista Giraldi, 151
Clark, Jaime, 197, 202, 203
Cloutier, Suzanne, 7, 8
Coburn, James, 206
Coleridge, Samuel Taylor, 86
Colman, Ronald, 179, 188
Colorado, 11
Columbine High School, 11, 79, 92
Comedy of Errors, The (Shakespeare), 107

Compleat Female Stage Beauty (Hatcher), 179
Compton, Fay, 36
Conan the Destroyer (Fleischer), 206
Condi, Giovanni, 35
Condon, Sir Paul, 81
Contarini dal Bovolo, Palazzo, 35
Coppola, Francis Ford, 206
Coriolanus (Fiennes), 87
Cortez, Stanley, 64
Coyle, Richard, 26, 83
Critchlow, Charles, 79
Croatia, 78
Crowther, Bosley, 56
Cruise, Tom, 206
Cukor, George, 14, 178, 179, 183, 190
Curtis, Tony, 99
Czech Republic, 78

Daileader, Celia, 2, 100
Danes, Claire, 187
Dantas, Daniel, 125
Davidson, John, 82
Davies, Andrew, 10, 12, 78, 81, 82
Davis Jr, Sammy, 48
Davis, Andrew, 205, 206
Day-Lewis, Daniel, 205
de Certeau, Michel, 177
de La Tour, Georges, 37
de Santis, Louis, 141
Dearden, Basil, 49
Deewaar (Chopra), 117
Delabastita, Dirk, 196
Demetrio, Mauro, 79
Dexter, John, 44, 47, 53, 55
Díaz Fernández, José Ramón, 4, 15
Disney, Walt, 13
Dobson, Gary, 81, 82
Dolan, Frances, 111, 112, 113
Domingo, Plácido, 50
Douglas, Kirk, 99
Dourado, Regina, 125
Drouin, Jennifer, 13
Duggan, Mark, 83

East India Company, 107
Eastwood, Clint, 206
Ebert, Roger, 97
Eccleston, Christopher, 32, 83
Eco, Umberto, 122
Edwards, Hilton, 60, 68, 70, 71
Elisofon, Eliot, 49
Ellis, John, 187
Ellison, Mark, 89
Enfants du paradis, Les (Carné), 16
Eraser (Russell), 207

CPSIA information can be obtained
at www.ICGtesting.com
Printed in the USA
LVOW10s1813200318
570521LV00014B/250/P